Something Completely Different

Something Completely Different

British Television and American Culture

Jeffrey S. Miller

University of Minnesota Press
Minneapolis • London

Published by the University of Minnesota Press
111 Third Avenue South, Suite 290
Minneapolis, MN 55401-2520
http://www.upress.umn.edu

Library of Congress Cataloging-in-Publication Data
Miller, Jeffrey S.
    Something completely different: British television and American culture / Jeffrey S. Miller.
      p. cm.
    Includes bibliographical references and index.
    ISBN 0-8166-3240-5 (hc.). — ISBN 0-8166-3241-3 (pbk.)
    1. Television broadcasting — United States.   2. Television programs — United States.
    3. Television broadcasting — Great Britain — Influence. 4. Popular culture. I. Title.
    PN1992.3.U5M49 2000
    302.23'45'0973 — dc21   99-40614

Printed in the United States of America on acid-free paper

The University of Minnesota is an equal-opportunity educator and employer.

11 10 09 08 07 06 05 04 03 02 01 00   10 9 8 7 6 5 4 3 2 1

To the memory of my parents

Contents

Acknowledgments

First and foremost, I wish to offer my most sincere gratitude to the members of my doctoral committee at Michigan State University for their careful attention, guidance, and support from the beginning of this project: Katherine Fishburn, Gretchen Barbatsis, Douglas Miller, William Vincent, and Gary Hoppenstand. One could not ask for a finer group of mentors, advisers, and friends.

Hillary Nunn and David Zauhar gave unfailingly of their time, good humor, and wisdom in their roles as readers of the work's first incarnations — their work made mine a good deal easier. Louise Desjardins's help in editing later drafts and indexing this volume has also been immeasurable. I am also grateful to Toby Miller for the guidance his careful critical reading and commentary have provided, and I owe many thanks (and a dinner as well!) to Roger Marshall for his comments and contributions to Chapters 2 and 3. Others whose contributions — intellectual, spiritual, and technological — deserve thanks and recognition include Janet Blank-Libra, Robert Bledsoe, Bernard R. Carman, Donovan DeJong, Thomas Doherty, Bonnie Dow, Sandra Looney, Richard Maltby, Rodney Marshall, John Murphy, Richard Panek, Nancy Pogel, John Raeburn, Margaret Roberts, Joseph Straub-haar, Tammy Stone, Lynette Tan, Tony Willson, Sherryl Wilson, and Frances Murphy Zauhar. Katie Knutson and Stacey Hesse provided valuable bibliographic and fact-checking help in their capacity as student assistants here at Augustana College. And I would be remiss in not acknowledging the many people with whom I watched these shows over the years and who in countless ways shaped my consideration of them here.

I am truly appreciative of the efforts of the University of Minnesota Press, especially Jennifer Moore, whose generous advice and good cheer have reminded me once again that good editors are good colleagues. Thanks also should go to Micah Kleit, who believed in this book before I did; Laura Westlund and Mike Stoffel, for shepherding it through production; and Judy Selhorst, who did the copyediting profession proud with her work here. In addition, I am grateful to

Roger Saunders of Python (Monty) Pictures Ltd. and Ron Mandelbaum of Photofest for their assistance in providing photographs for the book.

I am spiritually—although, I hope, not fiscally—indebted to Peter Levine, Rosemary Ezzo, and the American Studies Program at Michigan State University for their moral, clerical, and financial support of this work. The College of Arts and Letters and the Graduate College of Michigan State were also of great help through their monetary assistance, as was the Department of American Thought and Language. The Academic Research and Artistic Fellowship program at Augustana College also contributed financially to the completion of the project, for which I am very grateful.

Thanks also should be extended to the libraries and their staffs at Michigan State University and the University of Minnesota, as well as the Motion Picture, Broadcasting, and Recorded Sound Division of the Library of Congress in Washington, especially Rosemary Hanes; the Museum of Television and Radio in New York, especially Dina Consolini; and the British Film Institute in London, especially Bryony Dixon, Kathleen Dickson, and Mandy Rowson, for their help in the research phases of the project.

Finally, I owe more than I can say to Barb Ebeling, who took on the seemingly endless and assuredly thankless task of proofreading and checking the footnotes and citations, and whose patience and devotion saw me through all the inevitable breakdowns and detours on the long road toward completion of this project. Were it not for her love and support from before Day One, this book would not have been started, much less completed.

Introduction

"Here not there."

So the poet William Carlos Williams admonished his many friends and colleagues who flocked to Paris as part of the international migration that characterized American intellectual life in the 1920s. Rather than run off in search of the courtly muses that had defined the past, Williams argued, American poets and artists would be better off rooting themselves in their native soil and drawing their resources from the culture of which they were a vital part.[1]

This is a study of transnational communication that follows Williams's injunction. Although researchers and scholars of communication have traveled around the globe to examine the ways in which American media have affected other cultures, all too few have stopped to study the places that media artifacts from other cultures have occupied here in the United States. The reasons for this seem on the surface both simple and obvious: the American export of popular culture far exceeds its import from other societies, and because of the amount exported and the position of the United States as an economic and military superpower in the post–World War II decades, those films and records and television shows overwhelm the societies in which they are seen and heard. Both assertions, however, for whatever truth they may contain, act to obscure the significant role imports from other nations have played in American culture over the past half century. The paucity of research on topics ranging from the "art film" movement of the 1950s and 1960s to the British invasion in pop music to Hispanic sports broadcasting indicates the almost totally centrifugal pattern of American media scholarship. This is indeed an ironic development, given the concern voiced by writers (including Williams) throughout the history of the republic about the heavy burden imposed—or the welcome relief provided—by other societies on the establishment of American culture.

That is the imbalance I hope to address in some small way in this volume. Rather than popular music or film, however, I intend to focus on the medium that appears to be the most dominant internationally and the most impregnable domestically: television. Specifically, I am going to examine the ways in which British television programming made its way into American networks during the 1960s and 1970s, and the ways in which American audiences made sense of artifacts that represented a nation and culture different from their own. The time frame for this study is significant: the 1960s represented the peak of power for ABC, CBS, and NBC, as the commercial networks established a hegemony over the public airwaves that hewed more closely to the Marxist *realpolitik* definition of the term than to the postmodern revisions based on the work of Antonio Gramsci and presented most cogently by Raymond Williams. By the beginning of the 1970s, however, that hegemony began to disintegrate, with new Federal Communications Commission rules limiting network control of production and programming time and with a new emphasis on advertising demographics that meant the segmentation of the mass audience that had driven the medium through its first two decades. The recognition of audience segmentation as a programming strategy speaks explicitly to the economics of commercial American television; it also, however, addresses the cultural component of the medium. The deliberate breakup of a mass audience attracted to what NBC executive Paul Klein had defined as "least objectionable programming" revealed that meaning as disseminated by American television networks was a fabric woven out of many threads.[2] With segmented audiences, the battles for ratings to determine advertising costs showed American television to be the site of not only struggles of economic survival and supremacy but contests of meaning as well. Part of my intent in this book, then, is to trace the significant role British programming played in the development of these contests, particularly by exploring the ways in which that programming was, from its earliest import in the 1950s, shaped for a specific audience wealthy in educational, cultural, and, eventually, financial capital.

This is not to say that meanings viewers generated from British programs were necessarily those that the institutions, both domestic and foreign, shaping their reception intended or expected. As British television in the United States reveals the cultural intermeshings contained within the economic machinery of the medium, so it also reveals the variable readings possible with a given text. The most important legacy of the British spy shows of the 1960s, for example, was a character American women saw as a model for a new role in society — and a character American television producers saw as a model for re-creating their own crime series. But although these multiple readings demonstrate the power of specific viewers or audiences in creating meanings from a specific media text, the import of British television to the United States also demonstrates the limits of a theoretical approach based on the postmodern concept of polysemy.[3] British programming did indeed represent and was viewed as something different from domestic shows; that difference was often a key component of its popularity to given audiences. However, those readings were shaped by and at times purposively contained in American cultural and ideological structures in a manner that calls into play the notions of "absorption and domestication" that Todd Gitlin finds central to the functioning of media hegemony.[4]

What I hope to do, then, in this examination of British television and American culture, is to negotiate the distance between theories of unilateral media dependence and empowered active audiences, rejecting neither in toto but demonstrating the limits of each when applied to a specific historical practice. As such, the first part of Chapter 1 revisits the ur-argument concerning the American presence in transnational communication and culture: the thesis of cultural imperialism outlined by Herbert Schiller in his 1969 book *Mass Communications and American Empire.* Schiller's persuasive presentation of the United States as achieving global domination through its export of media and media artifacts has shaped research in transnational communication for the past thirty years and has yet to be displaced, either by other arguments in a political economy paradigm or by the postmodern active-audience paradigm.[5] My characterization of Schiller's thesis as a "myth" is not meant to suggest that cultural imperialism as he presents it is a fallacy; indeed, some of the conclusions I reach can be read to support his position. Rather, I mean to suggest that Schiller's presentation of American cultural imperialism, distilled from the social and intellectual ferment of the 1960s, is, like all myths, a social and historical construct, and, like all myths, it hides other social and historical processes in its construction. In this case, the assertion of a univocal and unilateral American cultural imperialism masks the presence in and influence on the United States of cultural artifacts from elsewhere—a presence and influence contradicting any notion of a unilateral relationship in transnational communication and culture.

To address the role of British television in American culture, I continue Chapter 1 by considering that relationship as representative of a cultural dialogue, following definitions established by Mikhail Bakhtin. Although language may help determine the meaning of a given "utterance," Bakhtin suggests, the actual meaning is "understood against the background of other concrete utterances on the same theme, a background made up of contradictory opinions, points of view, and value judgments—that is, precisely that background that, as we see, complicates the path of any word toward its object."[6] Meaning, in other words, is the sole property of neither a creator/producer nor a viewer/reader. Further, it is a commodity that undergoes a continual process of shaping and reshaping as it encounters other voices and visions in its journey from sender to receiver. The import of television programs from Britain and the complications arising when those artifacts encounter in America what Tony Bennett and Janet Woollacott refer to as "reading formations"—the specific social, historical, and ideological utterances that "bear in upon, mould and configure the relations between texts and readers in the determinant conditions of reading"—act as exemplars of Bakhtinian dialogue, I argue.[7] As such, in this volume I endeavor to establish the parameters of the reading formations in which American audiences derived meaning from imported British programs and the shifts occurring in those formations as utterances shaping them changed throughout the 1960s and 1970s.

In the concluding sections of Chapter 1, I begin that process by briefly discussing the place of other British cultural artifacts in American culture during the 1950s and early 1960s and the early British presence on American television in the 1950s. In Chapters 2 through 5, I then examine the place of British television in American culture by considering representatives of specific genres and the ways in which the relationship between those imports and their audiences were configured at specific times. I employ a limited amount of textual analysis—visual and verbal—in analyzing the place of a given show in this transnational dialogue. I also, however, follow Bennett and Woollacott's methodology in examining the placement of a specific media text in a general discourse through voices other than the text itself: advertisements, promotional devices, reviews and articles in the popular press, and the words of viewers themselves, in addition to government and industrial documents. I begin Chapter 2 by taking up the historical utterances guiding the reception of British secret agent series that appeared on American television starting in 1965. Articulated originally with the presidency of John F. Kennedy through the figure of James Bond, *Secret Agent* and *The Prisoner* represented both the utopian and, eventually, dystopian aspects of the "Camelot" myth that followed Kennedy's assassination. At the same time, the British imports, as well as American spy dramas crafted from the Bond cloth, functioned ideologically to turn the apocalyptic Cold War struggle between the Free West and the Communist East into a glamorous duel that was attractive to younger viewers. Of particular significance in that audience were young women viewers, for whom the most successful of the secret agent imports, *The Avengers,* provided something never before seen in American action series: a strong, physical female lead character. The way in which new American utterances concerning the place of women in society intersected with meanings available in and around the text of *The Avengers* to create a specific reading formation for young American women is the subject of Chapter 3.

This first wave of British programming ended in 1969 with the network cancellation of *The Avengers.* British television shows still found a place on American airwaves, however, through the channels of educational broadcasting. The success of the serialized historical drama *The Forsyte Saga* on American educational stations, discussion of which begins Chapter 4, coincided with the organization of those stations into the Public Broadcasting Service, designed as a cultural oasis in the "vast wasteland" of commercial broadcasting. To the Nixon administration, which oversaw the creation of PBS, however, the new service and its potential to criticize policy represented a threat to its political power, a threat that had to be neutralized by shaping American public broadcasting into a system following the original elite orientation of the British Broadcasting Corporation and featuring programs representing the best of the past, not the immediacy of the present. Foremost among those programs was *Masterpiece Theatre,* which presented a collection of imported serial dramas similar to *The Forsyte Saga* as a result of the corporate munificence of Mobil Oil. Mobil's effort to use British programming, especially the serial *Upstairs, Downstairs,* as part of a public relations campaign to improve its reputation and status among an audience of viewers rich in cultural capital is the subject of the latter half of Chapter 4.

Although historical, political, and economic utterances helped shape the reception of British programming in the United States, the aesthetics of the programs themselves also played a significant role in that reception, as I argue in Chapter 5's discussion of the popularity of British sketch comedies in the 1960s and 1970s. The BBC series *That Was the Week That Was* established in 1963 that comedy might be a profitable export commodity for British distributors. Although the NBC version of the show was produced in New York with mostly American performers and writers, the show followed precisely the verbal and visual format of its British progenitor and introduced American audiences to David Frost, one of the British show's stars. Frost in England, meanwhile, was working with a group of young comedians that would in 1969 combine to create the BBC show *Monty Python's Flying Circus.* By 1975, that series had become an unprecedented public broadcasting syndication success in the United States, thanks both to the shifting demographic patterns into which it was imported and to the way in which the comic utterances of the show spoke to its American audience.

Chapter 6 stays rooted in the 1970s but switches its focus from British imports and a general American audience to the single audience on whom British programming had its most measurable effect: American television producers. In his own dialogue with the domestic market, increasingly defined by specific demographic targeting, producer Norman Lear redirected utterances concerning race, class, and gender that had defined unexported British programs to create popular American shows, including *All in the Family* and *Sanford and Son*. At the same time, a number of other producers brought what Horace Newcomb and Paul Hirsch refer to as American "cultural elements with embedded significance" to British genres and formats that had already been successful in the United States.[8] Those producers became responsible for some of the most resonant voices of the televisual dialogue between Britain and America: *Three's Company, Saturday Night Live, Roots, Dallas*. In the final chapter of this book, I attempt to sum up that dialogue, revisiting the theories that inform the study as a whole and briefly addressing the role cable has played and will continue to play in the relationship between British television and American audiences.

Having outlined what this book is, I must also discuss what it is not. It is not an effort to create a new global theory in the study of transnational communication. Although I both use and respond to several theories dealing with the transfer of media texts between nations and cultures, my goal here is to provide a Geertzian "thick description," with the interpretation and analysis that description entails, of the historical, social, and cultural features defining a single relationship involving two major national media powers.[9] Extrapolating beyond that specific relationship to the whole of transnational communications defeats the purpose of this work—although I would hope that the arguments offered here might contribute to those larger discussions. In terms of method, as my reference to Clifford Geertz should indicate, I do not share Armand Mattelart's belief that media ethnographies help constitute a "universe of nonsense" in communication research.[10] I am, however, dubious of the appropriateness of ethnographic research in a project dealing with larger issues of politics, economics, and aesthetics in a historical context. Audience responses to imported media texts are essential in the apprehension of these larger issues, and I have attempted to include as many of those responses from the time as possible, whether in the form of established media commentary or letters from viewers. But to elicit comments twenty to thirty years after the fact from American fans of British programs of the 1960s and 1970s is to subject both the programs themselves and the contexts within which they were viewed to vagaries of memory that are more questionable and potentially more damaging than the obvious issues of gatekeeping and control raised by the use of popular media from the period.

Finally, in terms of the specific historical texts examined here, Anglophilic viewers and readers will note that this study is anything but all-inclusive. My primary focus is on prime-time entertainment programming; as a result, I do not consider British documentary or fact-based programming such as *Civilisation,* which played a considerable role in establishing a place for British programming on American public television. Nor do I consider, in the nonfiction line, the influential work done by David Frost as an interviewer and talk-show host in the late 1960s and 1970s, although I note at length his other contributions to the British-American dialogue. Within the context of fictional entertainment, I do not deal with the children's marionette programs created in Britain by Gerry Anderson (*Fireball XL-5, Stingray, Thunderbirds*), which were dubbed with American voices for overseas sale. In terms of prime-time entertainment, I omit the variety programs, most notably *This Is Tom Jones,* that constituted a large part of Lew Grade's "mid-Atlantic" production and distribution strategy between 1965 and 1975. More regrettably, I make short shrift of two major British science fiction imports, *Space: 1999* and *Doctor Who,* as the genre and its representatives are more weight than this study can bear. Similarly, I have to forgo for reasons of time and space the detailed discussions that the important comedy series *Doctor in the House, Fawlty Towers,* and *The Benny Hill Show* deserve.

As the wealth of material I am not able to include should indicate, the British presence and influence on American television during this period was a considerable one. And as the material I do include should indicate, that presence and influence has been one that has been unjustly ignored by media scholars. If this book allows readers to understand how and why British television programming occupied the place it did in American culture in the 1960s and 1970s, I will have succeeded in my most immediate goals. If it does something very, if not completely, different and opens the door to other studies of how transnational communication and culture have operated here, not there, I will have succeeded in the goals I hold most dear.

1. Here Not There
American Imperialists and British Invaders

Mass communications are now a pillar of the emergent imperial society. Messages "made in America" radiate across the globe and serve as the ganglia of national power and expansionism. The ideological images of "have-not" states are increasingly in the custody of American informational media.

— **Herbert I. Schiller**[1]

That huge English flow, so sweet, so undeniable, has done incalculable good here.... Yet the price The States have had to lie under for the same has not been a small price. Payment prevails; a nation can never take the issues of the needs of other nations for nothing. America, grandest of lands.... collapses quick as lightning at the repeated, admonishing, stern words, Where are any mental expressions from you, beyond what you have copied or stolen?

— **Walt Whitman**[2]

Although separated by more than a century, the words of Herbert Schiller and Walt Whitman address the same concern: the subjugation of young and weak cultures to global empires through an unimpeded "flow" of messages and texts.[3] That the United States would be the young and weak culture to Whitman and the global empire to Schiller says volumes about the changes in the world from the time immediately preceding the Civil War fought by Americans on their own soil to the civil war fought by Americans in Vietnam. Yet, as Whitman's own career suggests, it is possible for participants in a young and weak culture to break from the "custody" of a global empire and create something new and interesting that speaks to and for that culture — and that may in turn speak to at least some of the participants in an imperial culture.

Whitman, of course, is an exceptional case. One can hardly judge the ability of a Nigerian farmer, for example, to respond to the influx of American media in the 1950s and 1960s by the standards Whitman set in his response to the power of Britain in the nineteenth century. Whitman's place at the beginning of this study, rather, serves to cast Schiller's words and the notion of cultural imperialism in two significant new lights. First, as Whitman's poetry created what Ed Folsom has called "a sustained tradition" of other American poets calling on him and responding in their own work to his, so has Schiller's 1969 book *Mass Communications and American Empire* repeatedly called scholars of transnational communication back to address his thesis of cultural imperialism, whether to agree or to argue.[4] Second, at the very moment that Schiller was identifying and analyzing the role of American media in creating its "emergent imperial society," the domestic producers and consumers of those media were themselves experiencing a new "flow" of messages and texts from Britain. In examining the currents through which a growing imperial American culture should again pay the price, to use Whitman's terms, of British influence, it is first necessary to examine the thesis of cultural imperialism through which Schiller defined the role of the United States and its media in the world, as well as responses to that thesis that better address the "mental expressions" from Britain that would come to exert their own power in America.

The Myth of Cultural Imperialism

In his essay "Watergate and the Press," Michael Schudson presents the accepted story of the journalistic handling of the Watergate scandal as a myth. The notion, he writes, that brave, hardworking young journalists and their wise editors at the *Washington Post* succeeded in forcing an evil president to resign his office is distorted, ignoring the general complacency of the press, the role of government agencies in the demise of Richard Nixon, and the sheer luck involved. But, Schudson argues, that story contains a "kernel of truth [that] sustains the general myth and gives it . . . a larger truth that is precisely what myths are for: not to tell us in empirical detail who we are but what we might have been once, what we might again become, what we would be like 'if.' " These myths, he continues, "do not tell a culture's simple truths as much as they explore its central dilemmas. . . . For better and for worse, [the myth of Watergate] is the crystallization of the hopes and fears and confusions of American society about its own increasingly prominent news media."[5]

Schudson's term *crystallization* is particularly apt in its presentation of myth as being constructed from forces larger than its core elements.[6] The myth of Watergate brought together long-held understandings and questions about the role of the press in the United States with equally long-held understandings and questions about the role of the presidency—understandings and questions colored by an assassination of one president followed by grand social and military adventures, sponsored by strong presidents, that were at the time ending catastrophically. Those issues, as well as the economic reality of the recession over which Richard Nixon presided in 1973–74, were themselves shaped in the creation of the myth of Watergate by cultural forces: apprehensions of the world valuing individual tenacity, the rule of law, and the importance of freedom in a democracy.[7]

As Schudson finds the myth of Watergate to have become "the unavoidable central myth of American journalism," so has "cultural imperialism" become the unavoidable central myth of the study of transnational communication—myth taken to mean neither truth nor falsity, of which it may well contain both, but an exploration of problems inherent in the trade of messages and meanings between cultures. The "sustained tradition" of responses and arguments that the cultural imperialism thesis has engendered has been well described recently by scholars including Daniël Biltereyst and Colleen Roach.[8] To understand the significance of that tradition to a study of British media in the United States, therefore, one needs to begin with a brief consideration of the cultural imperialism myth as Herbert Schiller "crystallized" it for an American audience in 1969.

Schiller's *Mass Communications and American Empire* came out in perhaps the crucial year in a growing relationship between British television and American audiences: 1969. That year marked the end of a series of spy imports on commercial television, the beginning of broadcasts of *The Forsyte Saga* on educational television, the first episodes of *Monty Python's Flying Circus* on BBC, and the first pilot episodes for what would become *All in the Family* on CBS. That, however, was not a concern of Schiller, who was instead turning his attention to the growing presence of American media in a global marketplace—whether that marketplace wanted them there or not. The export of American media, particularly television, had become the tool of "an emerging imperial network" of government, military, and financial interests, to be used for that network's "defense and entrenchment wherever it exists . . . and for its expansion to locales where it hopes to become active."[9] The mechanized culture presented and represented by television offered a vision of American way of life, Schiller argued, that focused on little more than the consumption of material goods. And if the trade of those goods was the mechanism allowing a powerful economy to dominate a weaker one, then a free flow of information and communication "is the channel through which life styles and value systems can be imposed on poor and vulnerable societies."[10] "Free speech" and a "free market" become tools used deliberately by the military-industrial network guiding the culture industry in selling its products for ideological and profitable ends, particularly when those sales involved weak and poor nations as consumers. Moreover, it was not simply television shows and movies that were being exported, but entire systems of commercialized broadcasting that would create markets for American businesses and advertisers as well as *I Love Lucy* and *Bonanza*. The American economy needed to propagate itself through the development of foreign markets, and, Schiller wrote, "wherever big company influence penetrates, electronic communications are subverted to salesmanship."[11]

Schiller's argument was presented so forcefully, and the evidence concerning the power of the American media/culture industry, from Henry Luce to AT&T to Comsat and Intelsat, was so overwhelming that the assumption of a new (and malevolent) American communication empire seemed to be common sense. Yet, as Schudson suggests of the myth of journalism and Watergate, common sense is not necessarily verifiable. Schiller cited the work of researchers in Nigeria and Mexico who were appalled by the profusion of American programming and advertising on indigenous television networks as evidence that "everywhere local culture is facing submersion from the mass-produced outpourings of commercial broadcasting."[12] Schiller never indicated in his account, however, whether those researchers reported on how Nigerians or Mexicans may have responded to what they were watching or the purported influence that American-based television was having on their societies and cultures. As John Tomlinson points out, this leaves the impression that the American media/culture industry, to use Schiller's words, "envelops all viewers within the range of electronic impulses patterned after the American model," but it says nothing about what that envelopment might actually do or whom it might affect.[13] Indeed, although Schiller's greatest stated concern was with Third World nations such as Nigeria and Mexico, the societies he most clearly presented as being covered by an American media blanket included Canada, Finland, Hong Kong, and Britain — all thriving capitalist cultures.

Schiller's own subsuming of the differences between cultures in the economic and political ramifications of imperialism presented what Fred Fejes, among others, has identified as the great lacuna of the cultural imperialism thesis: its blindness toward indigenous patterns of belief that militate for or against any imperialistic intent of imported media. The simple commonsense power of the position taken by Schiller, Fejes argues, obscures the complex dynamics that exist between a native culture and an external culture.[14] In so doing, however, Schiller's work presented the forces at work in the United States in 1969 that crystallized the hopes, fears, and confusions of Americans over the place of their popular culture in the world into the myth of cultural imperialism. First and foremost in the political and economic realm was the real and observable expansion of American corporate and military interests in the years from the Truman administration to the administration of Lyndon Johnson. Indeed, the term *cultural imperialism* itself was introduced not by Schiller in his own work, but by a Johnson administration official who claimed that relationships between the First and Third Worlds in 1965 differed greatly from those "at the height of cultural imperialism" in the nineteenth century.[15] Writing in the decade following the Bay of Pigs, the invasion of the Dominican Republic, and the military "advising" in Laos that became the war in Vietnam, to say nothing of the corporate expansion he documented thoroughly in his text, Schiller spoke directly of a world in which the United States was in fact "dumping" an American way of life, in the form of napalm, bombs, and bullets, on poor and vulnerable societies.[16] He also spoke of a nation in which massive social changes, particularly involving black Americans and a growing student class, were redefining American life and culture. In his final chapter, Schiller presented both blacks and students (along with disenchanted professors and scientists) as forces capable of altering existing structures of power — including the communication and culture industries.[17]

Finally, as Schudson's myth of Watergate was shaped by cultural sources outside those explicitly definable as political or economic or social, so was Schiller's myth of cultural imperialism. Underlying his critique of an American "power elite" striving and succeeding to manage global communication for its own interests was a critique of media products themselves, born intellectually out of the work of Theodor Adorno and Max Horkheimer and culturally out of a post-World War II revulsion, on the part of academics and an American social/cultural elite, toward "mass culture."[18] Television lifted from its marketplace structure, he argued in his final chapter, would lead from what Federal Communications Commission chairman Newton Minow had called in 1961 "a vast wasteland" to broadcasts of government hearings, interesting educational programming, and cultural programming that would present "the best in the universe of national and international arts and humanities."[19] Schiller here seemed to offer a tacit acknowledgment that the walls of Fortress Mediamerica are not quite impermeable, but he presented more directly a vocal declaration of the elevating effect of external High Culture on common folk derived from the culture debates of the 1950s — a declaration that would be seconded, as I will discuss presently, by the mission of American public broadcasting.

Schiller's argument concerning the evident global power of American media thus was shaped into a statement, to return to Schudson's discussion of myth, that provided less in empirical detail about what America was doing than it did meditation about what America might have become. As such, it developed the generative power necessary for any myth to function, becoming the touchstone for those working in the field of transnational communication. First leading to strong efforts to quantify and exemplify the myth of cultural imperialism at work in the world, Schiller's work then led to a vital and ongoing debate among scholars working with him in the political economy paradigm concerning the relative weight given political and economic elements of the myth. Biltereyst characterizes this debate as one between scholars following Schiller, who advocated a dependency model, and scholars who viewed an uneven flow of media and cultural artifacts as obeying the natural processes of the free market.[20] Of particular note for this study are two works representing each side of that debate. Finnish researchers Kaaren Nordenstreng and Tapio Varis set out in the early 1970s to provide quantitative documentation, through the flow of media products, of the processes Schiller argued were under way in 1969. The results of their work, published in 1974, suggested that although other nations might also be considered media imperialists, in both global and regional senses, the American domination of the world market was so overwhelming that claims of an emerging empire were almost self-evident.[21] On the other side of the debate, scholars Colin Hoskins and Rolf Mirus, arguing that American dominance of transnational communications "follows naturally the characteristics of television programming, its production and trade," presented in 1988 their concept of the "cultural discount": "A particular program rooted in one culture, and thus attractive in that environment, will have a diminished appeal elsewhere as viewers find it difficult to identify with the style, values, beliefs, institutions and behavioral patterns of the material in question."[22] An American power elite was not conspiring to take other cultures into imperial custody through the export of television programs and other media artifacts; instead, the acceptance of those artifacts abroad was guided by market forces and the characteristics of both the artifacts and their foreign consumers.

Whereas the dependency versus free-flow arguments took shape in the political economy paradigm in the 1970s and 1980s, another response to Schiller's thesis, as Roach documents, developed out of British cultural studies in the latter decade. Influenced by the work of Stuart Hall and others at the Centre for Contemporary Cultural Studies and studies of British television audiences done by David Morley and Charlotte Brunsdon, a number of international scholars began to examine how audiences around the globe actually received, talked about, and acted upon American programming brought into their homelands. Following the prevalent early 1980s concern voiced in Europe about "wall-to-wall *Dallas*," the most notable of those surveys were performed by Ien Ang on Dutch women and Tamar Liebes and Elihu Katz on residents of the Middle East who

watched the adventures of J.R., Bobby, and Sue Ellen.[23] Their research discovered that local audiences read *Dallas* in a number of different ways that had little to do with either the intent of the show's producers or any presumed American imperialist agenda.

These responses to Schiller's thesis have numerous critical flaws of their own.
An understanding of television production, programming, and trade that considers
them as "natural" processes, as Hoskins and Mirus and other free-market theo-
rists argue, so divorces texts and artifacts from the individuals and institutions
that create them as to make culture meaningless. Active audience research, meanwhile, in its assertion of the absolute openness of transnational texts, similarly
strips the concept of culture of its power in the limitlessness of meaning, while
also stripping the vital political notion of "resistance" of its power in suggesting
that a local reading of a transnational text actively "resists" ideological elements
of that text.[24] Schiller himself has responded to his critics, arguing that the free-
market assertion that regional media centers (Brazil, Japan, Mexico) undercut
claims of an American empire ignores the imperial influence on those centers
themselves and suggesting that reception research "comes uncomfortably close
to being apologetics for present-day structures of cultural control."[25] Whatever
their flaws, all three positions are united in two key points: first, in demonstrating the continuing power of the myth of cultural imperialism; and second, in ignoring the possibility that the United States might be countenanced as anything
but an imperialist exporter. With a quiet but steady flow of cultural artifacts from
Britain making their way into American culture during the 1950s and 1960s, however, that possibility presented itself. And the consideration of what that influx
might mean to or for American media and culture requires some form of analysis that, while again addressing the myth of cultural imperialism, seeks to revise
and reorder the hopes, fears, and confusions crystallized in that central myth of
transnational communication.

So Many Uttering Tongues!

At first glance, the work of literary critic and theorist Mikhail Bakhtin seems
tangential to discussions of transnational communication. With his insistence on
multiplicity of meaning and the activity of both speaker and listener in acts of
communication, Bakhtin appears at most to provide theoretical support to the
position of those arguing from the cultural studies active-audience paradigm and
to say little about the issues of influence and control in communication between
cultures. A closer consideration of Bakhtin's ideas, however, particularly as found
in his essays "Discourse in the Novel" and "The Problem of Speech Genres,"

opens up considerations of and problems in transnational communication that build on (and around) the concerns voiced in the myth of cultural imperialism and that speak directly to the issues involved in the American reception of British media from the 1950s to the 1970s.

Two key terms emerging from the essays noted above are *heteroglossia* and *dialogue*. The former, as Bakhtin explains it, refers to "the social diversity of speech types...a multiplicity of social voices and a wide variety of their links and interrelationships."[26] This multivocality suggests that neither texts nor their producers or audiences can be thought of as unitary wholes blessed with a single meaning or intent. Similarly, the notion of dialogue as a "classic form of speech communication" presents and supports the idea that audiences are as active as producers in creating meaning from a given text: "The fact is that when the listener perceives and understands the meaning...of speech, he simultaneously takes an active, responsive attitude toward it. He either agrees or disagrees with it (completely or partially), augments it, applies it, prepares for its execution, and so on."[27]

Although heteroglossia and dialogue are important theoretical elements in an examination of transnational communication that finds fault with the Manichaean totalism of cultural imperialism, even more significant is what Bakhtin defines as "the *real unit* of speech communication: the utterance."[28] The utterance, according to Bakhtin, is the way in which speech obtains a concrete reality belonging to an actual subject. It is concrete because it has, in and of itself, absolute boundaries in the beginning of an individual's speech and its end. Dialogue comes out of those utterances, as a second speaker listens and then responds to the first. But, he continues, dialogue is not limited simply to the beginnings and ends of the concrete utterances that compose it. Before one begins a dialogue, one has to assume the existence of other utterances on the given topic. No utterance comes into being sui generis; rather, every element of discourse is itself a response, however indirect, to elements that precede or accompany it. This necessarily drains the speaker of any illusions of omnipotence—as Bakhtin writes, "He is not, after all, the first speaker, the one who disturbs the eternal silence of the universe."[29] Moreover, it destabilizes the "message" as well, as every utterance is shaped from its concrete beginnings by other points of view expressed in other judgments. Any awareness of other utterances, Bakhtin argues, "gives the speech a dialogical turn that cannot be produced by any purely referential theme with its own object."[30] And as the message and its speaker become enmeshed in a web of meanings beyond their immediate apprehension, so too does the respondent. The object of the utterance, Bakhtin argues, is already "overlain with qual-

ification, open to dispute, charged with value . . . enveloped in an obscuring mist—
or, on the contrary, by the 'light' of alien words that have already been spoken."
With both speaker and respondent—or producer and audience—having to address other thoughts, views, and arguments, in the present and the past, as part
of their dialogue, the utterance "enters a dialogically agitated and tension-filled
environment of alien words, value judgements and accents, weaves in and out of
complex interrelationships, merges with some, recoils from others, intersects with
yet a third group: and all this may crucially shape discourse."[31]

Bakhtin presents in his model a field of meaning(s) through which speaker,
utterance, and respondent all must move. Communication is not a straight line
from producer to audience—or from imperial power to subjugated culture—
guided by the intent of the former or the vulnerability of the latter; rather, it is a
series of vectors, eddies, collisions, reflections, and refractions that inevitably,
although unpredictably, result in dialogue. That model challenges the linear and
unilateral construction of Schiller's cultural imperialism thesis, just as it serves
as a theoretical tool for understanding its crystallization of hopes, fears, and confusions—utterances—concerning the place of American mass communication
in the world. But Bakhtin's ideas address not merely the structure of the cultural
imperialism argument but the heart of its content as well: the transfer of texts
between cultures. Bakhtin makes this connection clear in "The Problem of Speech
Genres":

> The unique speech experience of each individual is shaped and devel-
> oped in continuous interaction with others' individual utterance. This
> experience can be characterized to some degree as the process of *as-
> similation*—more or less creative—of others' words (and not the words
> of a language). Our speech, that is, all our utterances, (including cre-
> ative works), is filled with others' words, varying degrees of otherness
> or varying degrees of "our-own-ness," varying degrees of awareness
> and detachment.[32]

At first glance, Bakhtin here seems to describe a process through which a text
created in one culture enters another for any number of reasons (economic, political, social, aesthetic) and is then apprehended by any number of people for
any number of reasons. His concept of "utterances . . . filled with varying degrees
of otherness or varying degrees of 'our-own-ness,'" however, while allowing for
multiple voices and multiple meanings, grounds polysemy in the actual political, economic, social, and ideological statements that shape reception and meaning. At the same time, it grounds arguments defining transnational communica-

tion in terms of "natural" economic laws or processes in the real social processes conducted by people in constructing culture — including, significantly, language.[33]

Bakhtin's use of the term *assimilation,* however, with the creative and multivocal inflection he brings to it, also introduces two problems — one theoretical and one methodological — to this study. The theoretical problem concerns the relationship of assimilation to the process of hegemony derived from Gramsci's work and given a cogent explication by Todd Gitlin: "The hegemonic ideology of bourgeois culture is extremely complex and absorptive; only by *absorbing and domesticating* conflicting values, definitions of reality, and demands on it, in fact, does it remain hegemonic."[34] In many ways, the traditional definition of assimilation — one that allows for neither creativity nor multiplicity of meaning — and the definition of hegemony posited by Gitlin present the same model of a dominant set of meanings grabbing and devouring meaning introduced from a foreign source. Similarly, E. San Juan argues that the major flaw in Bakhtin's dialogic construction of communication and assimilation is that it fails to suggest the ideological limitations presented by internal power structures.[35] As such, Gitlin's and San Juan's consideration of assimilation and hegemony simply inverts Schiller's thesis, as the receiving culture exercises imperialism through its unilateral power to determine meaning in transnational communication — a power that evidently allows for only one possible construction within the whole of that culture. Their argument casts the terms along the same positivist lines of communication employed by Schiller; in so doing, Gitlin and San Juan fail to consider the concept of negotiation that Raymond Williams uses profitably in addressing hegemony:

> The reality of any hegemony, in the extended political and cultural sense, is that, while by definition it is always dominant, it is never either total or exclusive. At any time, forms of alternative or directly oppositional politics and culture exist as significant elements in the society. We shall need to explore their conditions and their limits, but their active presence is decisive, not only because they have to be included in any historical . . . analysis, but as forms which have had significant effect on the hegemonic process itself.[36]

Williams, like Bakhtin, suggests that both partners in the act of assimilation have something to say about the transaction; hegemony is not necessarily part and parcel of the act. Nonetheless, the relationship between assimilation and hegemony remains a charged one, and I will address that relationship at several points presently.

The methodological problem with Bakhtin's dialogism is simply stated: How does one accurately describe or do measurement in a system in which a speaker/producer is allowed intent but only with the understanding that the intent may not count for anything, in which a respondent/audience is granted activity but an activity that is not predictable in strength or direction, in which the message/text itself is bounced around other messages — personal, social, cultural, historical — of which either party may or may not be aware? And how does one bring such a model, which is based on individual communication patterns of dialogue, to a discussion of mass communication, much less mass communication that spans cultures?

One answer, particularly appropriate for the topic at hand, can be found in the work of British scholars Tony Bennett and Janet Woollacott, whose *Bond and Beyond: The Political Career of a Popular Hero* is almost Bakhtinian in its effort to consider the many utterances that shape dialogue and inflect meanings of a given text. Bennett and Woollacott base their study of James Bond on the notion that fictional forms such as "007" must somehow connect with popular experience. Understanding those forms through analyses, whether based on traditional aesthetics, cultural imperialism, or active audiences, that presume a single, immutable message/text from which meanings spring fails to speak appropriately to the social and ideological relations in which people live and apprehend those messages/texts. Instead, Bennett and Woollacott argue, the best way to understand the relationship between texts and their audiences is through what they call "reading formations":

> By reading formations here, we have in mind . . . those specific determinations which bear in upon, mold and configure the relations between texts and readers in determinant conditions of reading. It refers, specifically, to the *inter-textual relations which prevail in a specific context,* thereby activating a given body of texts by ordering the relations between them in a specific way such that their reading is always-already cued in specific directions . . . not given by those "texts themselves" as entities separable from such relations.[37]

The reading formation, in essence, produces both the text and the reader. Meaning can come only out of "intertextuality," which Bennett and Woollacott define as the relation between texts and readers in specific cultural and historical contexts. This is not, they argue, "so much a question of reducing text to context as an attempt to rethink the concept of context such that, ultimately, neither text nor context are conceivable as entities separable from one another."[38] To bring their theory into practice, Bennett and Woollacott use sales charts, marketing devices, reviews and interviews in the popular press, political history, genre analysis, and the books and films themselves to present the historical development of James Bond from the mid-1950s to 1980—a development that I consider in some detail in Chapters 2 and 3. In showing the differing constructions of James Bond at different times, Bennett and Woollacott present their subject as "a variable and mobile signifier," one that changes according to "the different sets of ideological and cultural concerns that figure [serves] to coordinate."[39]

Clearly, an understanding of the relationship between text and reader based on the ideological and cultural concerns surrounding both has great relevance to the transfer of texts from one culture to another. Indeed, the concept of the "mobile signifier" is directly applicable to transnational communication. Whereas Bennett and Woollacott present the mobility of "James Bond" in time, "James Bond" is no less mobile in space. They hint at this themselves by discussing the responses in other countries—the ways in which Bond is "assimilated"—following the release and export of the Bond films.[40] Whereas Schiller's thesis might see those developments as exemplary of British (or Anglo-American) cultural imperialism, an approach based on Bennett and Woollacott's ideas sees Bond not as (simply) a container of corporate capitalist ideology but as part of a complex relationship between text and audience defined by specific and determinant elements of the histories and cultures of those societies Bond entered in the early 1960s. And as the mobile signifier of "James Bond" suggests, perhaps the most interesting and complex of those relationships at the time was the one between Britain and the United States.

A Special Relationship

Although Bond, the Beatles, and the "swinging London" phenomenon in film, fashion, and art suggested briefly in the 1960s that Britain was the dominant partner in a cultural relationship with the United States, the period in that relationship from the end of World War II to the ascension of John Kennedy might seem at first to typify American cultural imperialism. Christopher Booker, writing in 1969, cited the "extraordinary sensitivity of the British to American 'imagery' " in the 1950s and 1960s, a sensitivity that gave rise to charges of the "Americanization" of Great Britain.[41] Even popular British imports to the United States could be seen as by-products of Americanization: British remaking and remarketing of American genres that had already made their way to Britain, frequently with the assistance of American money.[42] That this criticism downplayed the role of Britain's own heritage in popular literature, music, and film, as well as the significant gatekeeping role played by media organizations such as the BBC in holding American influence to a minimum, suggests the mythic dimensions of Americanization in crystallizing British hopes, fears, and confusions about Britain's place in the world after the horrors of World War II and the dissolution of its own empire.[43] Indeed, as Dick Hebdige and Dominic Strinati have argued, the American influence on British culture during the 1950s and 1960s was something assimilated in different ways by different groups, with young, working-class males in particular using American cultural artifacts to fill voids in their own social and cultural experience. The American influence was also accompanied by an influence in design and style from continental Europe, especially Italy, that was never countenanced as a new form of colonization.[44]

Similarly, the myth of Americanization, like the myth of cultural imperialism, has managed to obfuscate the sensitivity of Americans to British "imagery" in the 1950s and 1960s prior to the arrival of James Bond and the Beatles. Christopher Booker himself suggests that for whatever influences America may have had on Britain in that period, the cultural histories of the two nations move in not overlapping but parallel lines through everything from the emergence of rock and roll to student protests.[45] These lines extend across the Atlantic as well, with British imports coming to occupy a space in the United States during the Eisenhower and Kennedy years perhaps not as large but in some ways just as significant as that occupied by American exports in Britain.

As Whitman's concerns of the 1850s might suggest, it was literature and drama from Britain that exerted the most direct and interesting influence in the United States a century later. A British presence virtually defined American musical theater in the latter half of the 1950s, with Lerner and Loewe's *My Fair Lady* and *Camelot* presenting an idealized British past and the Bernstein-Sondheim *West Side Story* giving Shakespeare's *Romeo and Juliet* contemporary American faces and voices. The most curious, if not most direct, instance of the British influence, however, came in the furor surrounding D. H. Lawrence's 1928 novel *Lady Chatterley's Lover.* The extramarital affair at the core of the novel and Lawrence's frank sexual language had been bowdlerized in American editions prior to 1959, when Grove Press published an unexpurgated version of the text. Claiming that both the book itself and book club circulars advertising its availability were obscene material, U.S. Postmaster General Arthur Summerfield in April 1959 ordered the seizure of copies that had been mailed to retailers and forbade any further mailings of *Lady Chatterley* or any promotional material concerning its publication. Grove Press and Readers' Subscription book club filed a lawsuit against the U.S. Post Office, which they won in July 1959.[46] The publicity surrounding the case, however, resulted in a rush for the book, which sold some two hundred thousand copies between July and October of that year.[47]

American intellectuals read the *Chatterley* controversy as revealing the denatured quality of modern life, the mechanized structures of which had stripped passion, to say nothing of physical nature itself, from everyday American experience. "Lawrence's exultant, almost unbearably sensitive descriptions of the countryside can mean little to Americans, for whom the neighborhood of love must be the bathroom and the bedroom, both the last word in sophisticated privacy," wrote Alfred Kazin in his effort to shape an understanding of the British work for the audience of the *Atlantic Monthly*.[48] That much of the American interest in the book could be defined quite simply as that of an educated class with an officially forbidden treatment of sex by a noted author, something not necessarily confined to given national borders, was lost in the *petit mort* meditations on passion and American society. A similar controversy surrounding *Lady Chatterley* and British obscenity laws in 1960, ending with similar results, indicated the parallel concerns in the two cultures; Christopher Booker would note that the *Chatterley* cases "marked the emergence on both sides of the Atlantic of the same new 'permissive' moral climate."[49]

The issues American critics raised concerning *Lady Chatterley's Lover,* however, had also been raised in the American responses to a group of British writers earlier in the decade.[50] Lumped together in 1956 by the British press as the "Angry Young Men," novelists Kingsley Amis, John Braine, Alan Sillitoe, and Colin Wilson and playwright John Osborne, among others, shared really only their maleness, their youth, and their dissatisfaction with the status quo in Britain—a dissatisfaction that encompassed as many sources and as many solutions as there were writers to present them. Like their counterparts labeled "beats" in the United States, however, their general "dissentience" and the fervor with which they presented it enraged establishment critics and thrilled those who shared their unhappiness—particularly those in the educated, upper middle class.[51] It was the production of Osborne's play *Look Back in Anger,* an excoriation of the British class hierarchy and everything associated with it, that brought the movement its name in Britain; it was the New York production of that play in 1957, with the London cast and director Tony Richardson, that brought the Angry Young Men to America.

Again, the question of how British the British really were was raised in Osborne's interviews with the *New York Times,* in which he readily acknowledged the influence of Americans Arthur Miller and Tennessee Williams on his writing and the "professionalism and polish" of American films on his vision of the theater.[52] Although even Osborne's prototypical "angry" British play might be seen by some to fall into the embrace of Americanization, American theater critics, establishing a precedent that would be followed soon by television critics, were united in their understanding of *Look Back in Anger* as a definitively British work. Brooks Atkinson, writing in the *New York Times,* said that Osborne "has put into words an almost inarticulate point of view about the condition of British society today. For that specific reason the play is closer to the British than to us."[53] The critic for *Time* wrote that the play "jabbed some good spring cactus into the aspidistra drama of the English stage; on the other hand, it alarmingly echoed a new generation's call to disorder in English life."[54] And Harold Clurman in *The Nation* asked: "What is [protagonist Jimmy Porter] angry about? It is a little difficult at first for an American to understand. The English understand, not because it is ever explicitly stated, but because the jitters which wrack Jimmy... are in the very air the Englishman breathes."[55] While acknowledging the significant differences present in the British work, American critics were also curiously united in understanding what and for whom the play spoke: "the so-called 'working class intellectuals,' men who are given new teeth and a free education but nowhere to go," as David Dempsey wrote.[56] Given that Osborne himself had never attended university, this attempt to make *Look Back in Anger* understandable to American readers revealed more about the critics, their audiences, and the intended audiences of the play (as well as audiences in Britain) than about the work itself—something that would soon be seen again in American critical appraisals of British television. That commentary, however, also demonstrated how critical responses served as utterances helping shape an American apprehension of artifacts imported from another culture.

The cachet of the Angry Young Man readily carried itself from imported British drama and literature to film as well. Although the film version of *Look Back in Anger,* which deliberately opened itself up to an American audience by bringing jazz, racial prejudice, and Hollywood star Richard Burton into Osborne's play, failed to impress even American critics who liked the play, the screen adaptation of John Braine's 1957 novel *Room at the Top* fared exceedingly well, making a profit at the box office and collecting two Academy Awards in 1960. As was the case with Osborne's play, the critical response to the film spoke to its relevance for Britain; as *Newsweek*'s critic wrote: "[The film is] the first top-drawer British picture in a long time which presents British life as it is lived today rather than during England's finest hour or back in medieval times.... with *Room at the Top,* England enters the realm of topical films of social significance."[57] As Alexander Walker notes, however, that popular and critical reception came in large part as a result of utterances common to American culture. The hero of the book and film was a familiar representative of social mobility that, while more or less novel in the British class hierarchy, was little more than Jay Gatsby with a Yorkshire accent. At the same time, the rough-hewn masculinity represented in Laurence Harvey's character of Joe Lampton spoke to the burgeoning youth movement in American films, in which rebellious young men portrayed by Marlon Brando and James Dean earlier in the decade had already taken on iconic proportions. The sexuality of the film, which was released a month before the *Lady Chatterley* furor began, also proved to be an element attracting American viewers, Walker argues, in part because of its taboo-threatening frankness and in part because representations of virile men who themselves were threatened by the spiritual needs and/or physical desires of the women around them were hardly dangerous to American norms of the day (to say nothing of norms established by the Angry Young Men).[58] As *New York Times* critic A. J. Weiler summed up its American appeal, "Although [the film] takes place 3,000 miles away, it is as close to home as a shattered dream, a broken love affair or a man seeking to make life more rewarding in an uneasy world."[59]

The American success of *Room at the Top* led to the import and critical, if not popular, success of similar "kitchen sink" dramas—*Saturday Night and Sunday Morning, The Loneliness of the Long-Distance Runner, This Sporting Life*—dealing with angry young men trying to rise socially and score sexually in the moribund, repressive class hierarchy of postwar Britain. Based on works by such Angry Generation authors as Alan Sillitoe and David Storey, a number of those films were also produced by Woodfall Films, a company created by John Osborne and *Look Back in Anger* director Tony Richardson. The apotheosis of their work in Britain and the United States came with the 1963 adaptation of Henry Fielding's novel *Tom Jones,* scripted by Osborne and directed by Richardson, with a star—Albert Finney—already characterized for American audiences by one critic as possessing, in *Saturday Night and Sunday Morning,* "the humming animal vitality of Brando and the compelling abrasiveness of the young Cagney."[60] Adherents to the myth of cultural imperialism might point to the enormous success of *Tom Jones* in the United States, where it drew sizable audiences and won Academy Awards for best picture, best screenplay, and best director, as the result of American funding.[61] What is more important in that success, however, is the way in which what seemed on the surface to be an impenetrable eighteenth-century costume drama became accessible through utterances of class mobility, youth, and sexuality that had guided the American reception of the earlier books, plays, and films, topped off this time with bawdy physical humor. Although its comic elements had more to do with the slapstick of Chaplin and Keaton than with the verbal jests of *The Goon Show* or *Beyond the Fringe, Tom Jones* served as notice both that Americans were becoming increasingly familiar with British humor (a topic explored more thoroughly in Chapter 5) and that the sullen reactive anger of the late 1950s was transforming itself into a more joyful and active rebellion against the status quo.

Those same utterances acted, finally, to shape the arrival in late 1963 of the most public cultural transfer from Britain to the United States during the decade: the Beatles. Once more, the anxiety of American influence could be brought to bear on a British rock and roll band whose repertoire included songs by Little Richard, Chuck Berry, Carl Perkins, and Elvis; *Time,* in its first article on the group, published one month after the release of *Tom Jones* and one week before the assassination of President John F. Kennedy, noted that "Americans might find the Beatles achingly familiar."[62] Still, efforts to break the Beatles in the United States had at that time proved fruitless. Within three months, however, the Beatles were at the top of record charts, on the front pages of newspapers around the country, and genuine television stars following their appearance on *The Ed Sullivan Show.* "The one word that teenagers use over and over to describe them is 'different,' " *Time* commented in its feature article following the *Sullivan* performance, a "difference" that, like the acclaim for *Tom Jones* and the growing popularity of spy film hero James Bond, seemed to be connected directly with the Beatles' British origin — and inflected by the Kennedy assassination, an "utterance" the significance of which I will examine at greater length presently.[63]

With *Tom Jones,* the Beatles, and Bond leading the way, the British presence in the United States transformed itself from the dour miasma of the 1950s Midlands kitchen sink to swinging 1960s London, with British music, films, art, photography, plays, and fashion taking on a presence in American culture unprecedented in the twentieth century. Signifiers of youth, sexuality, and rejection of the status quo that had been seen as negative and angry earlier had become valorized during the Kennedy years; thus mobilized, they redefined British cultural imports for young, rebellious, and openly sexual Americans as desirable commodities: How else to explain the availability of a cologne for men called Pub? And while the importance of American corporate interests in marketing and, arguably, manufacturing those imports is clear, what is equally clear is that the audiences for those imports saw — and were told to see — them as artifacts at least somewhat different from what American culture had to offer. That would be the case for British television in the 1960s as well; a British presence on American television, however, had already quietly helped nurture the medium through its infancy.

Quality Time

One might plausibly chart the beginning of the British relationship with American television from the coronation of Queen Elizabeth on June 2, 1953, an event that saw the three major American networks (and the Canadian Broadcasting Corporation) involved in an almost comic air race from London to New York in an effort to be the first to show the proceedings to the American public.[64] That event, however, followed by almost five years the actual initiation of that relationship: the U.S. Supreme Court's 1948 *United States v. Paramount* decision. With the court mandating the breakup of the Hollywood studio system, the necessity of a relationship between the film industry and the upstart televisual medium became clear almost immediately. B-picture studios such as Republic and Monogram saw the number of hours available in the television market and realized that there was money to be made in opening their catalogs to local stations, which needed programming to generate ad sales.[65] After a short time, United Artists, Universal, and Paramount began leasing their older (and mostly lesser) films to broadcast outlets as well.[66] The dubious quality of many of the American films made available to television, however, and the voracity of local stations for the revenue available from running time-consuming movies helped create a niche for films created outside the industrial confines of Hollywood, a niche ideally suited for British films. The history of British films in the American theatrical market had been spotty at best, leading to a distribution pattern that left them out of the urban areas in which they might be expected to succeed; the opening of the television market, however, neatly reversed that pattern. British film magnate J. Arthur Rank saw this as an opportunity to act upon his belief in a profitable liaison between film and television by making a number of British movies available to American television stations. Meanwhile, American distributors who had handled British films in their American theatrical releases — most prominently United Artists, where renowned British producer-director Alexander Korda had once served on the board — found that those British offerings fit precisely the requirements for television release: small box-office grosses and pre-1948 playdates. This series of coincidences led to a television British ur-invasion, in which as much as 25 percent of the feature films presented on American television during the period 1948–52 were British in origin.[67] Even as late as 1956, Rank Organization imports accounted for 16 percent of the feature films shown on American television stations.[68]

The textual content of many of those films, which included historical and/or literary costume dramas (*The Private Life of Henry VIII, The Private Life of Don Juan*), Sherlock Holmes mysteries (*Murder at the Baskervilles, Study in Scarlet*), and adventures in empire (*The Four Feathers, Drums*), spoke of a rich and at times glorious past in which class, in all of its economic, social, and cultural connotations, won the day with wit, grace, and elegance. But with British movies being distributed to—or dumped upon—individual stations that could show them at any time of day or night, and with the often brutal cutting done both to add commercials and to fit the whole product into an arbitrary sixty- or ninety-minute time slot, it becomes difficult to suggest what meanings audiences of the time might have constructed from them, or to suggest what influence they might have had on American culture. In fall 1952, however, a British presence on American television spread from local stations to network broadcasting, as CBS's experimental magazine show *Omnibus* made its debut with Alistair Cooke as its host.

Cooke stands as an early example of the Bakhtinian processes of assimilation as they can be viewed in American television. A graduate student at Harvard and Yale during the early 1930s and a journalist whose BBC reports from the States during World War II had earned him attention and praise on both sides of the Atlantic, Cooke had in fact been an American citizen for eleven years when *Omnibus* went on the air. Nonetheless, the construction of "the text of Cooke" for his introduction to an American television audience foregrounded his Britishness in a discourse of difference that was both verbal and visual. A 1952 *Life* profile describes Cooke as "a witty, urbane ex-Englishman" whose "insight into the American scene has been so penetrating that he was recently given the Peabody Award." In the accompanying photos Cooke is shown, wearing a dapper Palm Beach suit, looking at gravestones "for an essay on colonial history" and talking to a Manhattan newspaper stand proprietor to learn "the man-in-the-street view."[69] Similarly, a 1953 *Newsweek* profile begins with an account of his BBC career and his accent, "which Britons consider American and Americans British." The article goes on to present Cooke as an elegant paragon of Popeian wit, noting his "carefully dressed" style on *Omnibus* and quoting Robert Saudek, director of the Ford Foundation Television-Radio Workshop, as saying that Cooke "has the intelligence, the urbanity and the curiosity that we want the show to have."[70]

This public construction of "Alistair Cooke" serves as another clear example of the processes of intertextuality, following Bennett and Woollacott's description of the same with James Bond: "[a text] produced in the constantly changing relations between a wide range of texts brought into association with one another via the functioning of Bond as the signifier[s] they have jointly constructed."[71] The magazine articles on Cooke produce those figures out of specific historical and cultural signifiers—Cooke's Cambridge and Ivy League education, his journalistic service in World War II—placed within a specific historical and cultural context: the development of American commercial television. Among those texts brought into association with each other in the case of Cooke, however, are ones that point out and exaggerate their differences from American norms: physical appearance, verbal facility, and—most important—British origin. The construction of Cooke as an Englishman abroad, as a result, is not simply different from those norms—it is superior. Cooke is gifted with "wit," "urbanity," and "insight" that the "man in the street" cannot possibly possess; he is the very model of a modern intellectual.

The association of Britain with signifiers of superiority embodied in Alistair Cooke speaks as well to Jane Feuer's discussion of "quality TV" in her analysis of the work done in the 1970s and 1980s by the MTM studio. Suggesting a relationship with a "quality" audience—upwardly mobile, professional, urban, and primarily white viewers—as well as the mass audience needed to win the ratings desired by both sponsor and network, quality TV as represented by such MTM shows as *The Mary Tyler Moore Show, Lou Grant,* and *Hill Street Blues* presents "a form of television... seen as more literate, more stylistically complex and more psychologically 'deep' than ordinary TV fare."[72] I will consider this definition of "quality TV" and its significance in greater depth in the discussion of British imports and American public television in Chapter 4; at this point, it is sufficient to note that it can be seen at work here in the image crafted for both the American *Omnibus* and its British host. Indeed, as Walt Whitman pointed out in 1856, the American concept of a "quality" cultural artifact as being one somehow connected to Britain long predates the arrival of television, much less MTM or PBS. As Matthew Arnold had summoned Hellenic art, whose power lay in its "fidelity to nature—the *best* nature—and on a delicate discrimination of what this best nature is," to bring sweetness and light to industrial nineteenth-century British culture, so Americans had turned to their linguistic forebears in England to lift them up from the horrific world around them from the time of the Puritans on.[73] Television was merely the newest frontier in which a cultivated British sensibility might help civilize the wilderness.

This configuration of "British as better" would continue to be developed as one of the vectors through which British television would come to be a part of the American video landscape by another source new to the industry in 1952–53. The magazine *TV Guide* in its formative years developed what Glenn Altschuler and David Grossvogel call "a vision of powerful and discerning viewers practicing dialsmanship."[74] American television, *TV Guide* founder and publisher Walter Annenberg and editor Merrill Panitt believed, offered a variety of choices; viewers from this democratic vista had the ability to select the best of what was available. Toward that end, however, their magazine championed the networks' "cultural" programming—plays, opera, concerts, as well as documentaries and educational programming, and, of course, *Omnibus*—often at the expense of the 1950s cultural critics who claimed that television was debasing and threatening.[75]

The magazine's attitude during its first decade toward British television per se was ambivalent. Annenberg and Panitt were highly suspicious of the "state-run" nature of the BBC, which denied the democratic potential of dialsmanship in its structure and its programming. A 1962 editorial on the Pilkington Report, an independent British study that attacked the vapid (and "American") programming of the British commercial network and argued for the establishment of a second BBC television outlet, concluded with a succinct argument for the development of an American system that offered more than the narrowly focused "uplift" defining BBC programs:

> How can [American broadcasters], under our system of free enterprise, live up to their responsibilities to us: to give us what the majority of us want and still give us what we deserve, which is the very best in programs of all types. Not pure entertainment, not all pure uplift, but an intelligent, carefully planned balance that will brighten our lives and nourish our minds.[76]

Despite its characterization of and concern over the BBC model of television, *TV Guide* immediately praised British commercial products when they first appeared in the United States in 1955. Imported as part of CBS's effort to present a "children's hour" between 7:30 and 8:00 p.m. each weeknight, *The Adventures of Robin Hood,* with its stories of heroes, heroines, and villains familiar to vast numbers of Americans, was a cheap buy for the American network and a needed source of income for its British exporter.[77] In *TV Guide, Robin Hood* came off as a blessing compared to standard kids' fare: "*Robin Hood,* as produced in England, could very well be the answer to a mother's prayer about Westerns, as produced in Hollywood. Appealing to both children and adults, this CBS show . . . comes as a welcome relief from the 'they-went-thataway' school of 'children's hour' programming."[78] Similarly, when NBC imported *The Adventures of Sir Lancelot* the following year, *TV Guide* praised it as a "fine combination of charm, swash-buckle and literacy." As with *Robin Hood*, the magazine contextualized the British import by noting that "the stories are not very different from our own Western yarns—good triumphs over evil." In an almost comical version of a British-as-better commentary, however, it also praised the locution of the cast: "It is such a relief to hear proper English properly spoken."[79]

Already by 1956, a discourse in which television programs "produced in England" were better than "standard fare ... produced in Hollywood" was being conducted in the pages of the single national publication devoted to American television. That discourse would develop throughout the 1960s in features on popular British programming and profiles of British stars by Robert Musel, as well as in the reviews of Cleveland Amory, who seemed never to meet a British accent he didn't think was worthy of an Emmy. The editorial stance of *TV Guide* continued the pattern, with the skepticism of the 1950s and early 1960s replaced by the middle of the decade with a respect for the secret agent imports, whose "invasion" was seen cheekily as comeuppance for the many and varied inferior American programs exported to Britain.[80] Even the early querulous criticism of the BBC was gone by the end of the 1960s: in the August 9, 1969, issue, *TV Guide* praised British television in its entirety for everything from picture quality to performance. "We should envy the British their prime time program balance," the editorial concluded. "It's what we need more than anything else."[81]

Although *TV Guide*'s initial praise of the 1950s adventure-costume dramas speaks to the cultural dimension of the arrival of British television on American shores, those imports can also be explained in terms of the political economics guiding the myth of cultural imperialism. British producers and their commercial television system gain needed funds through export sales; American sponsors and networks save money by purchasing preproduced programming. Those sales also provide economic validity to the new technology of video employed by both broadcasting systems. Although it is possible to see British commercial television itself, to say nothing of its American imports, as part of the process of Americanization, a British presence on American television can be explained in the same terms with which Nordenstreng and Varis define American cultural imperialism: American distributors control the global market by dumping preproduced programming into markets that cannot afford to produce their own; in so doing, they also define the technology necessary for those markets to make their own television programs.[82] Conversely, the mid-1950s British presence can also be seen to support the cultural discount side of the political economy debate, as *Robin Hood* and *Lancelot* both were shows that employed characters familiar to an American audience, presented them in a narrative form (the Western) also familiar to those audiences, and did so using "proper English properly spoken."

No matter how much influence American television may have exerted in the establishment of commercial broadcasting in Britain, however, *Robin Hood* and its fellow imports were presented to and perceived by American audiences as British. The United States did not possess medieval castles; Americans did not speak with those accents. And however proximate elements of the 1950s British shows may have been, they were also contained within an American political and ideological context that presented a significant "dialogical turn" to their reception. *Robin Hood* arrived in the United States at the moment in which the anti-Communist fervor of the McCarthy years was passing in what historians Douglas Miller and Marion Nowak would call "the era of conservative consensus."[83] Whatever problems may have existed in American society were pushed to the back of the collective consciousness in order to celebrate what seemed a golden age of peace and prosperity. That shift was visible in television programming, particularly at CBS: in its replacement of Edward R. Murrow's news/documentary series *See It Now* with *The $64,000 Question*; in its establishment of a "children's hour" that also moved the network news out of key evening viewing hours.[84] As potentially critical reporting and commentary began to fade quietly from American prime-time television, stories of knights and maidens and Merry Men from long ago and far away Britain, especially stories connoted as superior to what was being produced in the United States, served as worthy diversions from social and political problems of the day—a harbinger, as it would turn out, of British imports and American public broadcasting to come.

Although this first wave of British programming was short-lived, it demonstrated that 1950s American television, like American theater, literature, and film, was able and willing to open channels to Britain. Those channels might be defined and dominated by American interests, but the first television arrivals from Britain nonetheless offered something very different from a vision of an American way of life, especially in the way those imports, from Alistair Cooke to Sir Lancelot, were constructed by American media. However strongly those British imports might be classified as the products of either economic domination or natural economic processes, the fact remained that they encountered and were shaped by American social, political, cultural, and economic utterances that gave them a meaning—or meanings—superseding their existence as objects of trade. As those utterances acted to define British artifacts to an American public, questions concerning the nature of assimilation, dominance, and hegemony within a culture as well as without began to come to the fore. The import of British spy series accompanying the American success of James Bond would bring those issues into sharper focus, as they addressed the same hopes, fears, and confusions that Herbert Schiller crystallized in the myth of cultural imperialism. At the same time, they would open a dialogue into a particularly Whitmanian question: What payment would prevail as America again encountered an "English flow," perhaps not huge, but evidently sweet and assuredly undeniable?

2. Danger Men
Secret Agent and The Prisoner

I think the President likes my books because he enjoys the combination of physical violence, effort and winning in the end.

— Ian Fleming[1]

Drake is basically good, is unarmed, never kills and never has promiscuous relationships. Bond, I think, is a sort of cartoon-strip fantasy, with morals I find questionable.

— Patrick McGoohan[2]

Although on the surface a textbook case of political economics at work, the arrival of British television in the United States during the early 1960s represented a field of shifting and complicated cultural relationships typifying Bakhtinian dialogue. The British side of that dialogue developed as producers in the United Kingdom sought to take advantage of a burgeoning transnational trade in television programming. One of those producers, Lew Grade, hoped to make his fortune in the United States by giving American audiences British programming unrecognizable as such: shows that employed American actors, accents, and settings but that were produced in Britain, with American revenues returning to fund further production.[3] Grade's transatlantic strategy worked in industrial and economic terms; in terms of viewership, however, it fared less well. Only three of Grade's prime-time series — *The Saint, Secret Agent,* and *The Prisoner* — attracted interest enough to impress their American distributors. And that interest came less from Grade's formula than from another British import, spy hero James Bond.

The popularity of Bond in the United States, however, addressed specific historical and ideological concerns also embodied by an American given heroic trappings: President John F. Kennedy. Indeed, Bond's place in American culture was set by an endorsement from Kennedy that transcended national boundaries in ideologically linking the two figures, one barely more fictional than the other. Kennedy's assassination in turn brought to the fore the conspiratorial dangers of the world in which Bond worked, elevating both his heroism in triumphing over those dangers and the horrific nature of that world.

What started as an apparently simple economic deal to bring British television to the United States, in other words, turned out to be a complex transaction of meaning, with social, political, and historical utterances—including the element of difference itself—shifting that meaning from moment to moment. It was a dialogue the result of which could not have been predicted when it began, with the cherry blossoms unfolding on the banks of the Potomac in the first spring of America's Camelot.

Grade-A TV

On April 5, 1961, ten weeks after John F. Kennedy's inaugural address, CBS broadcast the first episode of a new British series that replaced the Western *Wanted: Dead or Alive*. *Danger Man,* unlike its British predecessors, was both of and in the modern world: "Patrick McGoohan stars in this half-hour filmed series as NATO special investigator John Drake, whose assignments take him all over the world," read the *TV Guide* description of the series.[4] Created in 1960 by Ralph Smart, who had worked on many of the British costume dramas exported to American television during the 1950s, *Danger Man* combined the action and adventure of those historical series with the thoroughly modern character of the secret agent. John Drake, like Robin Hood and Lancelot of old, traveled from scenic locale to scenic locale, encountering and besting villains ranging from IRA terrorists to brilliant master spies to Sicilian bandits to Communists, usually in a thrilling *mano a mano* fight. Instead of fabled swords or bows and arrows, Drake employed fabulous technological gadgetry in his conquests of evil. There were the occasional beautiful and grateful damsels as well, but for Drake, work always came first, even if there was no Marian or Guinevere waiting back home.[5] Explicitly compared by Smart and the show's other British producers to Ian Fleming's James Bond character, with many episodes borrowing elements directly from Fleming's work, *Danger Man* entered the American market with no such context.[6] Instead, the show's publicity foregrounded its Cold War elements, which allowed for the development of the character as a rugged individual hero, working within and without a bureaucracy, familiar to American audiences from Western and detective novels, movies, and television series.[7]

Although John Kennedy may not have played a signifying role in the arrival of this British series, another forceful and impressive presence most certainly did. Lew Grade, deputy managing director of the commercial broadcasting company Associated TeleVision (ATV), was coming to personify the British commercial television industry in a way that no single figure could the American broadcasting system. One of the foremost proponents of television exports, Grade launched a subsidiary company—Incorporated Television Company (ITC)—to handle overseas sales of ATV programs, including *Danger Man*. Overseas for Grade meant in particular the United States, which could provide money others could not, and which would in turn help fund British (i.e., ATV's) commercial production. *Danger Man*, with its overt referencing of East-West tensions and detective fiction conventions, as well as some rock'em, sock'em violence, represented an effort by Grade to ameliorate British accents and exotic foreign locations with elements addressed specifically to American audiences.[8] In a sense, Grade was willing to assist the American television industry in its absorption and domestication of his own work.

Even so, *Danger Man* came and went in six months with barely a trace, bringing to an apparently quick end the new British presence on American prime-time television.[9] But Grade was not about to give up on the American market. In 1962, having gained full control of ATV, he brought British actor Roger Moore, known to Americans as James Garner's replacement on *Maverick,* back to the United Kingdom to star in *The Saint,* a series based on the adventures of roguish detective Simon Templar, already familiar to American audiences from Leslie Charteris's books and a series of movies released in the 1930s and 1940s. ITC began syndicating the show the following year in a number of American markets, where it performed well enough to be picked up by NBC for three half-season runs (1967–69).[10] Grade's deliberate inclusion of structural elements in British programs that spoke to audiences in the United States increased as the decade progressed. His programs *The Baron* (ABC, 1966), *Court-Martial* (ABC, 1966), *Man in a Suitcase* (ABC, 1968), and *The Champions* (NBC, 1968) each offered a new take on the international agent working for the forces of good. Rather than the British protagonists and foreign settings used in his early programs, however, Grade cast American actors as the leads in all of these series and added American locations to *The Baron*, a World War II setting to *Court-Martial,* and a superhero device to *The Champions* to make even more obvious appeals to American audiences. All three series were canceled in less than half a season.[11]

The mid-Atlantic approach, while garnering Grade and ATV the sales and dollars both needed, clearly had its limits in terms of popularity, as the relative success of *The Saint* showed. Grade's 1965 decision to reintroduce *Danger Man* to the American market further complicated the issue, as it brought together elements of British and American cultures in a more complex and meaningful way than the mid-Atlantic formula allowed. Retitled *Secret Agent,* the show in its very name addressed American viewers with signifiers of a new popular hero, British in origin, who in turn signified and reconfigured a lost popular hero, American in origin. In their new, more vocal response to John Drake, American audiences also responded to James Bond, who by 1965 meant much more than when *Danger Man* first arrived in the United States; in responding to Bond, those audiences also responded to the man who made Bond what he was in America: John F. Kennedy.

The President's Agent

Although it was not until the week after President John F. Kennedy was assassinated in 1963 that the appellation "Camelot" was applied to his administration, even at the time of his election, the "text of Kennedy" available to most Americans had assumed a mythic quality that Norman Mailer assessed during the 1960 campaign as that of "a hero America needed, a hero central to his time."[12] The links between the American president and the British ur-myth that would define him for the ages, however, had a concrete foundation in the circumstances of Kennedy's own life. With his father serving as Franklin Roosevelt's ambassador to Great Britain in the late 1930s, Kennedy, as one friend later reported, grew out of his "anti-British elements [his Boston Irish background] . . . by the end you couldn't have found a more British person." He then channeled the experience and contacts gained in England into his Harvard undergraduate thesis, quickly published as *Why England Slept.* A study of Britain's response to Hitler that was highly critical of the "appeasers" led by Neville Chamberlain, Kennedy's work became a best-seller on both sides of the Atlantic.[13]

To Americans in 1960, the British elements of the "text of Kennedy" were not nearly as significant as those of his "anti-British" background, due largely to the controversy over his Catholicism.[14] Kennedy's British ties would quickly reassert themselves, however, in his renewal of America's "special relationship" with Great Britain and his own friendship with Prime Minister Harold Macmillan.[15] It would also reassert itself soon enough in American popular culture, in which the president and his family fast assumed a remarkable prominence. The Kennedys became almost regular characters in prime-time programs, serving as reference points on situation comedies, as the topics of sketches on variety shows, and as the models for what Mary Ann Watson calls "New Frontier character dramas"—shows such as *Dr. Kildare, The Defenders,* and *Mr. Novak* that focused on young professionals dealing with social problems in ways that demanded breaks from the past.[16]

Kennedy's most significant immediate contribution to American popular culture, however, was not to television. The March 17, 1961, edition of *Life* featured a report from Hugh Sidey titled "The President's Voracious Reading Habits." The article included a list of the president's ten favorite books, a list dominated by political biographies, many of which were British. The list, however, included a novel that seemed most curious, given the company: *From Russia with Love*, by Ian Fleming.[17] The book was one in a series following the adventures of British secret agent James Bond, a man who enjoyed golf, a good martini, and the company of beautiful women as much as he did thwarting evildoers intent on taking over the world. Fleming had been writing Bond novels at the rate of one a year since the early 1950s, but his success had been marginal at best on both sides of the Atlantic — until 1961.[18]

Kennedy's mention of the Bond novel constituted a massive investment of cultural capital, to use Pierre Bourdieu's term, into Fleming's work — enough to legitimate the paperback writer to middle-class and educated American audiences. According to Bourdieu, culture and accompanying "distinctions" of taste are controlled as capital in a given society by those who acquire needed cultural knowledge through education or inherit it through social origin. Kennedy possessed both the education and the social origin to manifest a wealth of cultural capital.[19] By including on his list of historians and highbrow authors a little-read spy novelist, Kennedy employed that capital in a way Bourdieu calls "affective investment":

> When he moves, as if by instinct, towards what is, at each moment,
> the thing to be loved, like some businessmen who make money even
> when they are not trying to, he is not pursuing a cynical calculation,
> but his own pleasure, the sincere enthusiasm which, in such matters,
> is one of the preconditions of successful investment.[20]

That investment made the British secret agent and his creator suddenly accessible and acceptable to a much larger American audience than the genre devotees who might have been previously familiar with either. With the president's endorsement, James Bond and Ian Fleming joined touch football, pillbox hats, and the Boston-inflected "vig-ah" as part of the Kennedy aura surrounding and suffusing American popular culture.[21] Sales of Bond novels began to climb, a rise boosted by an even more fortuitous development: Fleming's sale of the film rights to his books to British producer Harry Saltzman. The sale culminated a decade's worth of effort by Fleming on both sides of the Atlantic; indeed, the first filmed Bond was not the cinema's *Dr. No,* but a one-hour version of *Casino Royale* shown on the CBS anthology series *Climax* in 1953–54.[22]

By the time *Dr. No* had its American premiere in 1963, however, Fleming had become a household name, at least in the households of those with cultural capital, due largely to his legitimation by Kennedy.[23] With the president paying for his induction, Fleming's Bond entered American culture at last, becoming a text in and of itself that would both acquire and provide various meanings within that culture. As sales of the books took off, Fleming's other stories began appearing on a regular basis in *Playboy* and other magazines. Meanwhile, the first Bond movies did brisk, if not overwhelming, business. *Dr. No,* made in 1962 and released in the United States in 1963, made two million dollars in North America, doubling its production costs. *From Russia with Love,* made in 1963 and released in 1964, doubled the profit of *Dr. No.*[24] But it was *Goldfinger,* the first Bond film to be made and released after the assassination of President Kennedy and the beginning of the Camelot myth, that would make James Bond a powerful "British" signifier in the United States.

From Britain with Love

In their study of the "career" of James Bond, Bennett and Woollacott define several "moments" at which Bond articulated cultural and ideological concerns in Britain, two of which bear closer scrutiny in an examination of Bond in the United States. The first, following the Suez crisis of 1956, saw Bond as a definitively British hero fighting and triumphing over definitively Russian/Communist villains, as well as a male hero triumphing in battle and in bed over female villains and/or heroines. In the second incarnation, built around the Bond films starring Sean Connery, Bond shed both his Cold Warrior mantle and his veneer of traditional British class to battle more ill-defined global sources of evil and, at times, the old-fashioned class ideals and mores of the British Establishment. And as Bond freed himself from outdated political and social norms, so he and "the Bond girl" freed themselves from established, repressed norms of sexuality — although the Bond girl's "freedom" was defined by Bond's needs and desires.[25]

Those two "moments" of Bond telescoped into one when Bond entered American culture. As Ian Fleming's frequent appearances in *Playboy* might indicate, the "modernized," unrepressed sexuality of the Bond books and films was a representation of shifting sexual mores in the United States as well as in Britain.[26] But although the sexuality of Bennett and Woollacott's second Bond could be read by most Americans as part of the "text of Bond" from his arrival, James Bond remained, even at his most anti-Establishmentarian and even with the imprimatur of John F. Kennedy, a resolutely British figure in the United States. Certainly references to the British Secret Service and British luxuries in both the books and the films contributed to this positioning of Bond as outsider; the jux-taposition of Bond to the helpful but lesser American CIA agent Felix Leiter in *Dr. No* contributed as well.[27] But these obvious British signifiers, Alexander Walker argues, were assisted in the American reception of Bond by the casting of Sean Connery in the films. Producers Broccoli and Saltzman wanted to avoid using a familiar face like David Niven or James Mason (Fleming's choices); in choosing the little-known Connery for the part, they also got a Scottish accent that on the one (British) hand worked entirely outside of specifically English class linguistic distinctions and on the other (American) hand avoided the already familiar mid-Atlantic accent of Niven or Mason.[28]

Just as the text of Bond retained qualities of a British national character in America that Bennett and Woollacott see it losing in Britain, so it retained its Cold War elements. Two of the first three films — *Dr. No* and *Goldfinger* — rep-resented the United States as the target of foreign madmen associated with Cen-tral and Eastern European powers; the plot of *Dr. No* bore an eerie resemblance to the 1962 Cuban missile crisis, which preceded its American release by a matter of weeks. The third film, *From Russia with Love,* was, as already noted, Flem-ing's most blatant representation of Soviet-West tensions. In a 1963 *Saturday Evening Post* profile of Fleming, Geoffrey Bocca praised the author for his per-spicacity in pinning down many of the specifics of the Cold War before they happened: "We know now that the Russians *do* build missile bases in nearby Caribbean islands (*Doctor No*). They *do* plot carefully to get beautiful girls into the beds of Allied agents (*From Russia With Love*). Fleming said it first."[29]

The East-West conflict still imbued in American constructions of James Bond took on an added dimension after the 1963 assassination of John F. Kennedy, however. The Warren Commission's official investigation of the assassination, re-leased in September 1964, failed to answer many of the most relevant questions about the shooting and instead led to a profusion of conspiracy theories. The "trauma" created by the assassination was not healed by the investigation but rather opened up and left to bleed yet again.[30] This kind of trauma, John Cawelti and Bruce Rosenberg suggest, both created and fed a public anxiety and personal alienation that "makes the figure of the spy so compelling as a contemporary everyman hero."[31] Cawelti and Rosenberg, in their readings of spy novels, argue that what they call "clandestinity" — the ability to act in secret, the need to be-come invisible to do so, and the eventual sense of isolation involved in both — speaks directly to fears and frustrations about the powers of bureaucracies and massive institutions, including foreign governments and alien ideologies, to con-trol people's lives.[32] According to their formulation, James Bond, the individual

agent who takes on and defeats global conspiratorial organizations, at times necessarily going beyond the authority and technology given him by the bureaucracy
of Her Majesty's Secret Service, directly addresses the concerns of an era defined
by an individual who used clandestine bureaucracies against opposing powers
and whose end seemed to come at the behest of any number of powerful and secret institutions.[33]

The connections Cawelti and Rosenberg make between the popularity of Bond
and the events of the Kennedy years are borne out in the exponential growth in
the popularity of Bond following the assassination of the president. At the end
of March 1965, *Goldfinger* had made $10.4 million in its fourteen-week release
in the United States, a record-breaking total and almost twice as much as the
first two Bond films put together. "No other film in memory . . . has ever performed
with such speed for such a volume," wrote Vincent Canby. "The social historians of the future may study the James Bond syndrome to try to figure out why
Goldfinger in this particular year of the 20th Century struck such a responsive
chord."[34]

Notes of that chord were struck not because James Bond, as Bennett and
Woollacott suggest, literally became an American agent to American audiences,
but because the "text of James Bond" had been so articulated to the "text of
John Kennedy" as to make of a British hero an American one.[35] The American
president's position within a moneyed, elite Establishment, as well as his firm
resolve against conspiratorial agencies of evil, particularly Communism, were
present in an American reading of Bond. That reading, however, particularly in
Sean Connery's embodiment of Bond, also included the charm, sexuality, and
youthful vigor—shown at times in a willingness to fight against elements of the
Establishment he represented—that had signified Kennedy to a great number of
Americans. Indeed, the figure of Bond in America, through its articulation to
Kennedy, came to typify Fredric Jameson's definition of the functioning of American mass culture. Jameson argues that for mass culture to imbricate its consumers in its ideological purposes, it must also present meanings that oppose
those ideological purposes, presenting a world as it should be, not as it is. Those
meanings are quite visible in Kennedy's Bond, who at one and the same time
represented the contemporary corporate nature of the power elite at work in the
Cold War and the older, idealistic notion of the active, attractive individual fighting alone against all manner of arrayed forces in service of a better world for all.[36]

With the events of Dallas 1963, however, the latter reading of the "text of
Kennedy" lost its immediate utopian function. Instead, it became purposefully
reconstructed as "Camelot"—a utopia irretrievably lost, a tragic legend with

specific British overtones. This in turn enabled the "text of Bond" in America to be reconfigured further along its utopian lines: the noble individualistic warrior fighting for a better world—who succeeds and doesn't die in the end. Bond became, in Kennedy's sudden absence, the "hero America needed." The ties between Kennedy and Bond and the boom in the popularity of the latter following the demise of the former suggest the development of a further element in the assimilation of British cultural artifacts into American society: difference itself. To follow Cawelti and Rosenberg's argument, cultural difference gained power during the national "trauma" of the Kennedy assassination, when other messages and meanings lacked the cohesiveness they would have in calmer times. Internal anxiety took precedence over the anxiety of influence, further opening the door for artifacts from other cultures—in this case, the culturally proximate Britain, with which the United States shared a language (if not a complete vocabulary) and with which social, cultural, and political ties had been strengthened during the Kennedy years.[37] With Bond, as with British popular music, fashion, and films, Americans after the death of Kennedy were willing to let "otherness" override the "our-own-ness" of traditional American cultural utterances. Difference, in short, became one of the "specific determinations" guiding the reception of British television by American audiences in the 1960s.

Bond and Beyond: The Tube

According to Bennett and Woollacott, the "second moment" of Bond included not just shifts in signifiers of nationalism and sexuality, but the development of signifiers of commodity and consumption.[38] Those signifiers were always present in Fleming's novels; part of the Bond fan culture of the 1960s included compilations of catalogs detailing Bond's brand-name choices in both the necessities and the luxuries of life.[39] The shift came, Bennett and Woollacott suggest, when Bond himself became a brand name and advertising slogan.[40] In the United States, the success of *Goldfinger* brought a plethora of Bond products onto the market, ranging from toys based on the technological gadgets in the films to a line of Colgate-Palmolive toiletries (including Bond deodorant) to 007 golfing sweaters and trench coats.[41]

This emphasis on product identification and the development of Bond as a commercial property came at the precise moment of a paradigm shift in the commercial structure of American television, from individual production sponsorship to network spot advertising sales.[42] By making individual sponsors relinquish control of their series, the networks increased the importance of ratings services. Advertisers, looking for the largest possible audiences, sought to spend their money in the places where they could get the most return for their dollars. The mass audience, as a result, itself became a commodity to advertisers. And as the prices of commodities varied in a free market according to supply and demand, so the prices of audiences began to vary in "free" television, with highly rated shows commanding higher advertising rates. With this grand commodification of television, however, came an increasing understanding that as various groups of consumers would choose products based upon the needs or desires of that group, so might advertisers choose audiences based upon their own needs and desires for sales. The Nielsen company during the 1960s configured new survey tools that could measure the age, gender, ethnic, geographic, and socioeconomic locations of viewers; by the end of the decade, both networks and advertisers were speaking of demographics as the concept defining the commercial practices of the medium for the foreseeable future.[43]

Into all these changes floated the figure of James Bond. The evolution of Bond mirrored the evolution of television from the mid-1950s to the mid-1960s, particularly in the television genre the Bond films came closest to representing—the crime show. In its early years a genre represented by the sturdy male cop (Joe Friday of *Dragnet,* Dan Matthews of *Highway Patrol*) or the vigilant private investigator (*Peter Gunn, Richard Diamond*) taking on and episodically vanquishing (individual) sources of disorder, the crime show took an interesting turn at the end of the 1950s and the beginning of the 1960s. Instead of lone heroes consumed by their need to serve law and protect order, a group of shows produced by Warner Bros. for ABC—*77 Sunset Strip, Hawaiian Eye, SurfSide 6, Bourbon Street Beat*—featured agencies, teams of young, hunky private eyes who lived in then-exotic Sun Belt locales, drove fast cars, hung with hip crowds, and made out with the chicks between their various adventures in bringing down evildoers.[44] The Warner-ABC shows brought many of the signifiers of the "text of Bond"—youth, (male) sexuality, the joys of creature comforts—to American television in advance of Bond's arrival in the movie theaters. That they failed to articulate the significant British difference of Bond, as well as a concern with bureaucracy and conspiracy, that comprised an American reading formation of 007 is perhaps best measured by the fact that all had been canceled by 1964, the year of *Goldfinger.*

The short-term success of these American predecessors to Bond, inflected by the growing fascination with Fleming's character during the Kennedy years, would necessarily attract the interest of American television producers, ever attentive to social and cultural changes that might be shaped into new shows.[45] So it was that Norman Felton, producer of the prototypical New Frontier drama *Dr.*

Kildare, approached Ian Fleming in 1963 to ask for his help in shaping a first script about an American secret agent. Fleming, ever entranced with the possibilities of American television, was enthusiastic about the project, giving Felton the name of a minor character from two of his novels—Solo—as well as his blessings in making a series pilot. The networks, still skeptical, showed no interest in the project. Felton, along with writer/producer Sam Rolfe, reworked the concept he and Fleming had developed, giving Solo a partner (curiously eliminating the signification of the name) and an agency, and giving the agency a secret, conspiratorial foe bent on subversion and world domination.

The result of their efforts was *The Man from U.N.C.L.E.,* which NBC first presented on September 22, 1964.[46] U.N.C.L.E.—United Network Command for Law and Enforcement—was apparently a post–Cold War secret organization trying to maintain détente and world peace. With its headquarters behind the facade of a Manhattan tailor shop, U.N.C.L.E. possessed technological marvels and an arsenal of advanced weaponry that would have done the CIA and Special Forces proud. Agent Solo, a proud American played by Robert Vaughn, worked with a Russian, Illya Kuryakin (Scottish actor David McCallum); both reported directly to British organization head Alexander Waverly (Leo G. Carroll), thereby maintaining an iconic "British" superiority in matters of international spying that Fleming's novels and the Bond films had already established. Their dialogue also retained the wisecracking bravado that marked Bond's encounters with those for and against whom he was working. Although several of the early shows featured rogue mad scientists and Stalin wanna-bes, eventually the men from U.N.C.L.E. were regularly pitted against a malevolent bureaucratic opposite. THRUSH was derived from Fleming's SPECTRE, a secret organization composed of villains from around the globe removed from the direct control of the Kremlin—an elevation from historic to mythic that Fleming and film producers Albert Broccoli and Harry Saltzman believed would serve them well in the world market.[47]

Norman Felton's reconstitution of Fleming's adventuresome and droll spy stories for American television soon followed James Bond into popular currency.[48] David McCallum, repeating the instant celebrity accorded countryman Connery, proved to be the breakout star of the series in the United States, with teenagers writing the producers for photographs (McCallum was regularly profiled in teen fan magazines) and posters of him becoming best-sellers.[49] Other commodification and product tie-ins followed, although these were aimed more at the juvenile market than was the Bondware sold to *Playboy* subscribers.[50] And, like the Bond books and films, *The Man from U.N.C.L.E.* moved from an overt representation of East-West conflict to other concerns—modernization, commodification—while retaining the notion that the world was divided into large, secretive institutions of Good and Evil, constantly pitched against each other, with the lives of billions held in the balance. SPECTRE and THRUSH may have been mythic organizations of evil, but they still contained a core utterance of a conspiratorial Other—Communism—that for many could not be inflected out of existence. As one Kansas mother wrote to *TV Guide,* "Our two teen-age sons have pictures of Mr. Vaughn and Mr. McCallum in their room along with those of Barry Goldwater and Dr. Wehrner von Braun."[51]

Although the Bond films and *The Man from U.N.C.L.E.* represented a shift in signification concerning American-Soviet confrontation, that shift was eradicated in the slew of programs that came along in 1965 that drew from the popularity of Bond and *U.N.C.L.E.* and recombined elements of their success with other texts. *The Wild, Wild West* sent its secret agent team back to the post-Civil War frontier, as employees of the U.S. Treasury Department. *I Spy* continued *U.N.C.L.E.*'s multiculturalism by replacing Russian good guy Illya Kuryakin with African American good guy Alexander Scott (played by young comic Bill Cosby), sending him and fellow agent Kelly Robinson around the world explicitly to do the work of the CIA. Even Amos Burke, the dapper lawyer protagonist of *Burke's Law,* in 1965 gave up his lucrative practice in order to do his patriotic chores as a U.S. government secret agent.[52] These American cousins of Bond represented an important twist in the process Roland Barthes defines as "ex-nomination": the power of the ruling cultural class to naturalize its status by leaving itself a nameless universal while naming competing ideologies (Communism, to use Barthes's own example) as threatening Others.[53] In the political climate of the United States in the years following the assassination of President Kennedy and marking the escalation of the war in Vietnam, that process had to be reversed. The secretive, bureaucratic institution fighting for Good had to be identified as such to differentiate it from bureaucratic institutions of Evil whose power derived from their abilities to disguise themselves—the power of Communism in the United States as defined in and since the McCarthy era.[54] In so doing, those shows literally brought the ideological programs of the Bond films and *The Man from U.N.C.L.E.* home to American audiences.

In the four years since John F. Kennedy had welcomed and ushered him in, the British figure of James Bond had wrought a spectacular influence on American culture, linking that culture with new forms of commodification and reconfiguring Cold War tensions in a way that both mythified and rehistoricized those tensions. By the mid-1960s, a large part of American television culture had been recast along and between the lines visible in the text of Bond. A further recasting would come with the assimilation to that culture of one of Bond's stepbrothers: John Drake, Lew Grade's *Secret Agent.*

They've Given Him a Number...

With a proven track record and contacts at the network already in place, and with the now unprecedented success of *Goldfinger* and James Bond to add to their program's marketability, Grade and ITC sold twenty-four episodes of the new, hour-long *Secret Agent* to CBS in 1964. The deal brought ATV $1.25 million; more important, Grade said, it meant that "at last British product is getting a showing on an American network."[55] Beginning on April 3, 1965, *Secret Agent* made Grade's transatlantic hails immediately evident. The title sequence, using animation and graphics that, with fingerprints, bullet holes, and silhouettes, bore a distinct kinship to the opening credits for the Bond films, appeared onscreen backed by a song, soon marketed as "Secret Agent Man," featuring a twangy electric guitar, heavy drumbeat, and a vocal by American recording star Johnny Rivers. *TV Guide,* for its part, again linked the show to ongoing political concerns: "Based on the *Danger Man* series, this expanded hour-long program continues the adventures of urbane John Drake, a special security agent assigned to NATO."[56]

The premiere episode, "The Battle of the Cameras," undercut expectations that those moments might have created, however. The theme song may have been rock and roll, but the musical instrument featured most in the episode's background music was the harpsichord. And it became clear immediately that John Drake was not working for NATO but was instead connected with the British secret service organization MI9. In the first episode, the rugged individualist of *Danger Man* now receives assistance—albeit comically clumsy assistance—from another MI9 operative in his efforts to track down a villain dealing in stolen military secrets on the French Riviera.[57] In a further twist away from a strict Cold War construction, the villain Kent, who wears an almost medieval leather mask to hide an unfortunate earlier encounter with sulfuric acid, has nothing to do with the Communist Party in any way; rather, he is a corrupt capitalist out to sell the formula for a new rocket fuel to the highest bidder.[58] The episode, simply put, serves as a prime example of a polyvalent text, as signifiers of youth and an active individual hero central to American constructions of the Bond formula are combined with signifiers suggesting on the one hand a long-lost classical age and on the other a politically neutral agent of evil.

This is not to negate other elements of *Secret Agent* already present in an

American reading formation for the show. Whereas removing Drake from NATO auspices eliminated one obvious Cold War referent, the fact that he was now clearly a national government agent nominated the government bureaucracy as "the good guy." And *Secret Agent* was not loath to cite the dastardly Reds as villains when need be: in the fifth episode shown in the United States, "Yesterday's Enemies," Drake has to bust a spy ring in Beirut headed by a former British agent who freely admits that his past as a "fellow traveler" is part of the reason he is giving information to "the opposition."[59] That episode also features another element of the series that speaks to the issues raised by Cawelti and Rosenberg: Drake decries the tactics of his own bosses as "worthy of our enemies" when they eliminate the former agent after he has agreed to come back over and sell out his Eastern contacts.[60] The heroic individual agent, when confronted with bureaucratic treachery on his own side, sticks to his principles, even though he knows they are meaningless in the end.[61]

The dialogue between signifiers that exists in the text of *Secret Agent* reveals a difficulty in the concept of the mobile signifier as Bennett and Woollacott use it in their analysis of the popular history of James Bond. For them, the mobility of Bond is linear—from class-bound Cold Warrior to classless defender of détente to enactor of contemporary ritual; from conqueror of women to liberator of female sexual desire.[62] Clearly there is mobility as well in the "text of John Drake/*Secret Agent*" as it was constructed by an American audience, but it is mobility operating in several directions at once. The music moves forward to a mainstream acceptance of pop and rock and roll (itself inflected by the Beatles-led "British invasion") and with it the growing importance in the marketplace of a young audience; at the same time, it steps back to earlier significations of "British," accenting the heritage and class of the civilized, landed aristocracy. Ideologically, the show moves beyond Bond in suggesting capitalism as a source of global evil at the same time that it also overtly names Communism as "the opposition"; moreover, it extends from the construction of Bond both in valorizing individual morality as a response against bureaucracies of all stripes and in refuting its agency—literally—in the modern world. In a sense, then, the mobility of signifiers evident in *Secret Agent* as it became assimilated into American culture again speaks to the unpredictable way in which specific cultural utterances bend and shape the construction of meaning.

Not the least important of those utterances is what John Ellis calls the "narrative image" of the series. Ellis defines the narrative image of a film as "the cinema industry's anticipatory reply to the question 'What is this film like?' . . . it is the promise, and the film is the performance and realization of that promise."[63]

The narrative image, he continues, is composed of advance publicity and conversation about the film, as well as general public knowledge about the actors, director, producers, and other elements of the creation and production of a given film. Ellis goes on to argue that the concept of narrative image can apply only to media such as film that require single product differentiation, and not television, which relies on formula and convention. That British perspective, however, fails to acknowledge the demands of the commercial American television market, particularly in the 1960s, with each of its three networks seeking madly to differentiate its programming from the others, and the very real significance of narrative image in achieving success within that market.[64]

As previously noted, the post-Kennedy popularity of James Bond in the United States acted as a major vector in introducing the spy series to American television, and it was a significant part of the entrée given John Drake and *Secret Agent* to American audiences. As was the case in its first *Danger Man* incarnation in Britain, publicity about the series and its star, Patrick McGoohan, used Bond as a major referent; as was the case in Britain, that publicity sought to position *Secret Agent* and John Drake as a step beyond Ian Fleming's creation in some ways. In a *New York Times* profile accompanying the return of the series for its second season in 1966, William Kirtz presented McGoohan as a decent alternative to the decadent sensuality of Connery's Bond: "[He] is just as adventurous and virile as Bond, but the 37-year-old McGoohan insists that Drake owes more to the traditional virtues than he does to electronics, violence or animal magnetism. 'Drake is moral,' he emphasized. 'He's all business. Ladies might be an interest, for example, but he never reciprocates.' "[65] That "traditional virtue" was evident as early as the premiere "Battle of the Cameras" episode in 1965: the villain Kent has his femme fatale girlfriend, Martine, who is more than a little smitten with Drake, lure the agent to her "apartment" in order to seduce him and then slip him a mickey. Drake, however, is so aloof during the seduction that Martine finally whispers, "I've never met a man with such an icy surface before"—just before she collapses, having drunk the martini Drake switched with her own.

On one level, McGoohan, who had a creative and financial interest in the series, was engaged in product differentiation. Drake had to be like Bond yet unlike Bond. But that strategy also included the means for audiences to read around it. As Kirtz noted in his *New York Times* profile: "An English television magazine is currently printing his fans' various explanations of Drake's indifference to women. The actor admits to being pleased with this concern."[66] Although the "text of Drake" is explicitly defined as absent the sexuality that Bennett and

Like James Bond, *Secret Agent* John Drake held a certain attraction for beautiful women. But in star Patrick McGoohan's vision of the character, a look was about all they might hope for in return. Photograph courtesy of Photofest.

Woollacott find in the "text of Bond," that absence became a presence to many of the show's viewers—a presence that the publicity in turn exploited. Indeed, in a 1966 *TV Guide* profile of McGoohan, Robert Musel, while reiterating the moral rectitude of John Drake, concluded on a note less pure than prurient:

> There was a stampede when word first reached the secretaries that Mc-Goohan had come to film at Shepperton. His effect on women is remarkable.... The biggest stars have played at Shepperton, but you wouldn't have believed it from the stir his arrival caused. Pretty heads spun his way. Red lips smiled in his direction. McGoohan, the family man, paid them no attention.[67]

The publicity used to differentiate the program, in other words, serves as yet another example of the nonlinear mobility of signifiers in the apprehension of imported cultural artifacts: it deliberately presents signifiers that speak as directly to meanings concerning modern sexuality present in the "text of Bond" as its text speaks to opposite constructions.

While McGoohan and Lew Grade's companies, with the assistance of the American popular press, were playing out complicated market games, however, the more significant differentiation occurring with American audiences again was the one defined by language and locale. Following Bakhtin's definition of assimilation, *Secret Agent,* despite the "our-own-ness" of its rockabilly theme, Cold War context, and individual hero that shaped an American reading formation, still represented the "otherness" of Britain. As the "jolly good show" from the program's first fan letter indicates, the importance of the show's British heritage was a common theme in reader mail to *TV Guide.* One writer, responding to a satiric editorial comparing British and American television, accused the magazine of "trying to destroy Anglo-American relations.... Has chauvinism clouded your judgment against these imports, particularly the thrilling *Secret Agent?*" A second correspondent wrote: "By comparison, *Secret Agent, The Baron* and the older ones you also mentioned...are superior to the American programs."[68] And when resident critic Cleveland Amory chose McGoohan best actor of the 1965–66 season in his annual awards column, a reader concurred: "His selection is smashing.... How indeed do the British consistently produce quality shows that intrigue viewers week after week?"[69]

Members of the homes-using-television audience were not the only people asking similar questions. Following the strong ratings showing of *Secret Agent* in its first CBS run—a 20 percent increase over the performance of its predecessor, *Mr. Broadway—Variety* television correspondent Les Brown noted in a front-page column in June 1965 that American networks were starting to look to Great Britain as a potential major program source. The success of *Secret Agent* on a network and *The Saint* in syndication, Brown argued, proved both that British programming was "on target" with American tastes and that it was possible "to resolve the resistance here to speech differences."[70] Similarly, *Variety* reporter Roger Watkins noted in a November article that *Secret Agent* and *The Saint* had "firmly nailed a once-predominant notion that British production values are too sluggish for the U.S. 'big-league' broadcasters."[71] Again, both comments indicate the way in which American audiences in living rooms around the country and in corporate offices in New York and Hollywood had come to accept and welcome the differences evident in British television programs.

Those audiences, however, were not substantial enough to keep *Secret Agent* working past the summer of 1966—in part because the show was no longer different enough from American programs. The fall of 1965, as previously noted, saw a glut of spy and espionage series; it was then that *The Man from U.N.C.L.E.* rose from being a candidate for cancellation to enjoying a Top 20 ratings slot. When *Secret Agent* returned to CBS in December 1965, its competition was NBC's *Get Smart,* a spoof of the secret agent genre that had quickly established itself as a Top 20 show.[72] By February 1966, *Secret Agent* was rumored to be near cancellation, although its ratings were 35 percent better, according to one source, than those of the show it replaced that season; by May, the deed was done.[73] Les Brown, writing in *Variety,* attributed the demise of the import in some degree to a lingering concern about British accents and references by American programmers, but more importantly to the efforts of the American television industry to duplicate James Bond on their own terms and turf:

> With Beatlemania still in vogue, with James Bond the oversized hero of adolescent America, why haven't the British made it on American network TV? . . . like Japanese industrial producers, US telefilm series [producers] make marvelous copycats. In short, the British have a tough time trying to protect what may be their very own.[74]

John Drake was brought down in America, in other words, by a curious paradox: he was too different, yet not different enough, from the American Bonds.

That paradox, however, was not a problem for the many viewers who still watched the show—including *TV Guide*'s Amory, who called the program "easily the best, best acted and most believable of a dozen or more shows in its field" and referred to its cancellation as "idiotic."[75] Lew Grade's ITC distribution company used the massive amount of mail it received following the cancellation of

Secret Agent to mount a successful syndication campaign for the show.[76] There were evidently large numbers of Americans, many of whom were young and if not already well educated, getting there, for whom the differences in the "text of *Secret Agent*" remained attractive at the same time that they spoke to changes in their own society and culture. That audience helped convince those responsible for the show to elevate those differences to a higher level. The result was a program that no American "copycat" producer would try to remake.

. . . And Taken Away His Name

The extraordinarily long (two and a half minutes) introduction to *The Prisoner,* broadcast by CBS in the summer of 1968, presented a narrative of a man angrily resigning from some sort of bureaucracy and then being gassed into unconsciousness by unknown enemies. That narrative, however, was accomplished without spoken dialogue in a presentation that visually and aurally incorporated sophisticated cinematic techniques. This was, the silent film said, something very different from standard television fare. The narrative represented in that film, while linear, also left the viewer with several key questions that introductions usually answer: Who is the man? Why did he resign, and from what? Who is after him? Why do they want him? What happens after he passes out?

The only one of those questions ever to be answered directly was the first—and that required stepping outside the fictional text of the program. The man was definitely Patrick McGoohan, erstwhile *Secret Agent* John Drake and now executive producer, star, and frequent writer and director of *The Prisoner.*[77] As to who he was in the program, that was left entirely up to the viewer, in a deliberate move by McGoohan to create as open a text as possible.[78] The photo of McGoohan used in the introduction certainly looked like John Drake; one could plausibly assume that some form of intertextuality was in play, particularly given the sly reference to the previous series's best-selling title song in the first lines of dialogue from the premiere episode, "Arrival": Upon regaining consciousness, "Drake" attempts to use the telephone, only to hear a voice ask: "What is your number?" "Haven't got a number," he says. "No number, no call," comes the response.[79] He soon discovers that they have given him a number—Number Six—and taken away his name, a discovery that prompts the program's signature line toward the end of the episode, a line repeated in the first scene of each following episode: "I am not a number! I am a person!"[80]

"Arrival," which introduces the protagonist both to the viewer and to his new environment, a quaint turn-of-the-century seaside village in which every move is watched and/or dictated by a panoptic technological bureaucracy, further suggests a link between "Number Six" and "John Drake" in presenting the reason for his abduction: "It's acquisition of your imagination," Number Two, the visible head of the new bureaucracy, tells him. "The information in your head is priceless. I don't think you realize what a valuable property you've become. . . . They want to know why you suddenly left. I believe you—I do think it was a matter of principle." After being assured that his cooperation will mean a pleasant existence in the village, Number Six responds: "I will not be pushed, filed, shaped, indexed, briefed, debriefed or numbered! My life is my own!" The presumed "agent," in short, wants to regain his agency; each episode of the series recounts his efforts to do so by attempting to escape from the village. The only agency in the program, however, appeared to be that of McGoohan, whose disembodied head, zoomed to fill the screen over the village background, led into the show's commercial breaks.

The openness of meaning in *The Prisoner*, however, was immediately closed off for at least some of its American audience by publicity in the American press that set the show's narrative image by focusing on its single recognizable signifying element. In the *TV Guide* preview for the series, writer Joan Barthel noted that the abduction of the protagonist might be a bit more than expected of an employer upset with an angry resignation, "but this is no routine employer; this is the Government. This is no routine handsome fellow; this is Patrick McGoohan, wanting out of his intelligence-agent job."[81] Similarly, Robert Lewis Shayon told readers in his critique in *Saturday Review* that "*The Prisoner* is *Secret Agent* and *Secret Agent* is *The Prisoner*."[82] In *Time*'s review, most of the first paragraph was devoted to a synopsis and evaluation of *Secret Agent* as the lead-in to McGoohan's new series.[83] John Fiske argues that the amalgamation of the representational and the real as evident in these articles is "fun," as it plays with the reader's position in apprehending the "text" of McGoohan/Drake/"the prisoner."[84] Clearly, the possibility that Number Six was John Drake was one that McGoohan might claim to be one of the open "mysteries" he wished the audience to ponder; certainly viewers of *The Prisoner* have had fun over the years attempting to determine whether or not Number Six is actually Drake.[85] More important, however, the intertextual messages surrounding the program make an ineradicable connection between a text viewers had not yet encountered and a specific program (and genre) preceding it that is never directly borne out by the new text itself.

The willingness of the American press to foreclose meaning around the "text of McGoohan"—including his British background—was not the only attempt to inflect the program toward the perceived expectations of an American audience.

Is *The Prisoner* really John Drake? Only star/writer/director/producer Patrick McGoohan knows for sure—and he isn't talking. Photograph courtesy of Photofest.

Again produced and distributed by Lew Grade, *The Prisoner* was, aside from McGoohan's presence, free of the usual Grade-imposed American hails: the village (in actuality the Welsh resort Portmeirion) was, in its collection of tiny shops, formal gardens, and uniformed brass bands, as well as the accents heard there, distinctly British, and distinctly premodern British at that; the various Number Twos (with one exception—Australian Leo McKern, who also was the only Number Two to appear in separate episodes) were all British or Continental.[86] This did not, however, preclude Grade's concern for the American market. According to David Buxton, McGoohan's original plan for the series called for just seven episodes; Grade, however, ordered nineteen more, to give an American network a half-year series with the potential for renewal. The two settled on a compromise of seventeen episodes, a standard summer run.[87] CBS, where *Secret Agent* had enjoyed its American success, bought the show (which had just started production) in the fall of 1966 and began an effort to remove elements of the series that it thought might be problematic for Americans. CBS programming chief Michael Dann asked McGoohan to consider making his protagonist less troubled than he seemed in the first episode: "I told him that no matter how brilliant the production, the public likes to identify with a winner," Dann told *TV Guide*.[88]

Although McGoohan told the network that he wished to follow his own design for the series, Robert Lewis Shayon, in his *Saturday Review* article, argued that as the show progressed, the protagonist developed into more of a standard hero, not escaping himself from the village but enabling others to leave alive.[89] Whether part of his design or not, in episodes beginning at the halfway point of the series, McGoohan's protagonist indeed did begin to find others willing to cooperate with his plans to leave the village and assisted, via a mind-transfer operation, a scientist in escaping; moreover, he began to defeat the prison officials at some of their own games of mind control. Reviewers also tried to claw the series back into familiarity through references going beyond the McGoohan-Drake-Six conjunction.[90] *Saturday Review, Time,* and the *New York Times* all compared McGoohan's creation to the dystopia of George Orwell's *1984* in their critiques of the series. *Time,* for its part, described the village in familiar Cold War terms: "a detention camp for retired spies, defectors, nuclear scientists and others whose memories are weighted with state secrets. Among the purposeful ambiguities of the series is that neither the prisoner nor the viewer is ever certain which side of the Iron Curtain he is on."[91] And Shayon brought the show into the American political present with his description of Number Six: "The switch to the Nixon posture of the 'eternal loser' who refuses to quit but is in there fighting all the time was rather a refreshing stirring in TV's static world of the plot formula."[92]

The actions of both the producers and the distributors of *The Prisoner* in the United States, as well as the work performed by the American press in creating a narrative image for the show, seem to fill the hegemonic functions of "absorption and domestication," as the "our-own-ness" of meanings surrounding the text appears to overwhelm its "otherness." Although much of the publicity about *The Prisoner,* as the *Time* quote above indicates, allowed that McGoohan as author was attempting to create an open, multivocal text, the show's publicists and programmers at the same time pushed that openness into a framework defined in the United States by the secret agent genre in general, and by the British secret agent, call him John Drake or James Bond, in particular. Such an analysis fails to consider, however, the way in which the "purposeful ambiguity" of the series makes such closure impossible, leaving *The Prisoner* in America an example of what Raymond Williams calls a work that is "irreducible to the terms of the original or the adaptive hegemony, and [is] in that sense independent."[93] Indeed, that ambiguity served as a viable and meaningful difference in the program for many American viewers, as letters to *TV Guide* attested.[94]

McGoohan's dystopia and his trapped hero—which level the ideological and utopian functions Jameson identifies elsewhere in "mass culture"—typify not a static concept of the secret agent necessary for a hegemonic reading of *The Prisoner* in the United States but a mobility in the signification of that character, brought about by a shift in the reading formation of American audiences in the 1960s. Robert Shayon's connection of Number Six to what might be called the "text of Nixon" is most revealing in this respect.[95] Gone from this construction of the secret agent figure, in spite of CBS's efforts to construct it otherwise, were the references to John Kennedy that had so clearly defined an American response to James Bond and his various kith and kin, including John Drake. The vigorous youth, the cosmopolitan cultural consumption, the sense of privilege—all were drained. The sexuality remained, to some degree—as Joan Barthel's *TV Guide* description indicated, Number Six, if indeed he was Drake, had not quickly gone to seed—but it was an element of the "text of Number Six" that was much less overt than it had been with either Kennedy or Bond—or Drake.[96] What remained of the secret agent formula defined by Cawelti and Rosenberg and embodied by Bond and Drake was the lone individual, now typed as a prisoner, an "eternal loser," against an overwhelming conspiratorial bureaucracy, ever more dependent upon technology to conduct its repressive business.[97] As such, *The Prisoner* spoke not just to viewers who enjoyed the program's openness as a matter of aesthetic and intellectual taste but to viewers who found in that openness an ideological critique unavailable in any American television program.

David Buxton, in his analysis of *The Prisoner*, attempts to construct that critique as one speaking to the concerns of an inherently conservative upper middle class itself trapped in a new age of commodification and consumption, state intrusion into private lives, and the role of mass media in creating conformity.[98] Those concerns are evident to some degree in the response to the series that was printed in *TV Guide*, given repeated references to "intelligence" and "sophistication" indicating an audience possessing the cultural capital that defines an elite. In his description of the concerns of that audience, however, Buxton displays a rigidity in his conception of class structure that speaks much more to his own British culture and its audiences than it does those in the United States, and that oversimplifies the readings possible due to what he finds "peculiar" about the time in which the show was made and originally viewed.[99]

Buxton's analysis of the audience of *The Prisoner* as being representative of an inherently conservative bourgeois elides significant shifts in that class in 1960s America. Although elements of the program might indeed have appealed to such conservatives—Cold War ideologues and cultural critics of the 1950s—in matters both political and cultural, it also contained elements attractive to their children, who were at least for the moment rejecting the bourgeoisie and establishing new forms of political and cultural radicalism. Indeed, both groups are explicitly hailed in the final episode of the series, "Fallout." The final authority Number Six faces in the village identifies, in the persons of Number 48 and Number Two, the offensive forms of revolt that result in containment and punishment: "The first—uncoordinated youth, rebelling against nothing it can define. The second—an established, successful, secure member of the establishment turning upon and biting the hand that feeds him."[100] The "uncoordinated youth" of America's New Left followed the social and cultural critiques of their 1950s mentors, adding to them the belief in the power of individuals to act together in a participatory democracy to rid society of institutional repression; the radicals of the counterculture believed that repression was obviated through the discovery and cultivation of the individual spirit, frequently through the use of psychedelic drugs.[101] Buxton fails to consider the "peculiarities" of the show that might be considered by those new audiences. Its representation of state oppression via technology addressed those growing up in a world in which computers, view screens, and remote-control death were not fanciful science fiction, and its odd juxtaposition of visual elements and its cinematic style had a psychedelic flair.

Buxton's further assertion that the series allowed for a "resistance to commodified, mass-mediatized society" among its viewers both assumes a linear relationship between text and audience that can in no way be borne out and considers neither the way in which *The Prisoner* itself addresses commodification nor the relationship of its younger American audience to commodification and the mass media.[102] The show itself is open-ended in its depiction of consumerized postindustrial society: only the instruments of surveillance and death in Number Six's premodern prison village speak of technological advancement, and the "escape" for which he struggles propels him back into the world of Lotus sports cars, Carnaby Street fashion, and the commodified geography of travel brochures.[103] Nowhere in the program, meanwhile, are there the obvious endorsements for expensive or technological creature comforts that mark both the Bond films and previous television secret agent sagas. Young American radicals were equally mixed in their attitudes toward a consumer society, rejecting both consumerism and the affluence on which it was based on the one hand, yet buying and dealing massive quantities of a new culture — music, books, drugs — on the other.[104] However "trapped" any of these younger viewers might have considered themselves by American commodification and consumption, *The Prisoner* spoke to other, more immediate concerns than those represented by Buxton — or by previous British secret agents in the United States.

The openness of the text of *The Prisoner* in the end makes an analysis like Buxton's an exercise in futility — a problem he himself admits.[105] The multiplicity of meaning available in the show renders any sort of definition of its single "meaning" an inflection and closure similar to that performed by the American press and television industry upon its arrival from Britain. Examining the program and the responses of its viewers, however, in light of that specific process of assimilation reveals much about the peculiarities of the time. *The Prisoner* may have indeed spoken to concerns about commodification and consumerism in a British context; in the United States, however, the show addressed a time and a people for whom the dreams of a Camelot had passed, as domestic racial violence and the bloodshed of the Vietnam conflict had superseded whatever utopian sense of beauty, adventure, and glory might have been represented by the Kennedys. Although those dreams lived on for a while in the forms of James Bond, the men from U.N.C.L.E., and John Drake, the success of the lone noble knight errant against forces superior in number and strength became an increasingly dubious proposition as those forces became more global, more impersonal, more technologically advanced — and more and more seemed to include the castle to which the knight was supposed to return at mission's end. Buxton observes that part of the inherent conservatism he finds in *The Prisoner* lies in its definition of individualism as the total rejection of society; it was entirely possible in the United States of the late 1960s, however, to invert that definition: society totally rejects the individual, frequently violently.[106] Although it is a coincidence that the first episode of *The Prisoner* aired in the United States just four nights before Robert Kennedy was gunned down (eight weeks after the assassination of Martin Luther King Jr.), that coincidence made another potential meaning of the series evident: the dangers of the real world were too great for even the most noble men who attempted to fight them. Whereas Number Six had the existential misfortune of losing his name as the result of that fight, others had the primal misfortune of losing their lives.

The Prisoner served as a fin de siècle for all that John Drake had represented to American television audiences. When it came to its broadcast end in the fall of 1968, so did *The Man from U.N.C.L.E.* and *I Spy.* The Western-spy genre hybrid *The Wild, Wild West* remained on the air until 1970, as did the spoof *Get Smart,* but both did so with declining ratings.[107] Perceived forces of evil had become too organized and too surreptitious to be managed by individuals alone; they now had to be addressed by corporate crimefighters working as unquestioning apparatchiks of massive bureaucracies, both internationally and domestically: the Impossible Missions Force (*Mission: Impossible*), *The F.B.I.,* the LAPD cops of *Dragnet,* the San Francisco cops of *Ironside,* the Honolulu cops of *Hawaii Five-O,* even *The Mod Squad.*[108] And the fight could no longer be conducted by the British—one now could only trust one's own. The differences that had enabled *Secret Agent* and *The Prisoner* to speak to American concerns in ways that American programming itself could not were no longer of value—with a significant exception. One British program during the 1960s managed to continue the cultural dialogue represented in the secret agent genre by addressing an American audience and issue that the danger men in their prime could only briefly embrace and then toss aside: women.

3. Mrs. Peel Goes to Washington
The Avengers

I became an icon for the feminist movement in America. I still get people writing to me or coming to see me and saying "you were a role model for me when I was a girl" and all that. It's very sad that they had to take their role models off the television.

— Diana Rigg[1]

Though Lew Grade's spy shows made overt efforts to hail an American audience, they also included naturalized assumptions that made it all the more possible to respond. Perhaps the most naturalized of those assumptions was that the job description for secret agent, at least for the good guys, was male only. Women might be employed in Her Majesty's Secret Service, but, like Fleming's Moneypenny, they were assigned desk work — and were accused of being incompetent at that.[2] Female spies were employed by the enemy and accomplished their tasks with neither mental nor technological resources, but with the sexual use of their bodies — a more dangerous weapon than even the most creative of villains might dream up.[3]

The 1966 import to the United States of *The Avengers,* as a result, marked a paradigm shift in the secret agent series, in that one of its title characters was a woman. American television in the previous year had already produced a prototypical female detective, in the form of ABC's *Honey West.* As the Flemingesque name indicates, however, Honey relied far more on her sexual wiles and her burly, long-suffering male colleague Sam Bolt than she did on her limited organizational and analytic skills.[4] Publicity for *The Avengers* on its arrival in 1966 focused on its distinctive difference, secret agent Emma Peel, portraying her as tough but sexy — "kinky," to use a term employed in descriptions of the show. That publicity, however, turned on itself. Instead of creating an image of an Anglicized Mata Hari, American promotions and advertisements for the series, as well as the program itself, presented a strong and smart British woman who was in control of whatever situation in which she might find herself. Further inflected by the concomitant development of a new American feminism, *The Avengers,* a representative of a male genre aimed at a male audience, became in the United States a model of liberation for young middle-class women, as those women read around elements of its construction designed to contain it within patriarchal ideological conventions. That model, however, was closed down when the program's American distributor, ABC, misreading the dialogue represented in its success, contributed to the reshaping of the show in traditionally gendered secret agent genre patterns: *Honey West* redux.

Male Bonding

One of the most significant constructions in the "texts of Bond" during the 1960s and 1970s was the relation between the secret agent hero and "the Bond girl." In the novels and in the Bond films of the 1960s, the Bond girl represented a liberation from repressive sexual and moral codes in much the same way that Bond modernized male norms previously defined by class-based codes of chivalry and restraint. That liberation, however, merely re-placed the Bond girl in a patriarchal order, as Bond made it part of his "mission" to provide sexual healing to women who did not fit dominant codes of heterosexual femininity. Characters such as Honeychile Rider in *Dr. No* and Pussy Galore in *Goldfinger,* while free from traditional marital and domestic roles, are liberated only insofar as they pleasure Bond. Still, Bond's complicity in whatever liberation does occur and the notion of the Bond girl's exercising choice and free will, if nothing else, in the relationship, mark a significant ideological moment in the career of Bond. That moment passed by the time the Bond films of the 1970s were released, removed by a concern with the Bond girl's having gained too much freedom and power and needing to be put "back into her place." Those later Bond films and the publicity surrounding them suggested that although sexual liberation in the service of Bond was a good thing, taking that liberation into political and economic realms was a mistake requiring immediate correction.[5]

Though clearly a response to the women's liberation movement on both sides of the Atlantic, the textual shift in the significance of "the Bond girl" makes evident a naturalized assumption about the Bond books and movies: the implied reader/viewer is male.[6] Indeed, the whole secret agent genre, based on the role of the lone individual (male) in protecting and preserving the established social and political order by any means necessary, is one created by males largely for males. As such, the secret agent books, movies, and television programs popular in the 1960s mirrored the structure and flow of American prime-time television during the same period. Although prime-time programs have always attempted to attract as many diverse elements of the viewing public as possible, it has also been the case that those programs, particularly in the years surveyed here, have followed the circadian rhythm of a male-defined workday.[7] The fictional genres largely defining prime-time television during the 1960s—sitcom, adventure, professional drama—all began at a specific time, presented a specific single problem to be solved, and resolved the problem, often through physical strength and/ or action, to achieve closure. Although underlying problems—the unpredictability of children, the cruelty of nature, the threat of crime—remained from episode to episode, each prime-time show worked through its specific problem to a satisfactory resolution, much as the breadwinner could close the door behind him when he left the factory, store, or office at the end of the day.[8]

That women were a large part of the prime-time audience during this period speaks to the many meanings that were available in those programs; the popularity of such figures as Napoleon Solo and Illya Kuryakin suggests that some of the pleasures women and girls derived from looking at the medium were similar to those enjoyed by men and boys. Those meanings, however, were still circumscribed by the social definitions of American women and girls culturally represented in those programs: a teenager might hope to be a "Kuryakin girl," but she could not hope to be Kuryakin as the program's implied reader could. With the success of Bond and *Secret Agent* as proof that cultural constructions created outside the United States could now also speak to that audience of implied readers, however, ABC decided to see what would happen if it went to the same source for an update of the hip private detective series it presented early in the 1960s—an update that would give the sexy secretary brains and a gun.

M Appeal

The Avengers arrived in British homes in 1961 as a show tracking the adventures of domestic crimefighters John Steed and Dr. David Keel, whose wife's murder was the initial act to be avenged. Thanks to an intervening actors' strike, Dr. Keel was replaced for the show's second season by female anthropologist Cathy Gale, played by Honor Blackman. Gale, described in a producer's notes as "a 1960s version of Shaw's emancipated young woman," was a rising star in her field who had also developed impressive skills with firearms and martial arts while working in Kenya and Cuba. The freelance agents, Steed clad in dapper Edwardian suits and bowlers and Gale sporting a wardrobe defined by leather jumpsuits, dispatched villains ranging from computer saboteurs to gold smugglers to medical assassins over the course of two seasons. Their adventures, videotaped in black and white on studio sets that were as obvious (and, occasionally, as fragile) as those used in American soap operas, quickly drew a large cult audience, particularly among a young audience that was also starting to redefine British pop music and fashion.[9]

An unqualified success in its homeland, *The Avengers* was hardly an unknown quantity in the United States when it was first broadcast on March 28, 1966. A 1963 article in the *New York Times* introduced readers to John Steed and Cathy Gale (the latter seen judo kicking a villain off his feet) as the "knowing, cynical, rounded-out, experienced" heroes of a successful show that "revels in the sheer nonsense of the world of private eyes and special agents."[10] In May 1964, *TV Guide* European correspondent Robert Musel chronicled the ascension of the show's popularity as well as that of female star Blackman, who was leaving the series to star as Pussy Galore in *Goldfinger,* in the three years it had been broadcast in Britain.[11] Although Musel's article was directed to the American television audience, it also suggested the American television industry's interest in the show—an interest that had already been voiced to the British Associated Broadcasting Company by America's ABC network: a run of a filmed *Avengers* series in fall 1965.[12] Blackman's departure cast a pall on those plans; *The Avengers* made enough of an impression on ABC and independent producer Aaron Spelling, however, to lead the network to buy Spelling's *Honey West,* a show based on a series of pulp crime novels but that *Variety* television columnist Les Brown noted was "fashioned after" the British hit, for its fall 1965 schedule.[13]

While *Honey West* moved through preproduction toward being the first American representation of what *TV Guide* critic Cleveland Amory would call "Jane Blonde," *The Avengers'* British producers worked to recast their program in the hope of a future sale to the American market.[14] Steed's new partner was to be, like her predecessor, a highly educated widow with substantial experience in counterespionage. Literally a member of the jet set (her late husband was a test pilot), she drove only the coolest cars and wore only the latest fashions: one of the show's major marketing devices in Britain and Europe was to be the clothing designed specifically for the character.[15] At the same time, she was an expert in both martial arts and marksmanship. Called "Samantha" in early drafts, the character acquired another name by the time the series went into filming: according to popular mythology, a series publicist decided that the character had to somehow represent "Man appeal," which she shortened to "M appeal" and finally to "Emma Peel."[16] When the first actress hired to play Mrs. Peel failed to work out, producers Brian Clemens and Albert Fennell called in an actress from the Royal Shakespeare Company who also had experience in television. Diana Rigg's screen test immensely impressed both the producers and costar Macnee: the show had found its Emma Peel; now it could find the American market.[17]

"Agents extraordinary" John Steed (Patrick Macnee) and Emma Peel (Diana Rigg) in a classic pose: the unruffled British gent and the mod woman of action. Photograph courtesy of Photofest.

That search, however, required two major technical adjustments to the program. First, in order to compete with the visual quality of American prime-time programming, *The Avengers* had to switch from videotaping, which gave the show the cheap, flat look of American daytime serials, to filming.[18] Second, with the rapid development of color television technology, color would become a necessary component of any import hoping for success in the United States. These changes truly opened up the dialogue, on both the commercial and the cultural levels, between the show's British producers and audience and its American distributors and audience. In late 1965, ABC-UK offered ABC the right to purchase twenty-six filmed black-and-white episodes of *The Avengers*. If the show attracted an acceptable audience share, the American network would then have an option to buy a new, twenty-six-episode color series. ABC-US decided to take ABC-UK up on the offer, paying more than one million dollars up front. However, American executives attempted to control the dialogue even further, offering ABC-UK even more money either to add American elements to the show, à la Lew Grade, or to sell the format outright—an offer the British network refused, choosing to present its product in the United States as it had been in Britain.[19]

With the deal struck, a television program made in Britain for British audiences without content adjustments for foreign audiences would arrive in American homes early in 1966. The problem, then, for both British producers and American distributors, became that of shaping the program for the tastes and expectations of its American audience, of furthering the cultural dialogue established in the commercial realm. That dialogue would indeed develop at length and in surprising depth, but the efforts of both ABC and ABC-UK would play only a minor role, at least initially, in that development.

Both Eyes Peeled

ABC-UK announced its sale of *The Avengers* to the American market with a full-page ad in the January 26, 1966, issue of *Variety*. The top three-fourths of the page consisted of a head-on photograph of Diana Rigg/Emma Peel on a windy beach, wearing hiphugger pants, a low-cut metallic bikini top, and a jacket slung off her left shoulder, and pointing a gun toward the camera. The bottom left portion of the Rigg/Peel photograph was covered with an inset of a dapper Patrick Macnee/John Steed pinning a carnation into his lapel. At the bottom of the page, the ad copy announced, "ABC U.K. Sells to ABC U.S.A. for 1966," promoting the show as "combining toughness and fast-moving action with a glitter of sophistication and wit." Macnee, although first to be mentioned in the text, was described merely as "the suave bowler-hatted secret agent John Steed"; Rigg's character, meanwhile, was feted as a "cool, resourceful accomplice who fights fast, free and furious with every technique from judo and karate to a straight left to the jaw."[20]

The *Avengers* ad was nothing special in terms of space bought in *Variety*, where two-page ads replete with busty starlets were commonplace. In terms of establishing the show's narrative image for an American audience, however, the ad was of central importance, focused as it was on the body of its female star and protagonist. The photographic element reduced the male — the first-billed star and senior partner within the story — to an afterthought while presenting the body of the female star in full frontal display; the written copy accomplished much the same. The same image was used in the first major American journalistic publicity for the show: an article in the entertainment section of the Sunday *New York Times* of March 13, 1966, two weeks before the airing of the first show. The headline "From Lear to Leer" dominated the page, including the photo of Rigg/Peel used in the *Variety* ad running three columns wide and half a page high. A photo of equal size showing Rigg/Peel throwing a man down a flight of stairs introduced the copy, which was written by Stanley Price. "The lady is tall and shapely," Price began. "The combination of her natural contours and the white trouser-suit and the black peaked-cap are quite enough to turn the normally level heads of smart Bond Street shoppers on a chill March morning." After detailing an encounter Rigg had with a Jamaican man in London (whose English she did not correct) and outlining her switch from Shakespearean roles to "a hokey mixture of adventure and counter-espionage" intimated in the headline, Price returned to the body of his story: "[She] has worn just about everything except a long skirt, including the way-out leather ensembles, harem bras and panties, toreador outfits with bare midriffs, and indescribably modern outfits, half spaceman, half country-girl."[21]

Newsweek also participated in the construction of the narrative image for *The Avengers* in its April 4, 1966, issue. With the heading "Good-Chap Sexuality," an article announcing the arrival of the program to ABC-US devoted a quarter of its space to a photo of Rigg/Peel karate chopping a man across a boiler room, with the caption "Diana Rigg: Strictly for kinks." The show's "kinkiness" provided the story's lead, with Rigg identified as "the kinkiest thing" about it. In the article's fifth paragraph, Rigg herself was quoted: "I never think of myself as sexy....I identify with the woman in our society who is evolving. Emma is totally equal to Steed. The fighting is the most obvious quality." However, the following — and final — paragraph framed her comments by citing the *Times* of London's assessment of the program as "wonderful good-chap sexuality."[22]

Although possessing a stance and an outfit designed to attract the male gaze, Emma Peel also has a gun, and she knows how to use it. Photograph courtesy of Photofest.

The narrative image fashioned for American viewers of *The Avengers,* in short, follows Laura Mulvey's definition of the male gaze as central to the ideological purpose of "realistic" narrative film—and, by extension, television. That gaze, she argues, defines and controls—*styles* is the verb she appropriately uses—the image of woman on the screen: "With their appearance coded for strong visual and erotic impact... they can be said to connote *to-be-looked-at-ness*"—a quality immediately addressed in the American media focus on Diana Rigg.[23] The male gaze was also evident in commentary on the show in *TV Guide.* Cleveland Amory's review of the series, published in the May 14, 1966, issue, was headed with a Hirschfeld drawing of a leather-clad Rigg/Peel knocking down two bad guys. When Amory described Rigg/Peel in his column, citing publicity copy identifying the character as representing the "swinging girl of today and the forward-looking woman of tomorrow," his remarks followed a familiar path: "Pretty good, what? Well, make no mistake about it, she is both pretty and good. Furthermore, she not only dresses to the nines... but she also knows judo, karate and the score."[24]

Those comments were more than iterated when the show returned for its second season in 1967. An ABC ad in the January 14 *TV Guide* featured Rigg/Peel, again wearing a leather jumpsuit, standing front and center with a menacing look on her face, with the face of Macnee/Steed barely visible over her left shoulder, and the rest of his body off the page entirely.[25] The following week, Macnee and Rigg occupied the cover of the magazine as the prologue to a feature profile of the female star. Titled "En Garde!" and written again by Robert Musel, the article began with a full-page photograph of Rigg/Peel, holding a fencing sword, with the subheading "Britain's Diana Rigg is again after the American viewer."[26] Moving quickly from the threat to the "to-be-looked-at-ness" of the image, Musel began: "Diana Rigg is a tall, auburn-haired Yorkshire lass, perilously close to being beautiful, who is considered a character by her friends because she loses her keys several times a year and has to smash the window of her apartment with a milk bottle." This "kooky"—unthreatening—quality to the image was repeated throughout the article: she needs to get tipsy to relax for still photos; her casual approach to work as a fashion model was "unorthodox"; she is baffled by fan mail. At the same time, the visual pleasure of the image was also iterated: "Whatever her height, there is hardly an inch that isn't exactly where it should be and a computer could hardly have programmed a more fetching face," Musel wrote. "The eyes are brown, the cheekbones high; freckles dust the clear skin which needs no makeup... and the teeth are strong, white and serviceable."[27]

What was remarkable, however, in the American reception of *The Avengers* was not so much the program's narrative image or the significant employment of the male gaze in the construction of that image. Instead, it was the degree to which an American audience read around both, making *The Avengers* a secret agent drama appreciated by females as much as (if not more than) males, and moving the previously accepted "Bond girl" signification of women as subservient to men even when liberated to a different paradigmatic level entirely. Although that reading and the accompanying mobility in signifiers were accomplished to some degree by elements of the text itself, it was again the intertextuality involved in creating a public image of the show, as well as important extratextual shifts in American social and cultural norms, that inflected *The Avengers* away from the way it had been originally defined by both its British producers and its American distributors.

Boxed In

Historian Elaine Tyler May has described the decade of the 1950s in the United States as one defined by "domestic containment," a Cold War ideology that sought to create the middle-class home as a secure sphere of influence in which chaotic social and psychological forces could be tamed and adapted to the service of a prosperous and fulfilling life. Women were particularly shaped and defined by this ideology, May suggests, as the ones who were to be contained within the home: vessels of sexual pleasure for tired, overworked husbands; bearers and nurturers of the children who would carry forth both the family and the ideology; and household engineers, responsible for making sure that the home and all the gadgets therein worked as they should. This was supposed to be a small price to pay for the security and comfort provided by the home and family in a time of global insecurity and the threat of nuclear ruination.[28]

While an ideology of domestic containment seemed increasingly to define the place of women in American society, however, the cultural contradictions of capitalism began to exhibit their own power. Although apparently more and more consigned to day labor within the home, American women in the 1950s were going to college and entering the workforce in numbers never seen before: by 1960, 40 percent of all women over the age of sixteen held jobs, and the rate of married middle-class women joining the workforce increased almost fourfold in the decade between 1950 and 1960.[29] Most of the work done by these women was clerical and service oriented—these were jobs, not careers, as Sara Evans points out—but the involvement of these women in school and work outside the home meant that the energies and forces that were supposed to be contained within were seeping out.[30]

The problems and paradoxes created within both the middle-class home and American society as the containment model began to crack were given a name when writer Betty Friedan published *The Feminine Mystique* in 1963. An immediate best-seller, Friedan's book charged that domestic containment had created a "comfortable concentration camp" in which women were forced to give up the use of their minds in the service of a therapeutic norm and their bodies in the servicing of their husbands.[31] Friedan went on to argue that television was one of the most distinctive "comforts" of this concentration camp in a two-part essay for *TV Guide* in 1964. In the first half of "Television and the Feminine Mystique," Friedan spoke primarily to gendered television images that promote the passivity of women in general and denigrate the housewife in specific, turning her into a "stupid, unattractive insecure little household drudge."[32] In the second installment, however, she came down much harder on television's role in the ideology of containment: "Is it a coincidence that millions of real girls who have grown up watching television — and seeing only that emptily unglamorous housewife image of women — do not, in high school, have any goal of their own future except being a passive housewife?" Friedan went on to demand that television dare to improve itself and the place of the women it depicted by creating "more images of real women to help girls and women take themselves seriously and grow and love and be loved by men again."[33]

Friedan's polemic against television, even if, as later charged, representative of a middle-class bias, spoke directly to the way in which the male managers of the medium themselves constructed the middle-class housewife as their ideal viewer.[34] Early demographic surveys conducted by the networks found that viewers of daytime television were young women with growing families and incomes who lived in or near major market areas. Mrs. John Q. Public, producers and advertisers were told, managed a utopian workplace filled with "labor-saving devices," leaving her with the time to be concerned with her own appearance as well as that of her house, her spouse, and her family — and the time to go shopping to resolve those concerns. She was, in short, "a good customer" — precisely the sort of person toward whom advertising and the programs that surrounded it should be aimed.[35] Friedan's criticism of this construction and the perceived effect it had on female viewers was particularly appropriate in addressing the ways in which middle-class women were being mysticized and mystified by society in general and television in specific.

Indeed, although the ideology of domestic containment as May defines it had been realized during the Eisenhower years, at no point was that ideology more visible on television than during the Kennedy years of the early 1960s, the period in which Friedan was writing. In addition to daytime soap operas, which increased in number from seven to twelve in 1960, prime-time television kept women far away from the office, far under the still-concrete ceiling of the workplace, or completely out of sight and mind.[36] Women were, with the exception of *Gunsmoke*'s Miss Kitty and the profession that dare not speak its name, presented at best as secondary characters and more frequently written out of the Westerns that dominated the ratings during the Kennedy years.[37] Domestic situation comedies continued to burgeon, with June Cleaver (*Leave It to Beaver*), Donna Stone (*The Donna Reed Show*) and Harriet Nelson (*The Adventures of Ozzie & Harriet*), among others, perfectly embodying the feminine mystique. Several other sitcoms—*My Three Sons, Bachelor Father, The Andy Griffith Show*—followed the strategy of the Western and simply eliminated women as major characters. Those women who worked—the girls of the Warner Bros.–ABC detective series, Lucille Ball in *The Lucy Show*—did so in low-status, low-paying secretarial jobs, and more often than not with a remarkable degree of incompetence. The New Frontier workplace dramas discussed by Mary Ann Watson focused on men, with but one exception; *The Nurses* added supervisory males to the cast and changed its name to *The Doctors and the Nurses* when its ratings fell after two seasons.[38] Indeed, New Frontier dramas took previously accepted women's jobs—social worker and teacher—and gave them to men, in *East Side/West Side* (George C. Scott dealing with the economically distressed in New York) and *Mr. Novak* (James Franciscus dealing with the hormonally distressed in a high school).[39] Perhaps the most grotesque representation of containment came with the literally domestic comedy *Hazel,* which reduced Oscar-winner Shirley Booth to a comic strip (and acceptably white) maid for an upper-middle-class family.[40]

It was not until the year after President Kennedy's death that the ideology of domestic containment began to be addressed directly in an American television narrative. *Bewitched,* first broadcast by ABC in 1964, took explicitly as the situation of its comedy the efforts of a woman whose talents far exceed the housework that fills her day to make use of those talents, despite her husband's objections.[41] Samantha Stephens was in many ways the prototypical domestic comedy wife: feminine in appearance, happy to live and work in her home, bright but willing to accede to her husband Darrin's demands, the most forceful of which was that she not use her powers of witchcraft. Week after week, however, Samantha found herself in circumstances, frequently due to Darrin, requiring that she use the magic she knew so well. The result, as Susan Douglas has pointed out, was a deliberately polyvalent commentary on domestic containment and its discontents: Samantha is perfectly happy to do as Darrin asks and live the life of a suburban housewife; once there, however, she finds that it is far harder to let go of her abilities—her career, in a real sense—than she had imagined. She is willing to submit to patriarchal rules, but in using her witchcraft, she taps into powers the patriarchy can neither channel nor control.[42] The seven-year run enjoyed by *Bewitched* indicates the degree to which the multiple readings available in the show could address women working in the ideology of domestic containment as easily as it could women who, consciously or not, wanted out.

Bewitched was followed in 1965 by two other sitcoms that similarly addressed domestic containment. NBC's *I Dream of Jeannie* made containment a visual trope, as its title character, a beautiful (and curiously blonde) Persian genie worked her magic against the wishes of her astronaut "master" whenever she was released from her bottle. The spy series *Get Smart,* also broadcast by NBC, brought its lead female character, Agent 99, into the public world of espionage—which in her case meant acting as teacher, mother, nurse, and (eventually) wife to bumbling secret agent Maxwell Smart. The multiple meanings present in all three series make evident the cultural challenge to the dominant ideology of the day. In the two years between Betty Friedan's essays in *TV Guide* and the arrival of *The Avengers,* the United States witnessed the passage of the Civil Rights Act of 1964, including Title VII, ending discrimination against women as well as minorities in hiring. The Mississippi Freedom Summer of 1964 concurrently developed models of activism for college-age women to address oppression they observed and lived in American society. Friedan's own efforts to form a group to effect legislative and social change on behalf of women would come to fruition in 1966, as the National Organization for Women.[43] The social position of women in the United States was changing dramatically, and television's constructions of women were beginning to address those changes. Yet those constructions, built as they were within a system that both helped define and was defined by domestic containment, seemed unable to offer the direct critiques of that ideology being voiced by Friedan and others. It was into these swirling cultural currents that *The Avengers* was dropped in 1966.

"Agent Extraordinary"

In its one immediate textual concession to the American market, ABC-UK added a voice-over narration to the surreal introduction of the first exported episode explaining just who these "avengers" were: "Extraordinary crimes against the people and the state have to be avenged by agents extraordinary. Two such agents are John Steed, top professional, and Emma Peel, talented amateur—otherwise known as the Avengers." While the proper British male voice introduces the series, a man in a waiter's jacket crossing a giant chessboard falls face first, revealing a knife in the middle of a target on his back. Steed and Peel, on cue, walk out to the dead man and take the bottle of champagne he had been carrying from his hand. The next shots identify Steed's trademark umbrella and bowler, followed by Peel's pistol (carried in her boot) and her leather jumpsuit. The segment concludes as Steed pours champagne for himself and Peel, and the two, smiling, turn and walk off the chessboard.[44] While this opening deliberately hailed viewers familiar with the conventions of spy dramas, including the Cold War elements invoked by the reference to "crimes against the people and the state," it visually suggested that "the Avengers" were going to be involved in more fantastic, "extraordinary" circumstances than even those experienced by the men from U.N.C.L.E.

The episode that followed fulfilled the promise of the opening sequence. "The Cybernauts" begins as a tale of industrial intrigue, with several business executives being violently dispatched by someone of apparently superhuman strength. Steed and Peel discover that the executives have all been competing for the rights to new Japanese communication technology. Their investigation leads them to a Dr. Armstrong, the wheelchair-bound head of an automation concern, who has developed a corps of invincible robot killers; the communication technology enables him to control them anywhere through the use of a transistorized pen.[45] Peel is eventually trapped in the toy company warehouse by a "cybernaut" programmed to kill her, but at the last minute, Steed redirects the robot to attack another automaton. The cybernauts destroy each other and in the process accidentally kill their creator. The episode ends with Peel, driving her Lotus, encountering Steed sitting in his Bentley doing a crossword puzzle. She offers him a pen, to which Steed responds dryly: "I don't hold with those new-fangled things." Smiling, she zooms away.

"The Cybernauts," although only the first episode in the series shown in the United States, displayed all of the elements that guided the program's reception by American audiences. First, ironically, was the show's resolute Britishness. From the umbrella and bowler sported by Steed in the opening sequence to the automobiles featured in the closing tag, nothing and no one in the program spoke with anything approaching an American accent—even the foreign business concerns were Japanese. This was a deliberate strategy of the show's producers, who felt that success in the American market depended upon their offering something that "copycat" American producers could not imitate: England.[46] "We became terribly British," Brian Clemens later said. "A car is a car is a car, and not an automobile. A lift is a lift is a lift and never an elevator. It is this Britishness that fits the fantasy world so appealing to the Americans."[47] By retaining essential differences in signification between the two cultures, including language, while at the same time retaining narrative conventions and plot devices (and the ironic tweakings thereof) familiar to both, the producers of *The Avengers* wisely hoped to appeal to a culture still looking outward to the Mother Country as a participant in re-creating a web of meaning following the Kennedy assassination trauma.

Of those narrative conventions coming out of the Bond movies and other secret agent shows, none was more important, as "The Cybernauts" would indicate, than the menace of technology. David Buxton argues that *The Avengers* represents a discourse on the place of technology in accommodating modernity to the traditional British class structure. A danger when used by a nouveau riche class (including scientist/entrepreneurs such as Armstrong) without regard to a traditional elite, technology is equally problematic when used by aristocrats to defend the old order against the rising welfare state. The middle ground, he argues, is technology in the service of consumption and fashion, a middle ground American audiences already found themselves occupying, thanks to Bond, U.N.C.L.E., Drake, and other secret agents.[48] As Buxton himself points out, however, American readings of technology and consumption in *The Avengers* differed from those constructed in Britain: "It is certain that most of the class references . . . were lost on an American audience for whom the British series had a quaint charm in its juxtaposition of the traditional (country house, fox shooting) and the modern (robots, atomic power plants)."[49] Nonetheless, the narrative deployment of technology as the tool of evil, familiar to American audiences not only through previous secret agent movies and television programs but through their own fears of nuclear holocaust, became the central motif of *Avengers* plots, superseding the Cold War even in many episodes in which Cold War concerns were directly referenced.[50]

More than anything, however, the character of Emma Peel differentiated *The Avengers* from other programs on American television and helped direct the show to a very different audience from that which its creators had imagined. Neither contained nor domestic, the one scene in which she is shown at home visually foregrounds the fact that she is there alone, engaged in a purely leisure activity: doing the daily crossword puzzle. Home, for Mrs. Peel, is not a place

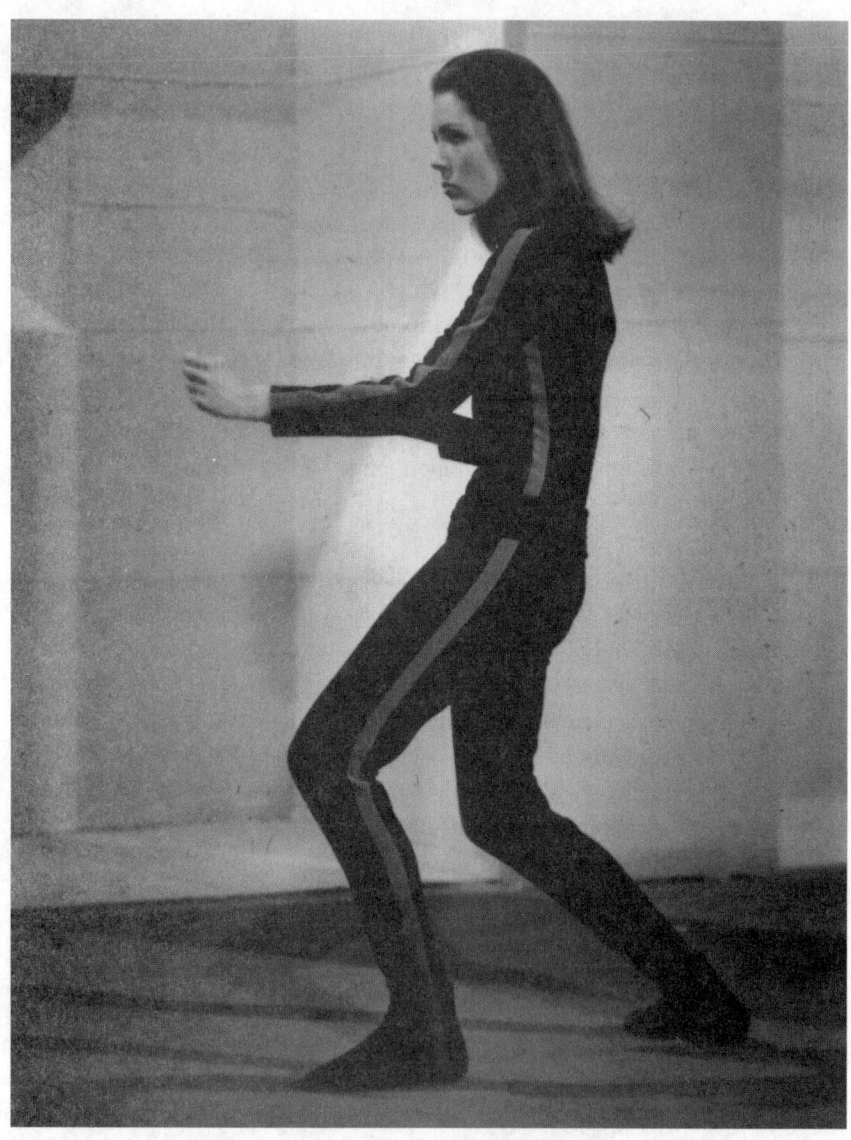

In one of her trendsetting Emmapeeler jumpsuits, Mrs. Peel embodies the dichotomy of a fashion model wanting only to be watched and a dangerous woman who can take care of herself in a man's world. Photograph courtesy of Photofest.

of day labor but a place of rest. That rest is disturbed, however, by her anxiety about not hearing from Steed, which finally leads her to bolt from the apartment to rescue her partner. She quite literally cannot be contained within domestic confines. Even more remarkable is the degree to which Emma Peel is depicted as an active, powerful woman who triumphs over the attempts of men to keep her "in her place." In a definitive scene early in "The Cybernauts," Emma goes to a karate studio to see if she can find a lead on the killer, who used karate to dispatch his victims. The bare and starkly lit training facility is occupied by four male students, a statuesque blonde woman, and the male teacher (*sensai*). When Peel inquires about taking a class, the *sensai* responds, "It is difficult for a woman to compete in such a category." "It's the idea of competition that appeals to me," Peel responds, to which the *sensai* ripostes, "Then I suggest that perhaps fencing will be more suitable for your purpose." Finally, he agrees to test Peel by pitting her against the blonde woman, "Oyuka—the immovable one." In a short time, Peel (dubbed "Obaki—the foolish one") subdues Oyuka, much to the surprise of both the loser and her instructor. "You attacked her as a woman," the *sensai* rebukes Oyuka, "but she has the skill of a man." To which Emma turns and leaves, flipping her shoes over her shoulder as she walks out.

This first episode of *The Avengers* aired in the United States reveals a shift in reading formations defining the relationship between the secret agent genre and its U.S. audience; at the same time, it reveals and begins to unravel what Janice Radway calls an "ideological seam"—a joining of a dominant ideology of domestic containment with the otherwise inflected utterances and practices of young American middle-class women, a joining that simply does not hold.[51] Emma Peel walking into a space defined by male power and triumphing over that power, rendering language itself meaningless in her silent departure, was a paradigmatic moment in American television, and a moment that American prime-time programs, still ensnared in issues of containment, could not yet present in their own cultural context. Indeed, the Britishness of *The Avengers,* coded in the program in everything from language to leisure activity to consumer goods, made Emma all the more powerful a role model to audiences of American young women. A contemporary American woman accomplishing Emma's deeds would have been seen as beyond fantasy, given the possibilities available in the ideology of the time. But a contemporary woman from a different place taking on those challenges and succeeding raised the possibility—within the text and without—that an ideology of domestic containment was something local, something temporal, and something that could eventually be transformed.[52]

This is not to say that the meaning of Emma Peel was constructed in the United States solely as that of an avatar of women's liberation. As Thomas Andrae suggests and Robert Musel's profile of Diana Rigg in *TV Guide* demonstrates, the character retained, for a significant part of the American audience, the quality of "to-be-looked-at-ness."[53] No less a bastion of the male gaze than *Playboy* defined *The Avengers* for its audience by containing the Rigg/Peel character within a well-established Bond girl formula. In a 1967 profile accompanying the show's return to ABC, the magazine said that Rigg "exudes more sheer sexuality than American TV has previously handled," and that the character of Emma Peel "is an erotic stylization, rather than a character, in pants suits, miniskirts and an incredibly kinky wardrobe."[54] And, as David Buxton argues, Rigg/Peel's secondary function within the show as a model for mod fashions marketed internationally adds another layer of "to-be-looked-at-ness" to the character: the "gaze of pop," in which an ideology of fetishistic consumption replaces the real world of social relations.[55] Emma Peel, in short, was still an object to be viewed for pleasure. But with that objective "to-be-looked-at-ness" in the character came the power, neither predicted nor discussed in Mulvey's concept of the male gaze, of looking back—a power evident not just in the series itself but in the narrative image created for it in its publicity: while displaying her body in the specially designed hip-hugging outfit in the photo used in *Variety* and the *New York Times,* Rigg/Peel is staring directly into the camera and pointing a gun at it. The object of the gaze becomes, in every sense of the term, an agent extraordinary.[56]

With the polyvalence present in the narrative image supported by that evident in the show itself, middle-class women and their daughters became particularly vocal partisans of the show. "Bravo to ABC for giving us *The Avengers,*" one woman wrote to *TV Guide.* "Now we can have at least one hour of excellent entertainment all summer long, hopefully even longer." Another woman correspondent commented in the same issue: "At last, a program with all the cheekiness of *The Man from U.N.C.L.E.* without being a direct take-off on same. I mean the zero-cool *Avengers.*"[57] "Amateur Avenger," a writer to *'Teen* magazine, the target audience of which is twelve- to seventeen-year-old girls, spoke to both gender and age in her comments after the first season of the show: "Let's get John Steed and Emma Peel back on television. 'The Avengers' was the only program that teens alone could understand. It had too much action for the older generation."[58]

Just as important as these letters in terms of revealing the significance of the Emma Peel character to a young middle-class female audience was the first American photo spread Diana Rigg did after the introduction of the series: for

Mademoiselle, a magazine whose audience of young middle-class women either in or on their way to college comprised precisely the "real girls who have grown up on television" about whom Friedan was speaking in *TV Guide* two years earlier. Presented in the July 1966 issue, the two-page layout, headlined "The Lethal Look," is every bit as polyvalent as the photographs used to establish the narrative image of *The Avengers.* On the first page, Rigg/Peel wears a jacket-brassiere-hiphugger outfit not dissimilar from the one worn in the earlier photograph—except this time the material is leather, with studs. Again, she points a gun, this time just to the left of the camera. The second photo features Rigg/Peel in a party dress covered with silver paillettes, looking over her shoulder toward the previous page, with her hands bound behind her back. The verbal text, again foregrounding the Bond connection, complements the pictorial contradiction: "Move over, James, the lady-killers are here, the fantastic females whose delicate fingers tap teacups one moment, pull triggers the next. The latest of the ladies to mix karate with pleasure is ice-cool-witted Mrs. Emma Peel (actress Diana Rigg) of ABC-TV's *The Avengers.*"[59]

The *Mademoiselle* layout represents the same dialectic present in the series itself and vital to changing constructions of women in American culture. Rigg/Peel is still forced to play captured princess (looking to herself for rescue, given the dynamics of the photo spread), yet she is in control of herself and her situation. As a fashion model, she embodies "to-be-looked-at-ness"; as the role model, however, that places her as fashion model in a magazine aimed at young women, she assumes that look and uses it as a source of power. And although the photographs emphasize her body to the point that the top part of her head is cropped off the page, they also suggest that the page cannot contain her. In short, the photo spread reveals the "lethal look" of the viewer while it grants Peel/Rigg a similarly lethal look. Like *The Avengers* itself, the Rigg/Peel *Mademoiselle* pages indicate the new fluidity of roles available to American women, particularly young middle-class American women, and help explain the appeal of the show to that group.

The Fall of Tara

Though never a Top 20 ratings hit in the United States, *The Avengers,* with its devoted core audience, performed better than average, which for ABC in the late 1960s was a major triumph.[60] After the show returned to the network's schedule in the middle of the 1966–67 season, ABC programmers assured its British producers that it would be brought back again at some point the following season. By that time, however, both parties faced a significant problem: Diana Rigg, exhausted with the weekly production schedule and with her character, had decided to leave the series.[61] Rigg's departure activated a new set of utterances that would both sew up the ideological seam her character had ripped open and exemplify the complex relationship between Bakhtinian "assimilation" and the process of "absorbing and domesticating" defining the hegemonic ideology represented by and on American television. American network executives, upon hearing of Rigg's resignation from the series, decided to hold her final appearances for broadcast in 1967–68 in order to string out the popularity of Emma Peel for as long as possible; at the same time, ABC-UK briefly removed producers Brian Clemens and Albert Fennell from the series to modify the show's entire premise. During their absence, the company chose the replacement for Rigg/Peel: Linda Thorson, a twenty-year-old ingenue, was selected from a casting call of more than two hundred actresses to play Steed's new partner, Tara King.[62] According to sources in the British press, reported in turn by *Variety,* however, that choice was made ultimately not by the show's British producers but by an ABC executive based in London.[63] Thorson's character was to be a different bird entirely from Mrs. Peel. Tara was young and single; her interest in Steed obviously extended beyond the professional, as did his in her. Her wardrobe was softer, more "feminine," than that worn by Mrs. Peel. And while she would still have the physical toughness of any secret agent, Tara was to rely more on her sexuality than on her knowledge of martial arts in vanquishing villains. In short, Tara King was conceived as a move away from the liberatory character portrayed by Rigg back to the model of the Bond girl: woman contained, if not in a home, in a role and image as object defined by the needs and desires of men.[64]

The narrative image fixed for Thorson/King in *TV Guide* before her American introduction to the series in March 1968 played the actress's own assertiveness about her portrayal of the character against more traditional elements of femininity and sexuality. Robert Musel's profile of Thorson, like his profile of Emma Peel, was preceded by a photograph of the actress in character. Instead of an intent woman holding a fencing sword, however, the image showed a crouching woman, wearing a jacket-miniskirt ensemble, peering out from behind a wall, with the larger, imposing figure of Macnee/Steed right behind her: the picture was one of containment. Musel's text again brought the male gaze to bear on the new character's body and sexuality, comparing Rigg's "lean and boyish figure, [with] her bizarre black-leather and mod outfits," to that of Thorson: "a notable 5-feet-9-inches tall and 38 inches elsewhere."[65] Thorson was presented as a spunky newcomer with her own ideas about who Tara King is; those ideas, however, conformed precisely to the expectations embodied in the notion of "to-be-looked-at-ness." She discussed how Tara should "have an affair" with Steed, how Tara would just as soon use a brick in her handbag instead of karate and her sex appeal instead of both, about the renewed fashion emphasis on bosoms: "[I saw] one dress with a top of yards and yards of chiffon, and nothing under it, that I'd love to wear. I hate bras."[66]

The creation of Tara King, the hiring of Linda Thorson, and the narrative image for *The Avengers* constructed around both represented a retrograde shift in signification similar to the one occurring in the Bond girl between the Connery and Moore films: a woman powerful enough to return the male gaze reverts to a character whose power lay in her willingness to accept men's sexual objectification.[67] Tara King was much closer in style and spirit to Honey West than to Emma Peel—no surprise, given the evident role of American network executives in seeing both characters come to life and the domestic cultural concerns to which they were speaking. With student activism over the war in Vietnam and urban riots at their peak in 1967 and 1968, American television producers sought to present a new model of containment, one that took representatives of dangerous elements of society—the young, African Americans, women—and put them to work preserving law and order under the tutelage of older male authority figures. Introduced by NBC's *Ironside* and perfected the following year on ABC by the Aaron Spelling-produced *Mod Squad,* this new model of containment allowed that women could work outside the home, even in dangerous occupations. But in so doing, those women worked only to uphold an ideological status quo that explicitly recognized them as a threat.

Tara King fit much more readily into this mold than did Emma Peel. To be doubly sure that the new definition of "the *Avengers* girl" would hold, ABC executives played a significant role in another major decision concerning the series: the addition of a superior officer to whom Steed and King would report. Although the agency chief, a large paraplegic man called "Mother," was to have appeared only in the Rigg-Thorson transition episode, ABC officials liked the character so much that they told the show's British producers to make him a continuing character.[68] Not only, then, had the role of the female agent been changed, but a new layer of authority had been added to the concept of the show itself, reintroducing the bureaucracy of earlier secret agent series and reducing another element of the show's significant difference from American product. Producer Brian Clemens nonetheless attempted to quell British concerns about an increased American presence in the production of the show, as well as concerns on the part of the show's American viewers about the changes being made. In an interview with *Variety,* he denied American involvement in Thorson's hiring and said that of twelve "suggested alterations" made by ABC-US, only three had been acted on.[69]

It quickly became clear, however, that no matter what Clemens might say, American audiences were less than pleased with the changes made in the series, whatever their origin. *Variety*'s own review of the first King episode, which acknowledged that Thorson was "a pretty dish," bemoaned the loss of the difference Emma Peel made: "It is obvious that Miss Thorson is going to be much more the femme foil and much less the strong and willful second hand portrayed by Miss Rigg."[70] Viewers who wrote to *TV Guide* were also less enthusiastic than Robert Musel about the change. "With Emma gone, *The Avengers* has lost its ap-peel," wrote one correspondent.[71] And with the return of Emma Peel in 1968 summer reruns, another writer commented: "One good thing about reruns with *The Avengers* — we get back the Peel instead of the lemon."[72]

The ratings of the eight shows broadcast in early 1968 before Rigg departed, however, were enough of an improvement over ABC's previous Wednesday-night offering, and the financially strapped network was desperate enough for any programming that might save money, that *The Avengers* was added to the fall schedule for the first time.[73] Programmers, recognizing the appeal the show had to an audience of young women, scheduled the show for 7:30–8:30 Monday nights, opposite CBS's aging horse opera *Gunsmoke*; they failed to recognize, however, that the character responsible for much of that attraction was gone, replaced by one targeted more for the men and boys who watched the CBS show.[74] *TV Guide* hardly made the situation for the network any better when it ran, barely a month before the beginning of the 1968–69 season, another Robert Musel profile of Diana Rigg, "She's Miss Rigg of St. John's Wood, Now." In response to letters from Americans that Musel brought with him to the interview, Rigg said: "I've come to realize the interest viewers have in television people. It's surprising — and touching — that nearly a year later so many should write that they regret my departure."[75]

With the absence of Rigg already contributing more profoundly to a narrative image of *The Avengers* in its new season than the presence of her replacement, ABC made matters more muddled in terms of its intended audience with its season-opening ad in *TV Guide.* Instead of Tara King, the familiar figure of John Steed, facing the reader, dominated the half-column photograph. King, like Steed in the earlier ads with Peel, appeared in a small inset in front of the male character, looking off the page.[76] Neither this nor any image constructed to promote the program, however, made any difference with viewers, given the programs NBC chose to present opposite *The Avengers: I Dream of Jeannie* and *Rowan & Martin's Laugh-In,* a sketch comedy show itself influenced by British television, which had become the most popular program in American prime time. Against this competition, as well as *Gunsmoke,* which now could attract an audience looking for something aside from the mod offerings of ABC and NBC, *The Avengers* ended up sixty-ninth among all regular series for the season; in early 1969, ABC canceled the series. Without import fees from the United States, and with falling ratings at home, ABC-UK announced that the conclusion of the thirty-three Tara King episodes would mark the end of *The Avengers.*

The Avengers marks a particularly significant moment in the cultural dialogue between British television and American audiences during the 1960s and 1970s. Beyond the direct American imitations it spawned—*Honey West* earlier, *The Girl from U.N.C.L.E.* later—*The Avengers* provided American television producers with the model for a female crime fighter they would then incorporate into their spy and police shows of the late 1960s.[77] The work accomplished by those producers in "adapting" *The Avengers* into American texts speaks directly to the fluidity of "the hegemonic" as defined by Raymond Williams, as that work recognized and incorporated the readings of an audience outside a dominant ideology of domestic containment in the framework of texts reconstituting a separate ideology of political containment.[78] At the same time, however, the efforts of producers, programmers, and promoters to reshape and reframe *The Avengers* following Diana Rigg's departure represent a limit to the process of hegemony, particularly as defined in terms of absorption and domestication. The character of Tara King represented a domestication of Emma Peel, contained if not in a suburban American home then in a patriarchal definition of an active woman. Yet many in the American audience of *The Avengers* rejected that construction, largely because of the way in which the character of Emma represented difference first and foremost through her Britishness—her lack of domestication. Williams argues that "any hegemonic process must be especially alert and responsive to the alternatives . . . which question or threaten its dominance."[79] In the case of *The Avengers,* however, hegemonic domestication meant negating the alternative—the appeal of the British Emma to young American middle-class women—in favor of another signification of patriarchal containment.

Again, it is Bakhtin's use of the term *assimilation,* with its multiple "utterances" and the creativity involved in addressing them, that better explains the way in which *The Avengers* made its way into American culture. Developed and exported as a representative of a genre created by males for a male audience,

The Avengers arrived from Britain at a moment when the ideological construction of the American woman was in flux. While the negotiation of its many "alien words and value judgments" meant that viewers could read the show as its initial promotion suggested it should be—as a male-oriented adventure—the character of Emma Peel opened up another reading for the young women of whom Betty Friedan had earlier spoken: that of the power of an independent woman who operated on equal, if not superior, terms with men in the "real world." The unwillingness, deliberate or otherwise, of American television executives to countenance this reading led to a retrenchment, a forced and false return to earlier genre conventions, that led in part to the show's demise, in both the United States and Britain. Finally, *The Avengers* amplified the argument, increasing in loudness, that British television was better than American television, and that it was the duty of American television, in the public interest, to present the best programming possible. The cancellation of *The Prisoner, The Saint,* and *The Avengers* in the same year seemed to mark an end to that reasoning. Soon enough, however, the argument would find a new channel.

4. Down the Up Staircase

The Forsyte Saga, Masterpiece Theatre, and Upstairs, Downstairs

Noncommercial television should address itself to the ideal of excellence, not the idea of acceptability — which is what keeps commercial television from climbing the staircase. I think television should be the visual counterpart of the literary essay, should arouse our dreams, satisfy our hunger for beauty, take us on journeys, enable us to participate in events, present great drama and music, explore the sea and the sky and the woods and the hills. It should be our Lyceum, our Chatauqua, our Minsky's and our Camelot.

    — E. B. White[1]

With the departure of the secret agent imports from the commercial networks in 1969, a second wave of British programming came to American airwaves — and with it, a shift in signification from a mod sense of contemporary consumption to a historical and literary sensibility of aristocratic noblesse oblige.[2] The BBC-produced *The Forsyte Saga,* which arrived on America's nascent noncommercial public broadcasting system in 1969, was followed by various programs presented as *Masterpiece Theatre* that were similarly based on canonical fiction and constructed as serial dramas. As had been the case with secret agent shows, American viewers found meanings in the differences represented in and by the new serial dramas that read around those prescribed in critical commentary. Those readings, however, were also shaped by the utterances of two institutional powers not previously encountered: the administration of President Richard Nixon, which sought to re-create American public broadcasting in the elitist image of the early BBC in order to defuse any potential political criticism; and Mobil Oil, which sought to use the British imports featured on *Masterpiece Theatre* as part of a public relations campaign to convince a cultural elite of Mobil's worth to the republic. Both succeeded in transforming the intent and purpose of American public broadcasting; neither, however, achieved the transmissive control it had imagined over American audiences.

It's Time to Get Things Started

If understandings of transnational communications based primarily on quantitative assumptions of economic domination held true, Lew Grade would have wielded considerable power over the United States during the early 1970s, given the numbers of programs he managed to get aired. Economics, however, as has already been amply demonstrated, is never the entire story in the relationships among television producers, distributors, and audiences. Whatever reception Grade's products may have enjoyed in sales was matched by the lack of public interest in them.[3] It was not until 1976 that Grade could claim a bona fide success in the American market, with a syndicated music hall variety show starring not a Briton but a group of fuzzy, made-in-America socks with googly eyes: *The Muppet Show.*[4] The popularity of Jim Henson's creation spoke not only to the efforts of Lew Grade, however, but to increasing public awareness and popularity of noncommercial American television, where Henson's Muppets had established a major presence as feature performers on the children's educational program *Sesame Street.*

Introduced in fall 1969, *Sesame Street* could not have arrived at a more propitious time for noncommercial broadcasting in the United States. For years a whirling nebula of tiny individual local stations, "educational broadcasting" became during the 1960s increasingly important to groups concerned about the spread of Newton Minow's "wasteland" under the now-dominant commercial networks. The Ford Foundation, for years the largest private funder of educational broadcasting, announced in 1966 that it would pay for the production of an hour-long program for the nation's some 170 educational television stations, as well as a linkup that would create working connections among all those stations. A month later, the Carnegie Commission report on the subject, *Public Television: A Program for Action,* was released. Although criticized by some for seeming to subordinate public television to the commercial network model and failing to create a definitive alternative to the networks, the Carnegie report impressed then-President Lyndon Johnson enough for his administration to sponsor a bill establishing goals and funding for American noncommercial broadcasting.[5] The Public Broadcasting Act of 1967 established the Corporation for Public Broadcasting (CPB) as a funding organization to facilitate the creation and production of national programming as well as the support of local operations and programming.[6] The act was designed to give educational television stability and to support an alternative structure to that of the network-affiliate relationship of commercial television; money would come at least initially from the federal government.

By November 1969, that structure had developed to the point that CPB formally incorporated the Public Broadcasting Service (PBS), a private organiza-

The Forsyte family gathers for a traditional British family photo, a visual representation, some American critics would argue, of a stability, order, and decorum lost in the tumultuous 1960s. Photograph courtesy of Photofest.

tion run by public station managers themselves, designed to connect those stations in something resembling a network.[7] With a distribution system in place, something to distribute had to follow. *Sesame Street,* which went on the air the same week PBS was incorporated, gave educational and public broadcasting both new recognition and new audiences.[8] Despite presenting acclaimed productions of theatrical plays and filmed documentaries, however, educational television had little presence in most American homes after the dinner hour. That too would change, however, with the broadcast, also beginning in fall 1969, of a series from Britain that bore neither the mid-Atlantic trademarks of Lew Grade nor the cheeky "kinkiness" of *The Avengers.*

Forsythia in Bloom

The import of *The Forsyte Saga* to the United States in 1969 both reinforces the most basic economic arguments about transnational communications and reveals the ideological underpinnings of American noncommercial television.[9] A twenty-six-episode adaptation of the novels of Nobel Prize winner John Galsworthy, mounted by the BBC in commemoration of the author's centenary in 1967, *The Forsyte Saga* depicted the rise and decline of an upper-middle-class British family during the late nineteenth and early twentieth centuries. At first the series focused on the feuding cousins Jolyon (Kenneth More) and Soames (Eric Porter) Forsyte, the former a disillusioned artist, the latter a rapacious lawyer; it rapidly expanded, however, to explore the affairs, betrayals, and chaos, romantic and financial, that their disagreements set off within and outside the family over the ensuing four decades. Chief among those affairs were those that brought the ambitious young women Irene (Nyree Dawn Porter) and Fleur (Susan Hampshire) into and out of the family struggles. By the end of 1968, the serial had become a record-breaking phenomenon not only in Britain, where evening church services had to be rescheduled in order to accommodate parishoners more devoted to the agonies of Soames and Fleur than to those of Christ and the prophets, but in dozens of countries around the world.[10] Those nations did not include the United States, where commercial networks would countenance neither a high-toned British historical drama nor a deliberately circumscribed series—especially one in black and white.[11] One American outlet, however, was interested in the program: National Educational Television (NET), the noncommercial programming service based in New York. With publicity about the show appearing already in trade journals, and with the BBC now trying to follow its British commercial rivals into American markets, NET purchased unlimited three-year broadcast rights to the entire series early in 1969 for $140,000—at a time when a single episode of *The Avengers,* a bargain by commercial network standards, cost $110,000.[12]

With cost the determinant factor in its arrival, and without the need for commercial product differentiation that spurred the deliberate development of narrative images for previous British imports, *The Forsyte Saga* began its broadcast history in the United States with little fanfare. *TV Guide,* which had previously introduced British programs to American audiences well in advance of their import, noted only in a brief July 1969 sidebar that the *Saga* was one of two programs that would replace the Ford Foundation's ill-fated *Public Broadcasting Laboratory* that fall.[13] Of all national media sources, only the *New York Times* offered an introduction to the series before its premiere—one that focused more on the broadcast and export history of the show than it did on the stars, characters, or plots thereof.[14]

Once NET began its weekly Sunday-night broadcasts on October 5, 1969, however, messages circulating in other media about the *Saga* would follow three clearly marked lines toward its American assimilation.[15] The first of those paths became evident on the morning of October 6, 1969, when Jack Gould wrote in

In one of the classic soap opera moments of the serial drama *The Forsyte Saga,* Fleur (Susan Hampshire), "assisted" by Soames (Eric Porter), prepares to marry a man she doesn't love. Photograph courtesy of Photofest.

the *New York Times* that NET would seem to be "the Sunday night home of upper-class soap opera. . . . If all goes well, as it so clearly did in its appeal in Britain, *The Forsyte Saga* might have a constructive influence on America's daytime deluge of serials."[16] Connections between the British import and the generic norms of American soap opera quickly became a common thread in commentary on the *Saga*. British novelist Anthony Burgess, writing for the *New York Times Magazine,* called the program "a great television triumph, since the Galsworthian conception has the near-coarseness, the near-melodramatic simplicity of superior soap opera."[17] American novelist James Michener, in a *TV Guide* feature article, called the serial "soap opera—at its glowing best."[18]

Significant in those comments is not just the genre identification each sought to create for the show but the stated belief that *The Forsyte Saga* was better than contemporary examples of American soap opera. That "superiority" certainly had little to do with the show's production values. *The Forsyte Saga* visually employed the same techniques and rhetoric as its American cousins: restricted camera movement, a large number of two-character scenes involving repeated use of close-ups, an almost exclusive reliance on interiors, careful attention to detail in props defining class status and/or plot action.[19] The first episode, in fact, included production accidents similar to those for which critics regularly mocked daytime serial drama in America.[20] Whereas daytime dramas, those critics argued, seemed only to serve the fantasies of everyday housewives, *The Forsyte Saga* supplemented romance-centered story lines with Galsworthy's "realistic" forays into male-defined worlds of business and politics.[21] As a result, the *Saga* acquired a cultural significance, coded as "literacy," to its critics that they transmitted to their readers in turn. As Michener, in the clearest example of the patriarchal upscaling of the program, described it: "In *The Forsyte Saga* the characters are differentiated, well-rounded and with universal application; the dialogue is literate; the problems dealt with are substantial; and over all there is high seriousness."[22]

The "literate" quality that Michener cited also constituted the second line shaping the American construction of the *Saga*. The fact that it was based on fiction by a British author was featured prominently in all the commentary on the television program; indeed, the series was enhanced, according to that commentary, by the way it improved on the original work. The "Galsworthian conception" of life portrayed in the nine novels of the *Saga,* Burgess argued, "has been waiting all these years to slide into its true medium—the leisurely, middlebrow television serial."[23] Margot Hentoff, writing in *Vogue,* agreed: "The *Forsyte* novels are good bad fiction at its best—admirably suited to the reduction of television since there is little complexity to be lost. . . . In fact, the shrinking effect makes Galsworthy seem far leaner and more witty than he was."[24] Even Michener, allowing that "almost every good line in the series comes from Galsworthy," went on to note that "the brilliance of the series does not stem from the books."[25]

The conflation of the television version of *The Forsyte Saga* conducted in the American press at the expense of Galsworthy's reputation circumscribed meaning in two ways. First, it created for a television text a single authorial figure born out of literature, whose intents and judgments, as both Roland Barthes and Michel Foucault argue, became the "final signified" from which viewers/readers could construct meaning.[26] Second, the authorial qualities Burgess, Michener, and Hentoff created to direct the reading of the television *Forsyte Saga* were such that the possibilities for deriving meaning outside Galsworthy's intent were virtually negligible. All three critics commented on the ability of Galsworthy and "his" series to convey external "reality," as opposed to "inner dreams."[27] Michener in particular praised the show's "real places," "real characters," "real people," and sets and costumes that "lend authenticity."[28] The emphasis on the literary realism of the novels and the series speaks directly to Barthes's concept of the "readerly text," developed for television studies by John Fiske. The "readerly text," Fiske writes, "is one that approximates . . . a 'classic realist text,' that is, one which 'reads' easily, does not foreground its own nature as discourse, and appears to promote a singular meaning which is not that of the text, but of the real."[29] Accessible to many, with meaning confined to what the author presents as "real," Fiske's "readerly text" seems to be well exemplified by a program that Margot Hentoff described as "the closest thing we have had to a 'good read' on television."[30]

Having first placed *The Forsyte Saga* into a familiar television genre and then addressed the text itself through the presence and qualities of its literary author, critics finally addressed its "singular meaning" in 1969 America as the third part of their effort to guide the program's assimilation. There was again unanimity in the belief that the *Saga* offered American audiences a somewhat wistful look at a time in which stability and order held sway in a society that could no longer exist. Hentoff, arguing as Michener and Jack Gould had, used an appropriate metaphor for her *Vogue* platform: "In our own time, we have more or less stopped believing in the continuity of anything. . . . As behavior becomes more generally erratic, our own erratic actions provoke fewer ripples on our society. What does one more rip mean to a tattered fabric? But in *The Forsyte Saga* rips matter."[31] In short, the critical view of the meaning of *The Forsyte Saga* was that ascribed later by John Caughie to all the "costume dramas of a simpler class hierarchy" exported by Britain to the United States: "a mild nostalgia for a lost community."[32]

Although they presented a remarkably consistent front in shaping an American construction of *The Forsyte Saga,* the arguments offered by Hentoff, Burgess, Gould, and Michener were followed only to a limited degree by the opinions of viewers cited in magazines of the day. One viewer quoted in a *New Yorker* piece on the series' popularity offered gratitude for its bringing back "many happy hours of my youth," while a South Dakota woman spoke of how she used the series as a means of getting together with friends: "I introduced them to the Forsytes with tea-and-sherry parties, and they've shared my enthusiasm ever since."[33] Similarly, a Minnesota professor interviewed by Michener scheduled *Saga* gatherings with other regular viewers in his town. A family Michener talked to watched the show together, afterward "discussing the Forsytes as if we knew them."[34]

What comes clear in the meanings circulated by the viewers of the *Saga* themselves is not so much a nostalgia for a lost community as a building of new communities around the experiences of a family from Victorian England — a phenomenon John Caughie notes in the British reception of serialized drama from the inception of the genre.[35] The "Forsyte phenomenon" represents in essence what James Carey defines as the ritual paradigm of communication, the archetypal case of which is "the sacred ceremony that draws persons together in fellowship and commonality."[36] (Given the British experience of *The Forsyte Saga* as sacred ceremony, it seems hardly a coincidence that NET chose to broadcast the show in the United States on Sunday nights.) The development of community out of the ceremony of viewing *The Forsyte Saga,* then, offers a new definition of the processes and products of communication in contemporary American life, running counter as it does to the messages transmitted by the show's critics about the messages they found transmitted in the show. As such, it also serves as another moment in which Radway's "ideological seam" shows, a moment in which the shock of something new from a different place reveals the operations of ideology in American television.[37] Taking meanings derived in this recouping of community from *The Forsyte Saga* in the United States as being resistant or liberatory in their own right would be an error: the ideological centrality of family in the "text of *Forsyte*" was little different from its centrality in American soap operas — or in the "containing" sitcoms and cop shows of commercial prime time.[38] The differences evident in the time and place of the *Saga,* however, along with the formal qualities of serial drama and the fact that both were being distributed by a "service" not defined by commercial capitalism, made for another moment in which dialogue between British television and American audiences — and resultant dialogues among those audiences — laid bare the processes that endeavored to control that discussion. It would only be a moment, however, as the meanings of British television in America were about to be redefined by utterances that made the industrial workings of hegemony seem as benign as a quiet Cotswold brook lapping its vernal shore.

Public Image Limited

The difficulties noncommercial broadcasting would come to face with the Nixon administration, and the role of British television in those difficulties, were set with the passage of the federal legislation that first began to organize what would soon be called "public television." The Public Broadcasting Act of 1967, for all it did in creating the institution of public television, did not create a source of funding outside the federal government itself.[39] In addition, the board created to govern CPB consisted of fifteen presidential appointees, ensuring that public broadcasting would represent the interests of the political party with the power of appointment. As a guard against already evident political pressure, Congress mandated that the corporation maintain "objectivity and balance in all programs or series of programs of a controversial nature," in essence requiring both CPB and local stations to maintain stricter standards than were required of any other broadcast or print media while leaving "controversial nature" an arbitrary term.[40] Enacted to "insulate" public broadcasting from external controls, the congressional provisions did far more to isolate it, making it all the more vulnerable to the political whims of the moment.

The arguments within and outside of public broadcasting as to the roles and limits assigned it lasted through the election of 1968, when public broadcasting's patron, Lyndon Johnson, was replaced in office by Richard Nixon, a man with a long-standing distrust of media.[41] With other matters preoccupying it, however, the Nixon administration would not become concerned with what were little more than splotches of gruel on the broad tablecloth of American broadcasting until November 1969, when CPB formally incorporated PBS. The new "service," as previously noted, represented the desire of local station managers to work together in determining the programming they wanted. It also deliberately reduced the power of New York's "controversial" NET as the distributor of programs to their stations.[42] Designed, in short, as another layer of "insulation" to protect local public broadcasters from political pressure, PBS instead immediately brought the entirety of public television under political scrutiny, as it both assumed a centralized role similar to that of the commercial networks and took on the duty of defining what was and was not "controversial."[43] This scrutiny came just when the Nixon administration, through a series of speeches made by Vice President Spiro Agnew, made clear its hostility toward the "controversial" news programming of the commercial networks, and just when public television was proving, through the daytime broadcast of *Sesame Street* and the Sunday-evening showing of *The Forsyte Saga,* that it could attract a national audience of both size and status.[44]

By the end of 1969, noncommercial broadcasting was beginning to feel the effects of the Nixon-Agnew hand, as programs and program segments were apparently added and dropped from PBS depending upon how they addressed governmental concerns.[45] The strict constructionism evidently employed by CPB and PBS with the terms *objectivity* and *balance* in order to appease the Nixon administration was observed with some jaundice in the press: *Variety* regularly referred to the two entities as "the Corporation for Patsy Broadcasting" and "the Public Blushing Service," and *Newsweek* would come to call PBS "the Nixon network."[46] Although the administration seemed content to use the carrot of funding and the stick of "objectivity and balance," along with the internecine squabbling they provoked, as benign ways to control a weak public broadcasting system, the creation of a CPB-PBS national news program and an attack on the FBI by NET's *The Great American Dream Machine* in summer 1971 served to make its hostility toward public television open and direct.[47] Soon afterward, Nixon administration officials directly threatened public broadcasters with denial of future funding, followed by a presidential veto of the first congressional effort to establish a long-range funding plan.[48]

The effort by the Nixon administration to force public television into line with its political program eventually failed, as it led to resistance among those it had hoped most to win over: local broadcasters and viewers.[49] Nixon's coercion of public broadcasting, however, did work in ways that those responsible might not have imagined. First, the Nixon mandate against centralization was essentially carried out with the approval of a 1973 funding bill that made PBS national programming dependent upon local stations' desire to pay for its production.[50] More significantly, the purpose of the rhetoric and funding threats aimed at public television constituted coercion in a special sense, as it never envisioned the appropriation of the system as a "propaganda machine" for President Nixon and his administration.[51] Rather, it sought to keep the negative use of the system to a minimum, to discourage the commissive sin of criticism by rewarding the omissive sin of silence. As such, it engaged in a public and political circumscription of meaning, keeping the boundaries of polyvalence as narrow as possible insofar as they might be seen with public television. And one of the key elements of that process became the small but significant success of an imported British series supposedly addressed to the contemporary lack of belief "in the continuity of anything," a series supposedly designed to satisfy "a mild nostalgia for a lost community," a series supposedly celebrating bourgeois values of stability and order in a time long ago and a country far away. With *The Forsyte Saga,* public television and its "cultural programming" began to move away from the threat of politically sensitive contemporary dramas, to say nothing of public affairs programming, and closer to the Nixon administration's vision for it, a vision best represented in Nixon's 1971 encomium to the British Broadcasting Corporation on its fiftieth anniversary:

> As one of the world's oldest and most respected broadcasters both at home and abroad, the British Broadcasting Corporation has set an inspiring example of objective and dispassionate news reporting. It has earned the widest possible reputation for credibility and integrity. On its fiftieth anniversary, the citizens of the United States join with countless other men and women in recognition of of its public service. On their behalf, borrowing from the words of William Shakespeare, I want to say that BBC has in its work over the past half-century mirrored the times in which we live, and that all the world has truly been its stage.[52]

With the words of William Shakespeare barely dry on the page, Richard Nixon would veto long-term funding of American public broadcasting two days later.

To Serve Mankind

As Nixon's birthday wish indicated, the British Broadcasting Corporation itself had, once its programs found an American audience through public television, become one of the most potent cultural and political signifiers of the British superiority to American television long seen in discourse about the medium. Granted its formal charter on January 1, 1927, the BBC was organized as a public corporation, supported financially by license fees on receivers instead of private commercial interests, and, as the recipient of a Royal Charter, operated outside of government influence by a board of governors acting as "trustees of the public interest in broadcasting."[53] Toward that end, the board worked to ensure the "great value" of broadcasting as a means of "disseminating information, education and entertainment" that maintained high standards of quality in content and that was both balanced and impartial in its news coverage.[54] Although the concept of "public interest" was left as deliberately open-ended as it was when the Communications Act of 1934 made "public interest" the basis of station licensure in the United States, the BBC's first director-general, John Reith, had a specific and Arnoldian definition of the term he intended to follow: "So the responsibility as at the outset conceived, and despite all discouragements pursued, was to carry into the greatest number of homes everything that was best in every department of human knowledge, endeavour and achievement; and to avoid whatever was or might be hurtful."[55]

Reith believed that broadcasting solely for the purpose of entertainment was "an insult to the character and the intelligence of the people." Instead, the BBC would present "the best" of music, of drama, of debate and conversation, all of which would further the goal of education, which he defined as "a systematic and sustained endeavour to re-create, to build up knowledge, experience and character." The educated, he believed, formed an "elect" that broadcasting could greatly increase; toward that end, he vowed that "vulgarity" had no part in the mission of the BBC: "It is occasionally indicated to us that we are apparently setting out to give the public what we think they need — and not what they want, but few know what they want and very few what they need." Broadcasting, in the end, by serving the public, became itself "a servant of culture."[56]

Reith's mandate for the BBC's public service was modified greatly by the demands placed on it, including the development of television technology, during World War II and the immediate postwar years. But his call for the BBC "to carry... everything that was best in every department of human knowledge, endeavour and achievement" — words that were in large part responsible for the creation of the serialized drama in Britain itself — would quickly and easily become the core of the American definition of public television, as well as Herbert Schiller's desideratum for the medium.[57] Indeed, E. B. White's invocation to the Carnegie Commission, however "vigorously diverse" it might seem, reflected in its call for "excellence," its summoning of the "literary essay," and its nominal qualifications of what "noncommercial television" should present — not vaudeville (the Berle or Gleason of commercial television) but "Minsky's" — the Arnoldian elitism voiced in Reith's early definition of the BBC.[58]

The name selected for the new system also followed that philosophy: it was not the Public Broadcasting *System* but the Public Broadcasting *Service.* Although chosen to avoid the already evident political concerns roused by the terms *network* and *system,* the *S* in PBS also spoke to the organization's relationship to its viewing audience, which John Macy, the first president of the Corporation for Public Broadcasting, would later define as "to create and deliver a message for the public good."[59] As C. T. Dornan notes in his critical commentary on the public service ideal of the BBC, the rhetoric of the terms *public service* and *public good* masks the ideology and power structure behind noncommercial broadcasting, one that necessarily stratifies the "public" and "serves" the "good" of those wielding power.[60] Macy's words unmask the similar function of CPB and PBS, regardless of any Nixon influence, in their early years: the organizations would indeed act as "servants of culture"—"culture," however, not as defined by a sharing of meaning but rather by the transmission of messages to "educate, enlighten and entertain."[61] Culture, in other words, came down from on high to elevate the low.

Self-improvement—and with it societal improvement—indeed was the specific function of PBS educational programs such as *Sesame Street.* Whether it was the purpose of enlightenment or entertainment—a term that, following Victor Turner, literally means "holding between" and implies a leveling of social strata—was another question, however.[62] That question would be answered by another apt phrase of John Macy's: "Hail to the BBC."[63] Though intended as a salute to British imports beginning with *The Forsyte Saga,* Macy's "hail" also articulates the ideology of broadcasting and culture represented in the "public service" character of those BBC shows to the still vague and unformed purposes of a public broadcasting service in the United States. That articulation also furthered the shift in signification of "British television" away from the ideological and cultural concerns of the Kennedy years that had shaped the reception of *Secret Agent* and *The Avengers* toward those represented by Nixon and Agnew. Already denoted as "better" than "standard Hollywood fare," American public television programs, beginning with the *The Forsyte Saga,* were also supposed to make their audiences better, to develop an "elect" through what Pierre Bourdieu calls the "generalizing tendency" to link the canonic works learned in school to other related forms: the television series was, as its commentators repeatedly noted without irony, John Galsworthy's *Forsyte Saga.*[64]

What was also clear in this generalization, however, was that the members of the "quality" audience of the *Saga* possessed educational and cultural capital that placed them, from the first episode, on a social stratum above many of the show's potential viewers, a fact visible in the location of intertextual messages about the show and about the network—the *New Yorker, Vogue,* the *New York Times Magazine,* and other publications aimed almost exclusively at an upscale audience.[65] In addition to being made better by public television, these viewers were "better" to begin with. The meanings to be constructed by American audiences from the new BBC imports were, then, inflected not only by political coercion and a philosophy of "public service" reducing a field of dialogic utterances to a line of transmissive dicta, but by an ideological configuring inherent in those imports themselves of the "public" to be "served."

As was the case with *service,* the term *public* received a great deal of scrutiny from the first discussions of a Corporation for Public Broadcasting. The 1967 Carnegie Commission report, recognizing that noncommercial television in the United States could never hope to equal the power of the commercial networks in drawing a mass audience, established that the goal of public television should be to "serve differentiated audiences"—in other words, to program for special segments of the "public."[66] Although the question of whether a specialized audience necessarily meant a small audience would be argued for years to come, the meaning shared within the American public television community was that public broadcasting should maintain a goal of creating and delivering messages for the public good of some of the people some of the time.[67] American public television, in short, seemed at its inception to be devoted to ideals of "cultural responsibility and social accountability" that Ang uses to define the "audience-as-public" paradigm—and that defined the BBC model of public broadcasting with which it became articulated.[68]

As Patricia Aufderheide and William Hoynes suggest, however, an "audience" does not a "public" make. A public, they argue, comprises individual citizens organizing and actively engaging in social dialogue to determine democratically their present needs and future aims; an audience is a group of people passively watching or listening to a spectacle—and in the case of commercial television, being manipulated to buy the products being advertised as part of that spectacle.[69] In calling viewers of its service an "audience" from the start, no matter how "differentiated" or "specialized," American public broadcasting in essence bought into the definition of viewership that the commercial networks had employed since the early days of radio. In so doing, Hoynes writes, it turned Ang's definition inside out: "In [American] public television, the more appropriate term is public-as-audience."[70] Those responsible for the creation of an American public television system may have hoped to define its relationship with its viewers as different from that of the commercial networks. The use of the word *audience,* however, suggested that American public television, developed under the poised boot heel of the Nixon administration and in the image of the BBC, regarded its viewers, as Ang puts it, "either from 'above' or from 'outside': from an institutional point of view which sees 'television audience' as an objectified category of others to be controlled."[71]

Ang's notion of the control of "an objectified category of others" inherent in the creation of American public television presents the vectors guiding the reception of *The Forsyte Saga* in the United States less as elements in a dialogue than as elements of James Carey's paradigm of transmissive communication. Nixon's criticism and coercion of the new system and the definition of "public service" employed by the noncommercial network shared a concept of communication in which meaning was embodied solely in the "messages" of texts delivered to an audience with the purpose of directing its behavior and/or beliefs. Utterances in the popular press concerning *The Forsyte Saga* also represented the transmissive paradigm, in their assignment of a specific author to the series and their derivation of a single "meaning" of the *Saga* to contemporary America: the search for a "lost community." Although viewers of the show were able to read beyond those transmissive qualities, their constructions of community were nonetheless limited by the way they themselves had been constructed as a specialized "public-as-audience" possessing an abundance of educational and cultural capital.

In short, although its American reception was linked to domestic events and social meanings unimaginable in its British production and reception, the saga of *Forsyte* in the United States was one in which a negotiation of "otherness" and "our-own-ness" was foreshortened in an understanding of television as a transmissive device, and of public television as a transmissive device created by and for an elite audience. This changed, however, as the success of *The Forsyte Saga* led to the import of other BBC programs based on historical and literary sources. The final moment in the assimilation of these British costume dramas into American culture was, ironically, a moment in which an "audience-as-public" would revert to the "audience-as-market" as conceived by commercial television—an audience pitched not the allegedly cheap knockoffs common to American television but the singular, the ideal: the masterpiece.

Mobil Signifiers

Whatever meaning may have been intended for *The Forsyte Saga* by its creators and distributors or that may have been derived by media commentators, the program's influence on the American television industry was enormous. As Horace Newcomb has noted, the *Saga* was the first program, with the earlier exception of ABC's *Peyton Place,* to bring soap opera conventions of memory, consequence, and change into the prime-time television cosmos.[72] That influence was further illuminated by the way in which the *Saga* handled the sine qua non of American television programming: the family. As Ella Taylor argues, the 1960s norm was that of "One Big Happy," whether in the domestic confines of suburbia or, increasingly, in the workplace. Generational and gender-rational differences were smoothed over—or contained, to return to Elaine Tyler May's term—in the interest of maintaining a seemingly happy and well-ordered consensus.[73] In *The Forsyte Saga,* however, that consensus did not exist: the Forsytes' saga was one in which betrayal and manipulation repeatedly shattered the ideal order of the family, part of the order that American audiences of the series were supposed to crave. Although many viewers of the *Saga* may not have seen the dysfunction of its core family as being central to its meaning, for an audience of American producers and programmers, both commercial and noncommercial, the Forsytes and their woes opened new and marketable vistas in entertainment for the coming decade.

While the conventional content elements of *The Forsyte Saga* revealed the evolving connections between American network and public television, an equally significant link was being forged in the consideration of viewers as audience each employed. The goal articulated by public broadcasting of "serving differentiated audiences" was developed at the same moment that commercial networks were beginning to consider what Ien Ang refers to as "streamlined," specialized audiences.[74] Meanwhile, the Nielsen ratings, which had little place in the Lyceum and Chatauqua E. B. White envisioned in public television, began to increase in importance to CPB and PBS, particularly given the response to *The Forsyte Saga*. While publicly denying that ratings were a concern, CPB released a "survey" showing that 3 percent of the homes using televisions in four major markets were tuned to the November 9, 1969, episode of the *Saga*—a small, "specialized" number, to be sure, but one now being placed in the context of the mass commercial market.[75] The differences between the relationships commercial and public networks engaged in with their viewers were gradually disappearing, a process that would accelerate in the fall of 1970.

On October 21 of that year, Manhattan celebrity barkeep Toots Shor played host to a press conference involving executives from the BBC, CPB, the Children's Television Workshop—and Mobil Oil. The oil company called the gathering in order to announce its grant of one million dollars to public television, with some six hundred thousand dollars to go to CTW to fund the production and distribution of material based on its *Sesame Street* to poor and inner-city neighborhoods, and some four hundred thousand dollars to Boston station WGBH, via CPB, to fund a new series of imported British serial dramas to be called *Masterpiece Theatre*.[76] In accepting the grant from Mobil for both his organization and WGBH, CPB president John Macy praised the oil company: "The leadership of Mobil is to be commended for its decision, which allows public broadcasting to dramatically increase its effectiveness."[77] Macy's words are important: the Mobil grant did not dramatically increase the *quality* of public broadcasting but its "effectiveness," a quantifiable term suggesting a directive relationship between the network and the public it was supposed to serve. Through its acceptance of the Mobil grant, American public television became, de facto, a network with commercial sponsors, while at the same time narrowing the gap between an ideal of "serving" a public and a praxis of following rating and demographic numbers.

Mobil itself, meanwhile, was able to use the grant as part of a new corporate program to employ culture in a campaign its public relations director Herbert Schmertz devised to reposition his company and the oil industry within what was seen as an increasingly adverse industrial and political climate.[78] Explored at length in Laurence Jarvik's thorough account of the Mobil–*Masterpiece Theatre* connection, Schmertz's strategy involved using strong issue-oriented newspaper and television advertising outlining the company's positions on energy and environmental issues as a public relations "bad cop" while using the corporate underwriting of "quality" entertainment as the concomitant "good cop." Central to the Mobil philosophy was the understanding of audience Schmertz brought to his strategy—an understanding exemplifying a shift from "audience-as-public" to "public-as-audience."[79] Both the advocacy ads, positioned on the op-ed pages of major newspapers, and *Masterpiece Theatre* would appeal to what Schmertz defined as the first of several audiences the Mobil campaign was meant to address: opinion leaders, or those, to use Bourdieu's terms, who possessed an abundance of educational and social capital.[80] As did the use of *theatre* (as opposed to the ignoble *television*) with its British spelling in the show's title, Mobil rhetoric about the "cultural excellence" and "quality" of *Masterpiece Theatre* employed terms already signifying a British superiority in entertainment to Americans in attracting the desired viewers to its program. First demographically segmenting and then differentiating the "public" that would view the series it would sponsor, Mobil then turned that public into the "objectified category of others to be controlled" that Ang defines as "audience."[81] In this case, however, the message transmitted by Mobil was not necessarily directing the audience to purchase a given product (although the company's research indicated that that might be a good side effect) but to buy instead the notion that Mobil was a good corporate citizen, interested in "uplifting" the society in which it worked.[82]

To make their desired audience even more receptive, Mobil and WGBH brought yet another signifier equating quality television with British origin into the picture. As NET's experience with *The Forsyte Saga* had shown, the fifty- to fifty-five-minute length of BBC shows did not fit into American television's regimented sixty-minute slots. Some appropriate filler, ideally providing historical and/or biographical background for the series and its production, was needed.

James Day's London interviews had filled that purpose for the *Saga,* and WGBH producers and their corporate benefactor believed that, with numerous historical dramas involving settings and characters unfamiliar to American viewers on the way, a program host would be necessary to set up and comment on what those viewers were seeing. One name headed the lists compiled by Mobil and WGBH: Alistair Cooke, the transplanted Briton who had been central in the construction of "quality television" and its initial association with Britain in the 1950s.

The intertextuality evident in the choice of Cooke as the voice of *Masterpiece Theatre* was also present in the first installment in Mobil's public broadcasting investment. *The First Churchills,* a twelve-part serial based on *Marlborough,* Winston Churchill's biographical account of the seventeenth-century lives and times of his ancestors John and Sarah Churchill, was broadcast in Britain in 1969.[83] Though previewed favorably in the United States, where *TV Guide*'s Robert Musel called it "spectacular and absorbing," the program had failed to gain the popularity of *The Forsyte Saga* in its native land.[84] Alistair Cooke himself would later refer to the series as "probably the worst [*Masterpiece Theatre*] has done."[85] These problems, however, were of little concern to the WGBH producers and corporate benefactors responsible for *Masterpiece Theatre.* Whatever difficulties *The First Churchills* might present for an American audience in terms of accent, costume, or history were more than offset by signifiers that directly addressed its desired PBS viewers. The show's title (it was not, after all, called *Marlborough*) spoke of a World War II leader more beloved in the United States than in his own country; in addition, it established the series as one telling the stories of a family, like the Forsytes who preceded it. Its serialized form and historical-literary content also followed those of the *Saga,* in part because it had the same producer (Donald Wilson) and director (David Giles). Most important, however, was the fact that Sarah Churchill was being played by Susan Hampshire, the actress who had made American reviewers dizzy in their search for superlatives to describe her performance as Fleur in *The Forsyte Saga.*[86]

It was Hampshire who would serve as the focus of the construction of the narrative image for *The First Churchills* in the United States. The *Los Angeles Times* announced the arrival of both *Masterpiece Theatre* and *The First Churchills* simply with a photograph of Hampshire in its January 9, 1971, edition.[87] The *Boston Globe*'s *TV Week* for January 10, 1971, featured on its cover another photograph of Hampshire in Sarah Churchill costume, with the caption: "A new saga brings that Forsyte girl back." An accompanying interview, headlined "Fleur Returns," by the paper's Elizabeth Sullivan, further reminded viewers of the connection: " 'You were a pert, saucy and independent creature in the *Saga,*' we reminded Susan Hampshire when she was in the Hub last spring. 'Wait until you see me in *The First Churchills,*' she chuckled. 'I'm worse!' "[88]

Although the narrative image constructed by Mobil and WGBH for *Masterpiece Theatre* and *The First Churchills* was largely built on meanings already in circulation from the success of *The Forsyte Saga,* that image took on a design not readily visible in the public reception of the latter. Just as the visual focus on Diana Rigg in the narrative image created for *The Avengers* five years earlier was enveloped in a male-defined discourse of sexuality, so did Susan Hampshire quickly become not merely a signifier of the British *Forsyte* heritage but of sexual content that went beyond what American television programs were offering at the time. The syndicated UPI review of the first episode began: "Susan Hampshire, aptly labeled the first sex symbol of educational television for her performance in *The Forsyte Saga,* returned Sunday in a colorful new series on the noncommercial network.... Miss Hampshire, of course, brings out the best in any man, and if you tune in Sunday or Wednesday nights, you will see why."[89] Similarly, Cecil Smith, writing in the *Los Angeles Times,* told viewers: "If you lost your Sundays last year completely to Susan Hampshire as Fleur Forsyte in *The Forsyte Saga,* be advised that you may well lose them again—for Sarah is played by Susan Hampshire, this time gloriously in color."[90]

Unlike the publicity for *The Avengers,* however, sexuality in *The First Churchills* was not represented simply as the fetishizing vision of a leering male gaze. In part, that decision can be attributed to the quality audience Mobil hoped to attract; in part, it can be attributed to the large numbers of women in the viewership of American serialized drama and the "feminine aesthetic" that relationship cultivated.[91] Indeed, the narrative image created for *The First Churchills* represented women as willing and powerful participants in the program's representation of sexuality: as the *Boston Globe* interview indicated, Hampshire herself was complicitous in exploiting the sexuality of her character. Instead of the "kinkiness" used to construct Rigg/Peel as an object of male desire, the narrative image established for *The First Churchills* was developed on its "bawdiness," an utterance that added a nongendered element of ribald sexuality to the serial that both distinguished it from American commercial programs and helped it appeal to American viewers uninterested in the political machinations of the court of Charles II. The *New York Times* brought this "bawdiness" immediately into line with already familiar signifiers of British television in the lead for its review, appearing under the headline "Bawdy 'First Churchills' Bows": "Even if *The First Churchills* weren't coming at us with humor, bawdiness and taste... the return of Alistair Cooke as a weekly TV visitor would be enough reason to rejoice at the British Broadcasting Corporation's latest export."[92] A second commentary, two weeks later, added another British referent to this "bawdy" construction of the show: "[*The First Churchills*] is centered on sexual intrigue of the court of Charles II and seemed intent on being true to the bawdy spirit of the time, a la *Tom Jones*."[93] *Time,* for its part, chose a slight variation on the theme in calling the show "a lusty historical chronicle of Restoration England."[94]

This focus on "bawdiness" was accompanied by a commentary that sought to link the new series inseparably with *The Forsyte Saga* in the two programs' mutual employment of the serial form. The *Washington Post* preview, written by William Woods, told readers, "The overall air of high-class soap opera is the same [as the *Saga*]. . . . In true daytime TV fashion, complications abound, nothing is resolved, and we end on a note of tension."[95] Molly Haskell, writing for *Vogue,* commented: "Proportions may vary, but the ingredients for the television serial remain constant, whether the subject is the Churchills or *One Man's Family*. The difference between a culturally ambitious project like *The Forsyte Saga* and a routine soap opera is one of degree—superior acting and dialogue—rather than kind."[96]

To Mobil Oil, this linkage of sex and soap to what were already circulating as signifiers of "quality" around its new program was a marketing godsend. Public broadcasting and Mobil had created an unprecedented promotional campaign for *Masterpiece Theatre* and *The First Churchills*; when overnight ratings in New York indicated that the first two segments of the series had attracted more viewers than two of the city's independent commercial stations and as many as the third, Mobil paid to publicize the fact.[97] It also paid for a half-page ad in the Sunday *New York Times* of January 31, 1971, that brought together every element of the narrative image for *The First Churchills*. Headlined "Who's Who in The First Churchills?" the ad featured photographs of individual characters arranged in a stairstep fashion down the page, employing the physical close-up central to the soap opera form, accompanied verbally by text that presented the "bawdiness" of the show and parodied the plot intricacies that defined its genre as well:

John Churchill definitely loves the temperamental Sarah.
But what was his relationship with Barbara, the seductive mistress of the bawdy, astute Charles II, King of England?
And what is Sarah's relationship with Princess Anne, daughter of the intolerant James, Duke of York?
Why did John fight Charles' illegitimate son, the Duke of Monmouth?

Was it because of the unscrupulous Lord Shaftesbury?...
How could the devious Robert Harley engineer John's downfall even
though Sarah's best friend was Queen?
Can no one help poor Sarah? Not even the honest Sidney Godolphin?

After requesting that viewers not miss a single episode, the ad reminded
them, "Host Alistair Cooke gives a brief run-down of previous episodes before
each new one."[98] In one space, Mobil Oil united every utterance, visual or verbal,
shaping an American reception of the series—the Churchill name, Susan Hampshire's face, the program's British historical background, its sexual content, its
connection to soaps, even Alistair Cooke. And to conclude the ad, it introduced
a final utterance it hoped would be as important in shaping that reception as
anything the producers or broadcasters might have suggested: printed in the
largest typeface on the page, the single word *Mobil.*[99] Schmertz, Warner, and
company had succeeded in linking the lowest form of American television culture to the "quality" of unfamiliar British imports at the same time they completed
the reconfiguring of an audience-as-public into an audience-as-market.

The Masterpiece Builders

With *The First Churchills* completing its run late in March 1970 a success for
both public television and Mobil, *Masterpiece Theatre* turned to what executive
producer Christopher Sarton would later say the series was "supposed to do...
serialized dramas of classic books."[100] BBC's serialized versions of Henry James's
The Spoils of Poynton, Fyodor Dostoyevsky's *The Possessed,* and Honoré de
Balzac's *Pere Goriot,* each steered toward American consumption by the prominent inclusion of the author's name in publicity and reviews and the introductions and benedictions of Alistair Cooke, filled out the first season. The cultural
elevation and political safety afforded by the import of British programming was,
after the success of both *The Forsyte Saga* and the initial run of Mobil-funded
Masterpiece Theatre episodes, finally something that American commercial networks could not ignore. In late March 1971, CBS announced that it had purchased the six-episode BBC series *The Six Wives of Henry VIII* for summer broadcast. Network publicity, perhaps reacting to fear that such a presentation on CBS
prime time might be perceived merely as *Search for Tudor's Morrow,* stressed
that the program was not, strictly speaking, a serialized drama: although the king
would indeed age, each episode was self-contained and dealt with the story of a
specific wife.[101] Nonetheless, generic ties to *The Forsyte Saga* and *Masterpiece
Theatre* provided a ready frame for the commercial networks and their audi-

ences and were exploited in publicity, including a *TV Guide* note that quoted a BBC official who found *Six Wives* "far superior" to *The First Churchills.*[102]

To enhance the "quality" of its presentation, CBS hired British actor Anthony Quayle to preview each program and provide necessary historical and cultural background.[103] Although public broadcasting might provide the production model as well as the cultural and political raisons d'être for CBS's broadcast of *Six Wives,* it would not provide the financial model. The commercial network, after announcing the procurement of *Six Wives,* could not find a sole corporate backer to pay off the network's reported investment of $800,000; instead, it relied on selling spot advertisements.[104] That backing would come for a different distributor, however, when CPB and PBS, which had already received in the summer a well-publicized new Mobil grant of $1.12 million for two more seasons of *Masterpiece Theatre,* would announce ten days after CBS began its broadcast that *Six Wives* and its sequel, *Elizabeth R,* would be added to the series's 1971–72 schedule.[105]

Despite its disappointment at not being able to find an equivalent to Mobil to sponsor *Six Wives,* CBS was able to use a narrative image developed largely from *The Forsyte Saga* and *Masterpiece Theatre* to promote the series with considerable skill and resources. Reviews praised the commercial network for taking on "quality" material that seemed to be the province only of noncommercial television.[106] The attention and praise heaped on CBS so interested NBC that it followed suit with its own six-part historical BBC import in February 1972: *The Search for the Nile,* a not-quite-serial, not-quite-episodic recounting of the efforts of nineteenth-century British adventurers to find the origin of the Nile.[107] NBC repeated that venture into "quality" with *America,* Alistair Cooke's thirteen-part "personal history" of the United States.[108] Whatever resonance the network may have hoped for with the *Masterpiece Theatre* audience was minimal, however: ratings for *America* were dismal, and the show eventually rejoined its creator on PBS.

The failure of British serial dramas and documentary series to attract large ratings on American commercial networks and their subsequent return to public television indicated that a gap still existed between the two systems' constructions of audience. The fact that programs such as *Six Wives* and *America* could travel back and forth between the two systems, however, demonstrated that the gap was narrowing, a situation that served the commercial purposes of Mobil Oil well. By providing and marketing the quality in *Masterpiece Theatre* from which the quantity-based commercial networks shied away, viewers who cared about that quality would turn from those networks, Mobil hoped, thereby reducing their all-important ratings and their power. In the end, Mobil believed, public broadcasting would gain viewers and support, *Masterpiece Theatre* would gain public attention, and Mobil would gain the philanthropic prestige it needed on the one hand to carry forth its political mission with the other.[109]

Although Mobil's plans for *Masterpiece Theatre* and public television were well conceived and charted, however, they did not come to fruition quite as the oil company had imagined. Along with WGBH, Mobil company attempted to build the show's popularity by using familiar authors (Balzac, Dostoyevsky, James), familiar performers (Susan Hampshire, among others), even familiar genre representatives (*Last of the Mohicans,* Dorothy Sayers's Lord Peter Wimsey mysteries). Nonetheless, the audience for *Masterpiece Theatre* declined rapidly after its showing of *Six Wives* and *Elizabeth R.* By the time *Vanity Fair,* starring Hampshire as Becky Sharp, made its American debut in November 1972, what had been an 8 rating in New York was down to a 1; similar drops in viewership across the entirety of the PBS prime-time schedule were noted in other major markets, including Washington, Minneapolis, and Los Angeles.[110]

Variety, as a matter of course, attributed the decline to the unadventurous programming PBS had to present in order to appease the Nixon administration.[111] More important, however, given the role Mobil wished to play in larger cultural and political arenas, was that the first seasons of *Masterpiece Theatre* coincided with ever-louder criticism of the oil industry for its part in the growing American energy crisis. When the Arab nations of OPEC imposed an embargo on shipments of oil to the United States and Western Europe following their war with Israel in October 1973, the response against oil companies, seen already as complicitous in the high prices and low supply of petroleum products, was so negative that Mobil sources themselves referred to it as causing "permanent damage to the credibility of the entire industry."[112] The drop in viewership on the service it funded so heavily may have been a symptom of the oil industry's rapid decline in trust and prestige; in any case, the need was greater than ever for Mobil to find a way to polish its public image, at least among the "opinion leaders" it most hoped to attract. It found what it was looking for in a British import introduced on *Masterpiece Theatre* in the middle of the embargo, a serial drama without literary antecedent that would come to stand as the crowning achievement of Mobil's vision and the ultimate moment in the domestication of quality BBC imports to the commercial model of American television.

For Whom the Bellamys Toil

As had so frequently been the case with British programming, news of *Upstairs, Downstairs* arrived in the United States well in advance of the show itself. *Vari-*

The Bellamys (seated) and their staff (standing) pose for their own traditional "family" portrait—a picture used frequently in Mobil Oil promotions for the PBS *Masterpiece Theatre* presentation of *Upstairs, Downstairs.* Photograph courtesy of Photofest.

ety ran a review of the program, which followed the lives of the upper-class Bellamy family and their domestic staff in Edwardian London, in December 1972, calling it "class merchandise, produced and played with style, conviction and sustained dramatic intent" and noting a "reported American pickup interest" in the show.[113] Leading British television critic Clive James, in a March 1973 article for *TV Guide* on British programming, referred to *Upstairs, Downstairs* as a "soap opera that rises above itself. . . . [It] should have no trouble running for the next century."[114] As James pointed out, however, there was a significant difference between *Upstairs, Downstairs* and other serialized costume dramas imported under the *Masterpiece Theatre* aegis: *Upstairs, Downstairs* was a product of British commercial television, not the BBC. According to Richard Price, chairman of London Weekend Television, the producers and British distributors of the show, its commercial background was anathema to executives of CPB, PBS, and WGBH. That was not a concern, however, of one other interested party: "Then Herb Schmertz of Mobil saw it and liked it. . . . The problems were solved when Herb convinced the US public broadcasters that it really was a brilliant series."[115] Given the Mobil imprimatur, CPB and WGBH purchased thirteen of the first twenty-six episodes produced by LWT for broadcast on *Masterpiece Theatre* beginning in January 1974.[116]

Anxious to reestablish the franchise upon which its public image effort was based, Mobil increased publicity for its new *Masterpiece Theatre* presentation. Whereas previews of the series focused on the ties between the new *Upstairs, Downstairs* and previous British serial dramas, Mobil's own advertising employed a very different strategy in creating a narrative image for the show. In an ad published the day of the first *Upstairs, Downstairs* broadcast, a formal photograph of a couple seated before a group of men and women wearing high collars, aprons, and bonnets sat atop the sentence, printed in large type, "Behind these sober faces lurk 13 weeks of sex, intrigue, jealousy — and just plain fun." The ad went on to identify Richard and Marjorie Bellamy as the "elegant" couple and their eight servants — the "downstairs staff" — as the other people in the photograph. "Everyone looks so starchy and prim," the ad continued, "you'd never expect the goings-on upstairs and down. And especially between 'upstairs' and 'downstairs.' " Having peddled the show as at least "lusty," if not "bawdy," Mobil's publicity then moved its British drama upstairs from the lubricious banality of American soap opera while peddling its own mission by telling viewers, "Each episode of the 13-week series is a complete play (and, often as not, a complete scandal)."[117] With utterances thus arranged to signify finally a quality British program and a quality audience to match — an audience interested in "complete plays," not TV shows — *Upstairs, Downstairs* began its three-year American run on January 6, 1974.

What American viewers saw in "On Trial," the first "complete play" of *Upstairs, Downstairs,* however, had little to do with what was described in Mobil's ad. The most overt discussion of sex or scandal came in Alistair Cooke's opening remarks about King Edward VII and his "enormous appetite for bed and board."[118] Aside from the opening scene, depicting the arrival of a young woman at a London household from the exterior, the entire show was taped using interior sets, repeating the visual motif and rhetoric of both the BBC imports that had preceded it on *Masterpiece Theatre* and American daytime soap operas. The "goings-on" between upstairs and down, meanwhile, were limited to exactly what one might expect from a master-servant relationship: courteous command on the one hand, courteous deference on the other. The plot of "On Trial," rather than considering salacious morals charges against Lord Bellamy for his assault on a staff member, deals instead with the "trial" faced by a new maid who is unwilling to accept the rigid class distinctions that define her place in the house and in society, and that other members of the domestic service not only accept but proudly uphold. The moment of greatest "intrigue" in the show occurs in the final scene, when the new maid, Sarah, has her hair brushed by Rose, the house parlor maid and the person with whom Sarah shares a bed. Whatever readings are possible from the setting, however, the scene exists primarily so that Rose can tell Sarah how she came to work in service and to allow Sarah to tell Rose that being a maid "is not so bad—it's safe. You know where you are and you know what's going to happen next. The world outside is dangerous."[119]

Whether they saw the program as frothy sexual intrigue, a realistic portrait of British class hierarchy, or simply an evening's entertainment, viewers responded to *Upstairs, Downstairs* in numbers that vindicated Mobil's belief in and promotion of the program. Overnight ratings in New York indicated that the show had attracted a larger audience than two of the city's three independent stations, and had done almost as well as the third.[120] *TV Guide* addressed its success quickly, with a Cleveland Amory review: "Ever since the BBC's *The Forsyte Saga* made such a smash, PBS has been casting about for another hit. And where better to look than good old England? . . . If *Upstairs, Downstairs* is good—and it is very, very good—it's because it's about old times but is not old hat."[121] More important, the magazine presented a profile of Jean Marsh, the actress who played Rose and cocreator of the show. As she told the magazine, Marsh and fellow actress Eileen Atkins were regaling each other on vacation with stories of their parents' work in domestic service when the idea dawned on them to turn those stories into a television series.[122] Marsh's anecdote quickly became incorporated into the publicity effort for the series, presenting the character of Jean/Rose as a metonymic figure for women who had advanced from domestic servitude (whether to the Bellamys or to the husbands and children of countless other home-based situation comedies) to important work outside the home—in the case of Jean/Rose, creating mass entertainment spectacles.[123] Jean/Rose became so central to the public image of *Upstairs, Downstairs* in the United States that Mobil's ads for the serial in its next three runs merely featured a drawing of the character with the announcement that the show was back for another season.[124]

"Downstairs" servant Rose, played by series cocreator Jean Marsh, became the focal figure in Mobil advertising for *Upstairs, Downstairs*. Photograph courtesy of Photofest.

The end of the serial's first thirteen-episode sequence on *Masterpiece Theatre* coincided almost exactly with the end of the OPEC oil embargo.[125] Mobil had survived its darkest hours in recent history, and the corporation saw its support of the PBS series in general and *Upstairs, Downstairs* in particular as central to its ability to fend off public and political criticism. "On the cultural front," an internal history later reported, "the highlight of this period was Mobil's introduction in January 1974 of the Bellamy family to the American public on *Upstairs, Downstairs*, perhaps the best remembered of all Mobil's television productions."[126] The wording employed by Mobil in its history, however, is revealing of both the company's consideration of audience and the conflicts present in how that audience was being guided to appreciate and understand the show. As Alistair Cooke noted in his introduction to "On Trial," *Upstairs, Downstairs* was as much about the servant staff, "a little, complete society of its own—a downstairs society intended by God, so its betters said, to minister for life to upstairs society," as it was about the patricians who employed them. Off-camera, Cooke would later say of the series: "I loved *Upstairs, Downstairs*. When I first saw it, my reaction was, 'I'll be amazed if this thing doesn't really hit the headlines. It's marvelous. It allows you to identify with the downstairs people while vicariously enjoying the life of the upstairs people.' "[127] Yet in Mobil's own understanding of the series, the downstairs society mattered little: it was "the Bellamy family" upon which that understanding focused, just as it was the contemporary American version of the Bellamys—societal leaders blessed with educational and cultural capital—that Mobil wanted to watch its program.

Those class-based readings of *Upstairs, Downstairs* were augmented by the way the series functioned on a third level: as a representation of distinctions in televisual forms. Not since the first Mobil ad for *The First Churchills* had the divide between the "upstairs" of "quality" British historical drama and the "downstairs" of soap opera been exhibited so explicitly in a *Masterpiece Theatre* program. The lack of a literary antecedent made the split all the more visible, as did the show's origins in British commercial television.[128] The task facing the viewer of *Upstairs, Downstairs* was therefore one of negotiating that particularly evident divide—a negotiation, to put the problem into terms established by Stuart Hall, between readings preferred both separately and jointly by Mobil and a public broadcasting service operating under Nixonian constraints and a reading rejecting the parameters of quality and public service in favor of the oft-benighted pleasures of serial drama.[129]

The processes of that negotiation might appear to be truncated in the instance of *Upstairs, Downstairs*, as the audience Mobil and PBS had attracted was as defined by quality as *Masterpiece Theatre* was itself, to say nothing of the writers that audience read in the *Times,* the *Post,* and other journals of record. An essay by Nora Ephron in another "quality" publication indicated, however, how that dominant framework might be restructured and how the split between quality British drama and tawdry American soap opera could be negotiated quite creatively. Written by an "upstairs" woman—as a popular essayist and journalist, Ephron was among Mobil's prized "opinion leadership"—for the "gentleman's monthly" *Esquire,* "Missing Hazel" presents a discussion of *Upstairs, Downstairs* involving three friends, written in the discourse of soap opera conversation:

> My friend Kenny does not feel as bad about the death of Hazel as I do. My friend Ann has been upset about it for days. My friend Martha is actually glad Hazel is dead. I cried when Hazel died, but only for a few seconds, partly because I wasn't surprised. About three months ago, someone told me she was going to die, and since then I have watched every show expecting it to be her last.[130]

Kenny, Ann, Martha, and Nora run through many of the plot twists of the past season of the series, offering their comments on many of the characters: James Bellamy is "a big baby"; Hudson the butler has become "a mealy-mouthed hypocrite"; but Rose, well, "Even Martha loves Rose." They also acknowledge the role that Alistair Cooke has played in their viewing of the series and allow as to how they already know that Hudson and Mrs. Bridges are going to get married because it "was mentioned in the obituary of the actress who played Mrs. Bridges."[131] In the end, the four devotees finally agree that Rose needs to find a man, that Lady Marjorie is missed, and that, most of all, "we all wish *Upstairs, Downstairs* would last forever."[132]

Ephron's humorous essay offers more insight about the appeal of *Upstairs, Downstairs* than do many serious analyses.[133] It demonstrates, first and foremost, the importance of the most basic conventions of soap opera to at least some members of the "quality" audience of *Masterpiece Theatre:* the multiple characters and stories (and the multiple readings/meanings they allow); the centrality of women; the recognition of the power of emotion, here tempered with its class constraints. It also points out the significance of what Fiske terms "secondary" and "tertiary" intertextuality (respectively, the obituary for Angela Baddeley and the knowledge gained from conversation with other viewers) in shaping expectations for the show, as well as the significance—or lack thereof—of the framing messages presented by Alistair Cooke.[134] As a collection of utterances concerning *Upstairs, Downstairs* that bounce back and forth between the conversants both reflecting and shaping their perceptions of the program, however, Ephron's essay notably lacks one significant utterance: Mobil Oil.

It is possible to view this lacuna as simply representing a naturalized knowledge of the sponsor. The whole thrust of Mobil's promotion of *Masterpiece Theatre* and *Upstairs, Downstairs,* however, was *not* for Mobil to be recognized merely as a sponsor but for the company to achieve a growing level of public awareness of its role as cultural provider—in other words, for Mobil to become a naturalized element of the new marketplace of public television. Ephron's article shows that although Mobil's choice of vehicle for its campaign may well have worked as an example of the seductive process of hegemony—Kenny, Ann, Martha, and Nora were, after all, consenting with glee to be part of the audience that Mobil wished to create—recognition of the corporation itself as patron, at least to some of its audience, was less important than recognition of the wine Hudson was serving with the evening meal. As such, Ephron's essay suggests that the construction of an audience as market, particularly one employing signifiers as radically opposing in terms of class, gender, and national origin as did Mobil's promotion of *Upstairs, Downstairs,* creates a space for negotiation with or around the transmissive message.

As *Upstairs, Downstairs* entered its final series in January–May 1977, however, commentary like Ephron's was replaced by more serious recapitulations of the show, similar to those visited upon *The Forsyte Saga,* frequently given a fin de siècle cast. Judith Martin of the *Washington Post* wrote: "As a modern viewer, you know you are being pulled toward a society in which great staffed houses can no longer exist. It is with a sinking feeling that one watches every sign of what we used to call progress."[135] John J. O'Connor, echoing Jack Gould's words about *The Forsyte Saga,* noted that the appeal of *Upstairs, Downstairs* lay finally in "the security of order" that it presented: "This concept of order may fascinate a good many Americans precisely because so much of our own history seems to be marked by disorder and chaos."[136] Syndicated *New York Times* columnist Anthony Lewis argued that the quality of the series lay not just in its presentation of the romance of an ordered class structure but in its evocation of the "realities" of World War I, the character of the English, and the hostilities inherent in the class system.[137] Even Jean Marsh joined the discussion, noting in a guest feature for the *Washington Post:* "The class structure in England is supported by all the classes. . . . I think this is partly what appeals to viewers in *Upstairs, Downstairs.* The sense of order and unquestioned authority has disappeared, and people adrift in today's world hanker for a discipline imposed on them whether by God or man."[138] Ephron's *Esquire* article had demonstrated, however, that it was not just a hypothesized yearning for order, fascination with class, or appreciation of historical mimetics that drew viewers to *Upstairs, Downstairs*. The pleasures inherent in the serial form—the apparently mundane concerns of character and plot, the intimacy with which they are presented, and the communal sharing of those concerns outside the text itself—kept viewers interested. In his farewell column, in addition to analyzing the show's popularity, O'Connor noted that his own viewer mail about *Upstairs, Downstairs* had been unprecedented. The mail he cited, however, dealt not with the drama's sociological aspects but with the effect of Hudson's heart attack on the Bellamy household and viewers' anger at having the plotline of the final episode revealed in a newspaper article.[139]

More significant than any of this, however, in attracting viewers to *Upstairs, Downstairs* was the work of Mobil Oil in publicizing the serial and *Masterpiece Theatre*. With the failure of the Nixon administration to support public broadcasting financially and the restructurings of the terms *public* and *service* embodied in the definition of PBS establishing the groundwork for their effort, Mobil succeeded, with *Masterpiece Theatre* as a whole and *Upstairs, Downstairs* in particular, in shifting American noncommercial broadcasting back to the paradigms defining commercial television. Nowhere was this more visible than in a two-page ad Mobil placed in the Sunday *New York Times* announcing the final season of the serial. The familiar drawing of Rose, this time headed with "*Masterpiece Theatre* presents the final, 'Roaring 20s' season of *Upstairs, Downstairs*," occupied the left page; the right page consisted of what was, in essence, a Mobil op-ed advocacy advertisement. Titled "A World Series Champion, 1974–1977," cleverly linking the popularity of the British series to American baseball, the ad brought together every element of the show's assimilation under Mobil's corporate logo. There were the references to the show as "literate television" as well as the familiar assertion that its success demonstrated "that there is an appetite among American television viewers for television drama of quality and intelligence." There were examples of mail from those viewers—mail grieving over the loss of Marjorie Bellamy in the sinking of the *Titanic* and mail furious that Mobil had allowed such a plot development to occur. There were the requisite quotes from "opinion leaders" who, aided substantially by Mobil's public relations department, wrote favorably about the show for quality newspapers and magazines, many of which ordinarily opposed the actions of oil companies.[140] There was a hearty clap on the back for Mobil itself, both for underwriting *Masterpiece Theatre* and for recognizing the merit of *Upstairs, Downstairs* when "many people claimed it would, as they say in broadcasting, bomb." There was a congratulatory plug for London Weekend Television, with a final reminder that *Upstairs,*

Downstairs had not been produced by the BBC. Finally, and most significant, there was the assertion that American commercial networks had, in their own broadcasts of serialized dramas, come to "acknowledge the appeal of serialized television drama in prime time." *Upstairs, Downstairs,* of course, was still the best of the lot.[141]

Mobil's ad, in short, represented *Upstairs, Downstairs* not so much as a triumph of public broadcasting but as a pinnacle of achievement for itself and, to some degree, commercial television.[142] The viewer involvement for which American daytime soap opera had so long been mocked was presented as proof of the quality of *Upstairs, Downstairs* and the literacy of its viewers. The fact that the commercial networks, against which Mobil's long-standing animus was still strong, were now trying to copy the serial's success merely indicated the degree to which Mobil and London Weekend Television had beaten them at their own game. *Upstairs, Downstairs* was no longer something very different, a tributary that trickled in from some distant and foggy peak—it had not only joined the mainstream, Mobil argued, it had redirected the course of the river. The corporation's sponsorship of *Masterpiece Theatre* had used the differences inherent in British television imports to foreground the shortcomings of American commercial networks. With *Upstairs, Downstairs,* Mobil further achieved the proof of the superiority of its British programs by foregrounding the series's success according to criteria set by those commercial networks: time on air; (comparative) ratings power; viewer response, both direct and indirect; commercial production base; and, finally, its use as a commodifiable product. Although toy store shelves were not occupied by Rose and Hudson dolls or scale models of the Bellamys' automobile, *Upstairs, Downstairs* did give rise to a thriving book industry, befitting the nature of its audience: novelizations of the show, cookbooks featuring Mrs. Bridges's recipes, Mr. Hudson's purported secret diaries. As those books indicated, the most easily commodified elements of the show were the characters themselves. PBS decided to capitalize on the familiarity of those characters by flying eight of the *Upstairs, Downstairs* cast members to Boston to take part in a special national fund drive for the network following the final episode of the series. Hosted by Alistair Cooke, the program included conversation with each of the actors and clips from the series while viewers phoned in pledges. To stimulate the donations, however, WGBH producers decided to rely upon American television's most blatant representation of the spectacle of commodity—the game show—as it pitted the cast members representing "upstairs" against those representing "downstairs" in a contest to see which could bring in the most money.[143]

Although the actors, now the assumed "prizes" of the competition, were evidently flummoxed by this turn of events, their effectiveness as fetishized commodity was unprecedented, at least for PBS: the network received pledges for more than $1.7 million in the hour.[144]

Orders of the Day

Two weeks before the premiere of the final season of *Upstairs, Downstairs,* WETA-TV in Washington, D.C., began presenting reruns of *The Forsyte Saga* on both daily and weekly bases. "[A] lot has happened to television saga-telling in those 6½ years," wrote the *Washington Post*'s Judith Martin in her appreciation of the series, but, to judge from her article, very little had changed.[145] The technology was different—one was black and white, one color—and where the *Saga* had the authorial presences of John Galsworthy and the BBC, *Upstairs, Downstairs* had the mythically common origin of two women sharing dreams in a swimming pool and the commonly denigrated origin of a commercial television studio. Otherwise, as two dramas about English families facing problems with the class and cultural distinctions that defined their society, as well as problems with "sex, intrigue, and jealousy" told in the visual rhetoric of the soap opera, not much had happened between *The Forsyte Saga* and *Upstairs, Downstairs* at all.

Although the texts themselves exhibited little change, much had gone on with the contexts in which they were presented. *The Forsyte Saga* came to the United States almost literally on a wing and a prayer, with next to no notice. *Upstairs, Downstairs* arrived as part of an established series, paid for and heavily promoted by one of the country's largest corporations at a time when that corporation was facing governmental and public approbation. The person most responsible for those changes had left his job in disgrace two and a half years earlier. *Upstairs, Downstairs* was as much a legacy of Richard Nixon's quest for an order in broadcasting that would suit his needs and desires as it was of the efforts of Mobil Oil. Without the former, expressed in the privation Nixon visited upon public broadcasting, the latter would not have been necessary. Thanks to Nixon, PBS was now institutionally beholden to its individual local stations for approval of programming, making public television much less a threat to its federal funding source.[146] And although the Public Broadcasting Act of 1975, passed after Nixon's departure from office, guaranteed federal funding at a greater level than any approved by his administration, it masked the fact that increased federal funding was only replacing relative losses in state and local funding that had occurred since the beginning of the decade. In the meantime, corporate finan-

ᵣrt for public broadcasting increased by more than 900 percent from ₁₉₇₁, when Mobil introduced *Masterpiece Theatre,* to 1976, just before the conclusion of *Upstairs, Downstairs.*[147]

British television became an inherent element of the Nixon plan to order public television in his image. The significance of British programming as quality television in the United States meant that public television, with its mission to provide the best in culture, was its proper home; that quality in turn kept it safe from criticism while at the same time limiting the ability of public broadcasting to criticize. Whereas British programs were thus guided one way toward American assimilation by the Nixon administration, corporations such as Mobil Oil saw the viewers who watched PBS British programming as a quality audience — as opposed to an active public — that could be targeted for messages representing those corporations as valuable political and cultural entities in American society. In so doing, corporations further truncated the varying utterances of otherness represented in that British programming as they brought the whole of public television into the "our-own-ness" of commercial American television.[148]

Whether or not Mobil "sold" the quality audience of *Upstairs, Downstairs,* its message of corporate worth was still debatable. Studies done by Mobil indicated both that the groups of opinion leaders it sought to attract had softened their attitudes toward the corporation during the first decade of its sponsorship of *Masterpiece Theatre* and that the general public had developed a greater recognition of the company as a leader in both oil production and cultural beneficence.[149] Readings that viewers, typified by Nora Ephron and by the mail cited in both reviews and Mobil's own documents, actually made of *Upstairs, Downstairs* indicated, however, that the political and economic orders being transmitted were far less directive than imagined by their institutional sources. The pleasures derived by audiences from the formal elements of the serial dramas, as well as their conversations about those dramas, represented very different utterances from those issued by the Nixon administration, public broadcasting, and Mobil, showing instead the importance of ritual in communication, of creating a shared meaning through conversation and dialogue as opposed to absorbing and following a given message. Whether such responses can be considered as deliberately "resistant" is another matter; Timothy Brennan, among others, has argued that political and economic institutions, by keeping their audiences talking about the treachery of Soames and Fleur Forsyte or the humble humanity of Hudson and Rose, effectively assume the control of social forces that those audiences relinquish.[150] Yet it can equally plausibly be argued, following the logic of Bakhtin, Williams, and Carey, that in their own ritual dialogues, American audiences of quality British serial drama acted, literally, out of order by not taking part in the prescribed agenda of powerful corporate and state interests. The formal qualities of a separate genre of British television would also allow a somewhat different American audience to read between the lines of institutional order evident in the medium, however, as signifiers of "quality" and the directive function of transmission would be met by the comic anarchy of *Monty Python's Flying Circus.*

5. (Naughty) Bits of Limey Eccentricity
That Was the Week That Was and Monty Python's Flying Circus

There was only one thing that we ever all agreed on, and that was that the show would never work in America.

—Eric Idle[1]

The relationship between British television texts and American audiences in the 1960s and early 1970s developed primarily along one line: whether action-adventure or serialized historical, the programs that made their way into circulation in the United States were hour-long dramas. Little in the way of "British wit," save for the clever and bitchy repartee of *The Avengers,* made its way to American screens. Some of that wit came to America in the early 1960s in the American reproduction of the British satiric revue *That Was the Week That Was.* After its demise in 1965, however, it would be another ten years before *Monty Python's Flying Circus* would claim a fanatically devoted audience in the United States with sketches that avoided topicality in favor of multilayered attacks on all manner of institutional authority, most specifically the institution of television itself. Although they represent distinctive styles of British humor, both of those shows would speak to an American audience first through revealing and criticizing the social and cultural processes in which they were created, distributed, and appreciated, and then through reaffirming those processes. Their success in the American market came as a result of this limited multivocality, which in turn addresses how they functioned as television and as comedy—functions at least somewhat different from those filled by British dramas.

Comedy Doesn't Travel (?)

That well-worn show business maxim is borne out to some degree by the history of comedy in transnational television trade, even when examined from the traditional aspect of the United States as exporter. As William Read has pointed out, situation comedies provided much of the traffic on the "one-way street" of programming flowing from America to the rest of the world in the early 1960s. The r sitcom format dictated relatively low prices, and nations building television technology and distribution systems could fill newly available broadcast time with shows such as *I Love Lucy* and *The Flintstones.*[2] The fact that those programs were sold to foreign markets, however, did not mean that large audiences in those countries watched them. By the 1970s, developing national television industries were creating, manufacturing, and even marketing their own comedy programs. Production costs for half-hour comedies were significantly lower than those for the hour-long dramatic series of the type imported from the United States (and Britain). As a result, the American programs that foreign distributors bought and overseas viewers watched became primarily action-adventure series and/or soap operas that were too expensive to produce domestically— just as the British programming presented by PBS in the early 1970s represented a genre that American commercial television at the time found too costly.[3] Action series and soaps also were heavily dependent on visual representations of violence and sex, which needed to cross fewer cultural barriers than did the content of American situation comedies. Producers found it easier to develop comedy programs that spoke to meanings circulating within their own cultures than to attempt to decode American sitcom imports.[4]

Yet some American television comedies—*I Love Lucy* and *The Flintstones* being good cases in point—did travel well, just as *Monty Python's Flying Circus* would travel well from Britain to the United States during the 1970s. The question becomes, then, How are the comic surprises visible in the common sense of one culture apprehended by audiences reading from a different set of codes and assumptions? Jerry Palmer, using the same theory of utterances as Bakhtin, provides a useful answer in his *The Logic of the Absurd.* Film and television comedy, Palmer argues, are based first of all on the *peripeteia,* the moment of visual or verbal surprise that deviates from a naturalized norm. Because those norms, however, are not universal but are defined by the specific "webs of meaning" spun by individual cultures, the *peripeteia* is dependent upon its context—context meaning both that of the comic performer, the audience, and the "butt" of the humor and that of the linguistic, social, and historical referents within which the humor occurs. The "meaning" of film and television comedy, in Palmer's words, arises from "the circuit of utterance," in which specific meanings are activated while others are ignored, depending upon the context in which the comedy occurs.[5] To describe that context, Palmer uses the term *plausibility* in defining an audience's participation in a comedic dialogue. If a comic utterance is implausible—if the norms being addressed by the *peripeteia* are still uncertain—the humor will not work. Conversely, if such an utterance is *too* plausible—if the norms present "reality"—the audience will also not "get it." Palmer further suggests that plausibility both influences and is influenced by the level of surprise involved in the comic utterance. Both too much and too little surprise— overwhelming the norms and letting the norms stand untouched—can render comic utterances meaningless.[6]

Although Palmer employs his plausibility-*peripeteia* schema to examine how individual examples of film and television comedy function, both the theory of utterances on which he bases it and the terms he employs are clearly useful in addressing the ways in which comedy can travel in transnational communication. The "circuit of utterance" is dependent upon the norms of a given culture that give rise to the surprises defining the comedy. Comedy can indeed travel when the norms of the culture producing the comedic text are recognizable to the culture receiving it—or when those norms can be translated into terms addressing the social and historical utterances of that culture. It would be the latter circumstance that would guide the initial arrival of British television comedy to American homes—a circumstance itself defined in each nation by a new generation of educated youth and the development of a form of comic utterance that spoke to the concerns of that generation by ridiculing the quotidian assumptions of its predecessors.

That Was the Week That Was, in a Way

One of the most visible responses to what was being called the "mass culture" of the United States in the 1950s was the rise of a new socially oriented, satiric style of comedy. Stand-up comics such as Lenny Bruce and Mort Sahl, publications such as *Mad* magazine, and theater troupes such as Chicago's Second City built careers and reputations out of poking fun at "commonsense" codes of politics, capitalism, and culture. As Todd Gitlin would later write, these satirists helped "pry open a cultural territory which became available for radical transmutation" by the young people growing up as part of their audience.[7] American prime-time television played a minimal role in the development of this satirical humor. Satire's foremost proponents, Sid Caesar and Ernie Kovacs, were banished by the middle of the 1950s, and situation comedies and even the more formally radical programs starring Jack Benny and Burns and Allen were about the business of containing the tensions of the time within representations of happy domestic life. NBC's late-night show *Tonight,* which went on the air in 1954 with Steve Allen as host, provided a small television home for the parody and satire seen in nightclubs. Allen's successor as *Tonight* host, Jack Paar, even allowed comics to plug their upcoming club gigs, thereby also allowing them to use the advertising they often criticized in their acts.[8] Nonetheless, *Tonight*'s welcoming of satiric material gave that material increased visibility into the Kennedy years.

While urban clubs, small improvisatory theaters, and late-night television were the breeding grounds for a new type of American comedy during the 1950s and early 1960s, British comedy was adding a new dimension from two old sources: the BBC and the theater clubs of Cambridge and Oxford. The BBC was the home of *The Goon Show,* a radio comedy program running throughout the 1950s that de- and reconstructed the staid music hall sketches and formulaic situation comedies of the prewar era into a pastiche of parody, satire, and violent nonsense that shocked, for better and for worse, millions of listeners every week.[9] Among those most electrified by the antics of the Goons were a group of students coming of age in the most elite bastions of British higher education. The Cambridge Footlights Club and similar, less institutionalized groups at Oxford had for a number of years presented comedic revues for audiences around the country. By the end of the 1950s, the influence of *The Goon Show* and the changing sensibilities of those growing up in postwar, post-Empire Britain were becoming evident in the university revues. Four veterans of those revues—Alan Bennett, Peter Cook, Jonathan Miller, and Dudley Moore—collaborated in 1960 to present their best material at the Edinburgh Festival. Their show, *Beyond the Fringe,* included parodies of Shakespeare, Benjamin Britten, and war films, jests at the upper class and issues ranging from capital punishment to apartheid, along with a wicked imitation of Prime Minister Harold Macmillan, all presented on a bare stage with no costumes. The troupe was immediately lauded as the harbinger of a new form of British satire that was, in critic Bernard Levin's terms, "real, barbed, deeply planted and aimed at things and people that need it."[10]

The reviews, as Alan Bennett would later explain, "got the show a name for being topical and satirical in a mode at that time associated with American standup comedians—Lenny Bruce, Mort Sahl, and Nichols and May."[11] Bennett's comment makes clear a knowledge of, if not a debt to, American comic utterances; with that connection and with an established audience and market for both satire and British theater in the United States, it would not be long before *Beyond the Fringe* crossed the Atlantic. The show, with nothing changed from its British incarnation, opened in New York on Saturday, October 27, 1962; by Monday, October 29, it was a smash hit. Comedy might indeed travel, it appeared, even with what Alistair Cooke (this time in his guise of expatriate commentator for the *Guardian*) cited as "the quartet's decision not to adapt their material to American themes, or their strangulated tripthongs to the ears of a people to whom a vowel is a vowel is a vowel."[12] Peter Cook suggested that the cultural differences presented in the show provided a sort of "snob merit" for well-educated and well-off American audiences. Jonathan Miller, again pointing out the significance of difference in transnational communication and culture, said, "There were things which the Americans liked because they *were* English, and they were getting a sort of ethnic 'buzz' out of little bits of Limey eccentricity."[13] Although both arguments contain elements of truth, Jerry Palmer's scheme for understanding comedy in terms of utterance shines a brighter light on the success of *Beyond the Fringe:* the plausibility of comic utterances ridiculing a British politician or a socially determined aristocratic point of view on capital punishment is greatly enhanced when the culture into which they are introduced itself is rife with comic utterances lampooning its own leadership (as Vaughan Meader's hit comedy album called them, "The First Family") as well as socially determined points of view on any number of issues.[14] Similarly, the "strangulated tripthongs" and references to historic Britain featured in the revue provide moments of *peripeteia—* comic surprise that would not be present in an American version of the material.

With *Beyond the Fringe* establishing British collegiate humor as a marketable theatrical commodity on both sides of the Atlantic, television seemed to be the next logical outlet for the satire and parodies of the Oxbridge revues. The medium offered a particularly ripe opportunity for Cambridge graduate David Frost, who hoped to turn his experience as a self-styled "new Peter Cook" during his time in the Footlights Revue into a theatrical career. Although his credentials were less than stellar, Frost's Cambridge degree and the topical material he was writing and performing brought him to the attention of BBC producer Ned Sherrin, who was mounting a new satirical comedy show to help rejuvenate the public image of a doddering "Auntie Beeb."[15] Sherrin was impressed enough with Frost to hire him as the moderator of his revue-styled program *That Was the Week That Was,* which made its first regular BBC appearance in November 1962. Sherrin, Frost, and the show's other writers and performers brought the insouciance of the Oxbridge revues to bear on the most controversial issues and personages of the day.[16] The parodies and musical numbers that were at the heart of the theatrical revues were used to mock politicians and entertainers for a national television audience; monologues and improvisatory interviews brought television techniques to the theatrical form of the revue. To give the show's "behind-the-facade" verbal cheekiness a visual counterpart, as well as to accommodate its fast pace, Sherrin produced *TW3,* as it quickly came to be called, in a bare-bones open studio, allowing viewers to observe the technical machinations of the production as it was going on. *That Was the Week That Was* quickly gained a large and vociferous British following in its initial run of twenty-three episodes. Almost as quickly, it gained attention from the American television industry. In a December 5, 1962, review, *Variety* called the show "hardhitting, witty, pungent and brilliantly conceived. . . . with cameras in full view, [it] established an appropriate clinical atmosphere, as of devilish work in progress."[17] Two weeks later, the trade journal presented a feature article about the controversy the show had already engendered in its home market.[18] The "small band of young offbeats led by actor David Frost," *Variety* noted, was pleasing the BBC, if not the government, with its satirical commentary: "The BBC's attitude is now quite clear: 'That Was the Week That Was' is adult, if controversial and provocative, and because it is performed by highly talented performers, it is being done without unnecessary pure insult."[19] Given the acclaim accorded the imported *Beyond the Fringe* and the still-opening market for domestic satirists and parodists, NBC

Singer Millicent Martin proves more adept at balancing copies of the *That Was the Week That Was* coffee-table book than the BBC was in balancing the show against complaints from offended viewers and politicians. The cast of the British show, from left: David Frost, Roy Kinnear, Lance Percival, Kenneth Cope, Alan Mancini, Irvin C. Watson, David Kernan, Martin, producer Ned Sherrin, and William Rushton. Photograph courtesy of Photofest.

contacted the BBC and obtained permission to produce its own American version of *TW3*.[20]

The initial result of the arrangement was broadcast on November 10, 1963. Featuring the "open studio" of its British progenitor, the hour-long pilot episode of the American *That Was the Week That Was* began with the same musical device: a song featuring comic lyrics mocking and linking the particularly ridiculous events of the previous week. Structurally, the show also followed the revue style of the BBC version—a series of sketches and songs dealing with topical issues and personalities, including civil rights, Republican presidential candidates, and Nikita Khrushchev. The hip satirical team of Mike Nichols and Elaine May was also on hand, performing "The High Cost of Dying," a routine about contemporary funeral practices. But although NBC had aped the formal elements of the BBC series well, the content of the show was another matter. Most visibly, the moderators of the American version were not brash young representatives of a new style of humor, but veteran movie star Henry Fonda and equally veteran radio comedian/game show raconteur Henry Morgan. The other performers seemed to have little to do with the sketches in which they were acting; those sketches in turn seemed largely to strain for the satiric effect they hoped to achieve.[21] Nonetheless, public and critical response was strongly positive, and NBC put the series into production for a January debut.[22]

That debut, however, was reshaped dramatically by the assassination of John F. Kennedy less than two weeks later. While American television ceased broadcasting its regular program schedule to follow the events of the assassination, the BBC moved up its regular Sunday night presentation of *That Was the Week That Was* to Saturday, November 23. The show began with David Frost saying: "It was the least likely thing to happen in the whole world. . . . that Kennedy should go, well, we just didn't believe in assassination anymore, at least not in the civilized world." What followed was a somber tribute to the slain American leader, with the show's performers reminiscing and discussing his family, his trip to Britain, his successor. Singer Millicent Martin performed a funereal spiritual, "His Soul Goes Riding On." Dame Sybil Thorndike read a poem, "To Jackie." David Kernan, with tears in his eyes, called Kennedy "much more than a father figure, and much more than Ike ever, ever was"; Lance Percival continued, "He was simply and superlatively a man of his age . . . who put all of his own energy and the best brains of his country into solving its problems—by doing the right thing at the right time because he'd gone about it in the right way." Frost concluded the abbreviated twenty-two-minute program with what turned out to be, given the events of the following decade, a prescient benediction: "The tragedy of John Kennedy's death is not that the liberal movements of history that he led would cease; it is that their focus would become blurred and that the gathering momentum may be lost. That is the aftermath of Dallas, November 22. It is a time for private thoughts."[23] As hagiographic as anything constructed by domestic media in the same time span, the BBC's *That Was the Week That Was* for November 23, 1963, was all the more of interest to an American audience as a text representing the grief of a different culture. NBC flew a tape of the program to the United States to run on Sunday, November 24. At its conclusion, some one thousand calls came into the network's New York switchboard praising the show and NBC for airing it. Following coverage of the president's funeral and burial on Monday, NBC presented a repeat broadcast of the BBC program. The network eventually received thousands of requests for excerpts from the show, including one from Senator Hubert Humphrey requesting that its entire transcript be reprinted in the *Congressional Record.*[24]

Whether or not NBC obliged those requests directly, it addressed the outpouring of praise for the British show when its own version of *TW3* began in January 1964: gone was Henry Fonda, and in his place were Broadway performer Elliot Reid and David Frost, appearing as "Our London Correspondent...by special arrangement with the British Broadcasting Corporation."[25] Although his role on the American program was not as substantial as that in his native production, Frost's presence on the new *TW3,* made possible in large part by the BBC's cancellation of the British original at the end of 1963, was perhaps the final connection between British and American culture made directly as a result of John Kennedy's presidency.[26] In articulating a British grief over Kennedy's assassination, Frost also became articulated to the popular image of Kennedy—young, bright, and glib, with a bent for attacking the musty doctrines of an established order not to bring down that order but to make it responsive to a new group of participants. As was the case with the "text of James Bond," the "text of David Frost" in the United States acquired a level of signification that was defined by and inseparable from the fallen president: critic Jack Gould, after all, had used the most Kennedyesque of labels in citing the "vigor and compassion" Frost and his cohort had shown in their BBC memorial.[27]

As was true with Kennedy, however, although David Frost and the comedy he and *TW3* presented and represented might challenge the status quo, it never threatened to eliminate that status quo. The comic genre, as Steve Neale and Frank Krutnik point out, is one that is neither inherently subversive nor even inherently progressive, particularly when that comedy considers and tries to replicate familiar

The NBC version of *That Was the Week That Was* replicated the "open studio" look used by its British parent. From left: hosts Elliot Reid, Henry Morgan, and, "by special permission of the BBC," David Frost; singer Nancy Ames. Photograph courtesy of Photofest.

constructions of everyday life.[28] If comedy seeks to destroy those norms, the plausibility and surprise necessary for Palmer's "logic of the absurd" to work vanish with them. Only in the rigid formula of the domestic situation comedy is the maintenance of the status quo more significant, then, than in topical satire. Whatever their differences, satire and parody both require familiar constructions of language, ideology, culture, and aesthetics in order to exist, much less be effective; in a sense, then, the form of comedy Frost and *TW3* offered was one that was framed by the "real"—the utterances defining, refining, and confining culture.[29]

In the case of the American version of *That Was the Week That Was*, the most significant utterances were the ones defining the system of commercial television. Although the British version, as noted, had had run-ins with political officials and BBC authorities, it never had to satisfy sponsors who were supposed to pay for its existence. Sponsorship, however, was a major problem for the American version, as the cigarette, cosmetic, and car companies that might sponsor a traditional sitcom were reticent to spend money on a program that might make fun of their products.[30] By the time the first episode of the series was broadcast on January 10, the network had arranged sponsorship deals with Brown & Williamson (a subsidiary of British-American Tobacco), Clairol, and Speidel. However, the sales effort went far beyond what NBC had anticipated; one network official indicated that the *TW3* matter was the final proof that the old definition of product sponsorship had ended.[31]

Whether the result of concern over commercial sponsorship, the sudden adjustment of an established roster of writers and performers to a new colleague with a proprietary interest in their work, or both, the first show in the regular series of *TW3* failed to live up to the expectations created by either the pilot episode or the British version. Although it retained, in its thirty-minute form, the always-reworked title song, the open studio format, and the parodies and sardonic one-liners about people in the news, much of the material, including a brief monologue by Frost, was flat and poorly received by the studio audience.[32] Critical reaction to the new *TW3* was merciful only in its swiftness. *Time*, comparing the show to its British progenitor, called it "bland and unfunny.... Instead of savage young malcontents, the American program is largely staffed with familiar commercial personalities... flinging around nightclub material that would be tossed out of the thinnest of topical revues."[33] *Variety*'s reviewer noted that the episode "was as humdrum and pedestrian as the 'sneak preview' was delightfully impudent," blaming the problems on bad writing and "the mistaken impression that just because you're gagging up the political scene it comes out satire."[34] Cleveland Amory, in his *TV Guide* review, wrote, "Even David Frost's performances, often with dreary material, merely serve to point up that what was obviously a fast and funny show on the other side has become, over here, a labored succession of smart-alecky collegiate skits."[35] Indeed, a *TV Guide* article on the series in its first season suggested that the show's problems reflected a cultural clash between the "London Correspondent" and his colleagues. Frost, then-journalist Peter Bogdanovich reported, was at odds with the rest of the staff throughout the week's writing sessions and rehearsals over targets that seemed inappropriate, jokes that seemed too rude or racy, and sketches that seemed too British for the American writers and performers.[36]

Still, as the article pointed out, *TW3* was drawing a devoted following in its Friday-night time slot, with ratings approaching those of competing shows on ABC and CBS. With that in mind, NBC renewed the show for the 1964–65 season, moving it to Tuesday night, where it no longer had any relation to the calendar week that was but a very strong relation to its lead-in show: the British-inflected *Man from U.N.C.L.E.* And however battles between Frost and the Americans on staff may have transpired the previous year, Frost was clearly the winner, assuming his familiar British role as host. Frost's increased visibility and other moves, including the hiring of younger cast members, gave the program a greater appeal to an audience of his age group; these changes, however, came to naught, thanks to an intrusion of politics similar to the one that had brought an early end to *TW3* in its homeland. In the United States as well as Britain, 1964 was an election year, when major political parties purchased network time to present their points of view. The first show of *TW3*'s second season was to have been presented on September 22; the show's writers and performers, however, found themselves that evening watching a paid political program from the Republican National Committee. *TW3* did air the following week, but more messages from the Republicans preempted the program for three of the next four weeks, with election coverage itself wiping out yet another Tuesday broadcast.[37] Many involved with the show felt that the preemptions were the Republicans' revenge for material that they felt (probably rightly) struck at Republicans more than Democrats; Frost himself was skeptical of NBC's assertion that *TW3* was the only half-hour time slot available to the Republicans.[38] By the time the show returned for its second broadcast, a week after the presidential election, its opposition on ABC, *Peyton Place,* had become the most popular new show on the air. The final American *That Was the Week That Was* aired on May 4, 1965.

The history of *That Was the Week That Was* in both countries exemplifies the multiplicity of meanings available in a text relying upon the "logic of the absurd." The comic utterances expressed by Frost and the other writers and performers of both *TW3* editions, based upon constructions of "reality" that recognize established social institutions and cultural codes as a status quo to be ridiculed, were necessarily apprehended in different ways by different segments of the audience. Individuals identifying with those institutions and codes were angered by what they perceived as unwarranted attacks; individuals looking for a change in the status quo enjoyed the ridicule. The context of the jokes themselves, and the contexts in which the audience receives them, as Palmer points out, determine the effectiveness of the comedy. Letters, telegrams, and phone calls sent by viewers, both in support of the program and in angry opposition, also provide measurable evidence of the activity of audience members in deriving their own meanings from the text—and then acting in a literal fashion to respond, to conduct a dialogue.

Although *TW3* does seem to support the notion of active audiences, the fate of the program also convincingly demonstrates the limitations of that activity, both institutionally and textually. In the former case, the actions taken by the BBC and NBC in response to the complaints of political partisans indicate the way in which both networks would allow criticism of organized ideologies only to a point—albeit a fairly surprising point, given NBC's allowing the American *TW3* to present a sketch that attacked a sponsor's product. Once powerful interests made known their organized opposition to the program's satire, however, each network took the ultimate coercive measure: it eliminated the problem, much as public broadcasting eliminated programming that provoked the Nixon White House and potential corporate sponsors. This construction of *TW3* as a threat to the established order was a particularly curious one, however, given the conservative nature of the show's humor. As Neale and Krutnik point out, film and television comedy based on representations of a recognizable reality necessarily validate the existence of that reality. To eliminate the norms upon which that verisimilitude is based is to eliminate the source of the comedy. Despite their complaints, then, British Tories and American Republicans were actually well served by *That Was the Week That Was,* as the show's gibes merely validated and reinforced their central positions in each culture—just as the show validated and reinforced the norms of the Cold War through its gibes at Castro, Khrushchev, Mao, and other Communist figures.[39]

The relative safety the humor of *TW3* afforded its targets was also evident in the relationship the show established between its creators and viewers—a relationship again similar to that established by American public broadcasting some years later. Those responsible for the original British version of the show were primary possessors of cultural capital: from at least upper-middle-class backgrounds and educated at the nation's finest public schools and universities. As Bernard Hollowood, editor of the British humor magazine *Punch,* wrote in an explication of both *TW3*s for the *New York Times:* "It was rather like a family game of charades. Dad's leg was pulled, but the right people were pulling it."[40] The American version may not have had quite the pedigree of the British original, but it did have a redoubtable amount of cultural capital behind it. The addition of David Frost, moreover, added an Oxbridge patina to the program and with it the "snob merit" Peter Cook and Jonathan Miller found in the American reception of *Beyond the Fringe*. Both programs in turn made a point of showing off their wit through political and cultural references that only those who were well-read, in current events and in English lit, might understand.[41] In short, the audience the program's creators had in mind in both countries was an elite one that, like themselves, had accrued the most benefits from the institutions and codes they were supposedly threatening.[42]

That Was the Week That Was was, for all its reputation as groundbreaking television comedy in both Britain and the United States, a conservative form of comedy, upholding the norms it supposedly skewered and presenting a dialogue between its creators and its audience based on utterances that represented the privilege both enjoyed within those norms. *TW3*'s conservative nature was the primary reason it could so easily be adapted from one culture to the next, just as the conservative nature of the sitcom would result (as will be seen in Chapter 6) in the assimilation-through-adaptation of British representatives of that genre in the 1970s: simply substitute norms, and find the people with the appropriate cultural capital to ridicule them.[43] The presentation of *TW3* on organized television networks augmented its conservatism. As delimitors of meanings through their own systems of rules and codes, as well as through the power of controlling access, the BBC and NBC could and did keep the program within what each considered proper cultural boundaries. For television comedy to become something truly threatening in a national or transnational context, it would have to examine the "real" norms from which its textual deviations and *peripeteia* developed, the social and cultural contexts of its creators and audiences, and the ways in which it was distributed. British comedy in the United States would soon address all of that, in large part through the offices of David Frost.

From Frost to Flying Circus

The conservative vision of the comic presented by Neale and Krutnik and, implicitly, by Palmer in his construction of the "logic of the absurd" has its counterpart in Robert Stam's analysis of film and television comedy in his *Subversive Pleasures*. Working off of the theory of the carnival developed by Bakhtin in *Problems of Dostoevsky's Poetics* and *Rabelais and His World*, Stam argues that much in film and television comedy presents and represents a ritual and oppositional culture similar to that found in medieval and Renaissance carnival festivities.[44] In Stam's own words, the "carnivalesque" in film and television comedy offers a view of the official world as seen from below... a symbolic, anticipatory overthrow of oppressive social structures. On the positive side, it is ecstatic collectivity, the joyful affirmation of change, a dress rehearsal for utopia. On the negative, critical side, it is a demystificatory instrument for everything in the social formation which renders collectivity impossible: class hierarchy, sexual repression, patriarchy, dogmatism and paranoia.[45]

In his discussion of carnival and comedy, Stam argues for the resonance of many voices and meanings in a given text or cultural artifact. He contends that an understanding of Bakhtin's notion of carnival is meaningless without a consideration of his philosophy of translinguistics, one based on the notion of the many voices available in an utterance and the "interpretive grid" through which one makes meaning of those voices.[46] Although in his analysis of film comedy Stam avoids any discussion of the role of the audience in making meaning or of the circumscribing functions played by the film industry and the culture at large in containing those meanings, in his brief consideration of the television medium he is more aware of the need to consider the ways in which given utterances are shaped for and by specific audiences. A proper understanding of television, he suggests, "eschews both the elitist pessimism of manipulation theory and the naive affirmative celebrations of the uncritical apologists for mass-mediated culture." The goal of that understanding, he continues in language reminiscent of Jameson's consideration of popular culture, should be "to discern the often distorted undertones of utopia in mass media, while pointing to the real structural obstacles that make utopia less realizable and at times even less imaginable."[47]

Stam's willingness to consider television as a polyvalent medium, in which many meanings may be called but few can be chosen, reflects a more synthetic stance toward the paradigms he defines here than he presents in his discussion of the comic genre as a whole. More to the point, however, is that Bakhtin himself presents the comedy of the carnival as "ambivalent" and "dualistic," addressing both birth and death, destruction and renewal, the flesh and the spirit.[48] Given that, it becomes a good deal more plausible than in Stam's initial account to see television comedy working ambivalently, functioning both to reinforce the norms upon which it is based and to liberate its participants (the viewers) from those norms.[49] Todd Gitlin's comments concerning the importance of those who "spoke through the boob tube about its own boobery" to young radicals of the 1960s stand as a clear example of that ambivalence: "In a world that adult ideologies had defined as black and white—America versus totalitarianism... obedience versus delinquency, affluence versus barbarism—they did help establish the possibility of gray."[50]

Using the analyses offered by Stam and Bakhtin, an understanding of the ultimate failure of *That Was the Week That Was* in both Britain and the United States takes on a shading not provided simply by Neale and Krutnik's definition of the comic. The elite origin of the satire and parody involved, however circumscribed it might have been by the networks through which it was disseminated, created a condition in which the satirists, whether their laughter was mocking or friendly, were above the objects of their jests—and much of the audience that might have laughed with them. Those objects in turn, as specific representatives of the "real" norms of the time, both embodied a verisimilitude that, as Stam as well as Neale and Krutnik suggest, further limited the liberatory function of the comedy and revealed the show's elitism: to get the joke, one has to get the reference.[51] Given that, following the "logic of the absurd," a certain amount of verisimilitude is necessary in order for comedy to work and that elitism is a necessary part of satiric comedy, the question faced by the comedians of the early 1960s became one of finding the proper proportions of each to ensure the participatory laughter of millions.

That was certainly the question facing David Frost when he returned to Britain after the American *TW3* closed shop in 1965. After a failed reprise of the *TW3* formula, *Not So Much a Programme, More a Way of Life,* Frost decided for his next project to modify at least the specificity of the targets of its comedy.[52] *The Frost Report,* which was broadcast by the BBC in 1966 and 1967, used a specific topic—"Youth," "Crime," "Class"—as the theme for each show; two long sketches and several short ones on that theme, along with appropriate music from American singers Tom Lehrer and Julie Felix, were linked by Frost's "Continuous Developing Monologue": the "report," in other words. With a theme to consider each week, *The Frost Report* broadened its appeal and masked its elitist origins by becoming less dependent upon specific topical references than its predecessors and more reliant on archetypal representations of the norm being addressed. Both viewers and critics praised the show, which went on to win the Golden Rose for best program of the year at the 1967 International Television Festival.[53]

Even with that international recognition, however, *The Frost Report* did not make a transatlantic jump, although it did give its star his first practice in the talk-show format he would employ with great success into the 1990s in both Britain and the United States.[54] The importance of *The Frost Report* in this narrative comes from the talent Frost brought in to write and perform the program.

In addition to introducing British audiences to American satirist Lehrer and veteran native comedian/writer Marty Feldman, *The Frost Report* marked the first meeting of five veterans of the Oxbridge comedy revues: Graham Chapman, John Cleese, Eric Idle, Terry Jones, and Michael Palin.[55] Chapman and Cleese had written and performed in shows at Cambridge together just after Peter Cook and his colleagues had left; they were part of a touring revue from Cambridge that played in New York in the fall of 1964.[56] With connections established in the Footlights Club, Idle got his first job as a writer on *The Frost Report*. Jones and Palin were concurrently getting their degrees from Oxford, writing and performing together in various revues that swung more to "zany," absurdist humor than to the satire coming out of Cambridge.[57]

Of the five, Cleese was the only one regularly featured as a performer on *The Frost Report*—although while that show was being broadcast on BBC-TV, he and Chapman were working as regulars on a BBC radio sketch comedy program, *I'm Sorry, I'll Read That Again.*[58] All five, however, quickly went on to achieve greater success as performers as well as writers in other sketch programs: Cleese and Chapman on an absurdist revue produced by David Frost for commercial television, *At Last the 1948 Show* (1967), and Palin, Jones, and Idle on the BBC's *Do Not Adjust Your Set* (1968), a children's program whose fantastic humor quickly attracted an adult audience as well.[59] In addition to the three Oxbridge performers, *Do Not Adjust Your Set* also featured contributions from American-born artist Terry Gilliam and musician Neil Innes, whose Bonzo Dog Doo-Dah Band performed silly rock tunes that appealed more to children age twenty than children age two. It would not be the last of their collaborations.

Like *The Frost Report*, neither *At Last the 1948 Show* nor *Do Not Adjust Your Set* was exported to the United States. Both are, however, key moments, in Bennett and Woollacott's schema, in the mobility of signifiers surrounding and defining "British comedy," particularly the comedy created by "the Oxbridge Mafia" seen from an American point of view.[60] The "text of British comedy" early in the 1960s, which emphasized the elite backgrounds and cultural capital possessed by its writers and performers, was defined by the topical satire of *TW3*.[61] In each of the later programs, however, topicality and specific cultural references came to have less and less significance. Instead, the sketches came to present absurd surprises in everyday events: a madman doing ant imitations in a bus queue, the trial of a sheepdog, a visit to a psychiatrist who turns out to be sadistically cruel. Although the comedy again followed Palmer's "logic of the absurd," with *peripeteia* coming out of cultural norms, the norms were no longer given specific names and/or newsworthy situations, and the *peripeteia* as a result were all the more surprising.[62] In addition, the comedy of these later shows increasingly represented as part of the quotidian the mass media of which it was part. *TW3* was groundbreaking, in this sense, in its device of deliberately showing the home audience the means through which it was produced; it did not, however, make fun of those means in and of themselves. *At Last the 1948 Show* was devised as an early TV variety show to make fun of BBC executives' predilections for letting shows they had produced sit on the shelves until they could find appropriate times for them; *Do Not Adjust Your Set* regularly mocked other television forms, including old superhero serials.[63]

Simultaneously, then, the post-*TW3* programs became both more conventional, dealing with the everyday in a sketch form that had by this time on British television become a formula, and more liberatory, shedding to some degree the superior attitude of the earlier satire shows and welcoming more viewers—including children—into sharing their absurdist and irreverent attitudes. This is not to suggest that an elitist attitude had been completely eliminated, however. The verbal wit displayed in many of the sketches, along with the *peripeteia* introduced to the everyday world those sketches represented, still conveyed something of the cultural capital the jesters enjoyed—as did the way in which a network built on connections made at Oxford and Cambridge defined the form and controlled access to it. But by the end of the decade, when Chapman, Cleese, Idle, Jones, and Palin reunited, that elitism and the topicality it originally spoke to and for had mutated into something that for Americans would indeed be quite different from what had preceded it.

And Now, It's . . .

Monty Python's Flying Circus was introduced to British audiences by the BBC in October 1969, the same week *The Forsyte Saga* was introduced to American audiences and five years prior to its being aired across the Atlantic. This contextualization is significant in that it demonstrates the lack of concern the BBC had at the time for an American audience. *The Forsyte Saga* was the first BBC television series to achieve any measure of popularity in the United States, and that reception came more than two years after its original British production and broadcast. Only when the *Saga* achieved *succès d'estime* status did the BBC begin to consider the United States seriously as an export market for its entertainment programming.[64]

The British members of Monty Python were not ignorant of an American audience, however, nor were they unknown quantities to that audience before the arrival of their show in 1974–75.[65] As previously noted, John Cleese and Graham Chapman had appeared briefly in New York as part of a touring Cambridge production; Cleese stayed on for a year after it closed, performing on Broadway and working for *Newsweek*. He and Chapman returned together to the United States in 1969, via a special produced by David Frost for syndication by Westinghouse, *How to Irritate People*.[66] And although they would not be seen on camera, Cleese and Chapman also played a role in the successful (running from 1970 to 1973) syndicated sitcom import *Doctor in the House*, for which they wrote the premiere episode and then returned, during a *Monty Python* hiatus, to write several episodes later in the series.[67]

Soon after the BBC reunited Gilliam, Idle, Jones, and Palin with Chapman and Cleese in *Monty Python's Flying Circus*, the troupe began to become familiar to an audience in the United States, raising the questions involved in the establishment of a narrative image that would indeed be answered by the series. Broadcast late on Saturday evening—"fringe time"—on a staggered schedule around the country, the first group of thirteen *Python* episodes shown in Britain nonetheless attracted a substantial audience, strong critical praise, and a firm commitment for more shows from the BBC.[68] The comedy team turned a number of sketches from the first series into an eponymous record album; it would proceed to do the same with sketches from its other series (*Another Monty Python Record*, 1971; *Monty Python's Previous Record*, 1972; *Monty Python's Matching Tie and Handkerchief*, 1973). The albums began to make their way to the United States via tourists and import shops, as did collections of humorous essays, scripts, and drawings (*Monty Python's Big Red Book*, 1971; *Monty Python's Brand New Bok/Papperbok*, 1973–74).[69]

While these products began to trickle in, a more substantial familiarity with *Python* was developing elsewhere in North America, as the Canadian Broadcasting Corporation began to run the program in 1970, making it available to Americans living close to the Canadian border. The popularity of the show in Canada led the troupe to make a live tour of the provinces in 1973, stopping off at the end for a brief visit in the United States to perform on *The Tonight Show*—an appearance that, although less than wildly successful, further validated the troupe to an American audience.[70] The most significant introduction of Python comedy to an American audience, however, came a year earlier, with the release of the theatrical film *And Now for Something Completely Different*. A collection of sketches from the first two series of *Monty Python* programs reproduced for the film medium, *And Now* was the idea of Victor Lownes, manager of the London Playboy Club, who believed that Monty Python would be immensely popular with a young American audience.[71] He would turn out to be right, but *And Now* was not the vehicle through which that popularity would be gained. The movie failed to recover even its advertising costs in the United States, despite a glowing review from John Simon in the *New York Times.*[72]

Perhaps the largest surprise, then, when American public television stations, beginning with Dallas's KERA, started to broadcast *Monty Python's Flying Circus* in 1974 and 1975 was the way in which it attracted viewers at least somewhat different from the audience addressed by Simon and by the stations to which it was syndicated. This is not to suggest that the American *Monty Python* audience was one bereft of status. But although the program's audience in urban, urbane New York grew threefold in the first four months it was broadcast there, moving WNET ahead of the three commercial independent stations in ratings, *Monty Python* was extremely popular in Iowa, where a two-week period without a *Python* broadcast resulted in flooded switchboards, bags of mail, and a petition drive demanding its return.[73] This response was not, however, coming from the audience for *Masterpiece Theatre* serials. *Monty Python,* as Victor Lownes had predicted two years earlier, appealed most specifically to college-age viewers—an audience that, in acquiring educational capital, might have some appeal for public television stations already defining themselves, through their relationships with Mobil and other "sponsors," in terms of just such an elite audience.[74]

Several utterances of "our-own-ness" outside the text of *Monty Python's Flying Circus* present themselves as explanations for the show's American assimilation. Distribution is assuredly one element in the growth of the show's audience, as its availability for "free" in its original form in markets where audiences had to pay to see *And Now for Something Completely Different*—or never received the film at all—necessarily helped develop a relationship between the program and its American audience. Some measure of intertextuality also plays an organizing role, given the appearance in the United States of Monty Python artifacts and commentary thereon in small but significant amounts prior to 1974. Contributing to that intertextuality was the domestic development of a new style of comedy, descended from the topical satire of the early 1960s but speaking more directly to domestic political and cultural issues. Individual comics such as Richard Pryor and George Carlin turned out chart-topping albums in the early 1970s featuring material on political figures, race relations, drugs, and sex in a form and with language that was not acceptable at any hour on American television of the time.[75] Meanwhile, various groups of comedic writers and performers, similar to Python, were making renewed marks in nightclubs and college halls (Second City, the Committee), records (the Firesign Theatre), film (*The Groove Tube*), and periodicals (the *National Lampoon*) employing the same style of topical comic dislocation.[76]

The growth of this form of comedy also spoke to the growth, in pure numbers, of its intended audience—the audience that would in turn appear to constitute the major part of the viewership for *Monty Python*. In the fall of 1965—just after *TW3* left the air and just before *The Avengers* arrived—American colleges and universities enrolled slightly fewer than 6 million students. By the fall of 1969, when *Monty Python* was first broadcast in Britain, the number had risen to slightly more than 8 million. Five years later, when *Monty Python* arrived on American television, some 10.3 million students were enrolled, an increase of 73 percent in less than ten years.[77] The products of the peak years of the postwar baby boom, in short, reached college during the years that *Monty Python* was becoming a hit in Britain and that were marked in the United States by the climax and eventual denouement of the continuing tragedy of Vietnam, the violence and dissipation that overcame the civil rights movement and the New Left, and the election and downfall of Richard Nixon. The members of that generation, as Gitlin suggests, developed through the events of their youth a rude, raucous comic sensibility that embodied the communal, liberatory, and carnivalesque functions of humor directed at ruling classes and institutions presented by Bakhtin and discussed by Stam.[78] At the same time, however, that baby boom sensibility also filled the conservative function of maintaining those classes and institutions—of which they were becoming a part through attending college—by affirming them as cultural norms, both within the comedy itself and in the commodified products through which the comedy was available.

It is this last dichotomy that begins to explain the appeal the British series *Monty Python's Flying Circus* had to an American audience on a textual level. As was the case with other imported shows from *The Avengers* to *Upstairs, Downstairs,* difference itself—or the varying utterances of otherness—was attractive, especially to an audience angry with or weary of the cultural norms that were the sources of American comedy. That attraction was heightened by the fact that the program appeared almost exclusively on television stations operating outside the norm of commercial American broadcasting. As previously noted, however, public broadcasting in the United States was a system becoming defined by the eliteness of its audience—an eliteness as visible in the educational credentials of that audience as in the wealth it might possess. *Monty Python* viewers working their way through the American educational system were precisely the viewers who would financially support the future of PBS.[79] That the writers and per-

Military officials, whether British, German, or Icelandic, were among the many targets of the antiauthoritarian humor of *Monty Python's Flying Circus*. Photograph courtesy of Python (Monty) Pictures and BFI Films.

formers of the show regularly displayed their Oxbridge backgrounds through highly literate sketches invoking, for instance, various schools of Marxist theory, debates between Oscar Wilde and George Bernard Shaw, or the ability to summarize all seven books of Proust's *A La Recherche du Temps Perdu* in less than a minute, also contributed to the elitism of the cultural dialogue. Getting the joke (the irruption of high culture and philosophy into the commonplace norm) meant knowing the references, which in turn meant owning the appropriate educational capital.[80] Again, liberatory and communal laughter becomes laughter that reinforces a hierarchic status quo.

Sketches that specific in required knowledge, however, were more the exception than the rule on *Monty Python,* a rule that helped develop the dialogue between the British show and its American audience. As both Wilmut and, later, Neale and Krutnik note in their analyses of *Monty Python,* the comedy in the program largely avoided topical satire that named specific names and/or issues; instead, it focused on institutions of authority familiar to both national cultures —

the church, the military/police, the legal system, governmental bureaucracies, and so on.[81] This is not to say that the members of Monty Python shunned specific comic attacks. A particularly vicious sketch directly mocked their former employer, David Frost, portrayed (by Eric Idle) as unctuous celebrity "Timmy Williams," who is too preoccupied with his "super" acquaintances and photo ops ("They syndicate these photographs to America!") to help out a desperate old friend.[82] Even in that sketch, however, the ways in which the comic *peripeteia* address the norm of "Unctuous Celebrity" are funny regardless of whether one knows the specific identity of that celebrity, just as sketches on lecherous vicars, upper-class twits, and Ministries of Silly Walks might be funny regardless of what one knows of the Church of England, the landed gentry, or the structure of British government.[83]

Although the appeal of *Monty Python's Flying Circus* to a young American audience in the 1970s may well have been due to the program's willingness to make the norms of institutional authority the source of its comedy, that appeal was enhanced further by the institutional authority most constantly and reflexively referred to throughout the series: television itself.[84] As had been the case with sketch comedy shows since the 1950s, *Monty Python* made parodies of game shows, talk shows, beauty pageants, and the like a regular part of its comic repertoire. American audiences who had grown up with and thus had a trained knowledge of the forms, if not necessarily the specific referents, being mocked could find the comic surprises in their treatment both appropriate and plausible. This standard sort of mocking, however, was surpassed in the Python treatment of the medium, which directly addressed not just generic forms but the way in which television as a whole was constructed as a transmissive and authoritative device. Several devices regularly used by the troupe—the intrusion of opening and closing credits at inappropriate places in the show, the use of captions and other graphic material, the foreshortening of sketches by characters in those sketches who decide that they are not funny and so should end—are discussed at some length by both Wilmut and Neale and Krutnik.[85] What is significant in each instance is the way in which the comic surprise develops not out of an unexpected twist given to a specific genre but out of the audience's expectations and knowledge of the way television is "naturally" supposed to be and work. Indeed, the ultimate humor of "Timmy Williams' Coffee Time" works in much the same way, as the sketch reveals, through offscreen voices, camera pullbacks, and a credit roll, that what appears to be an everyday meeting in the life of the Unctuous Celebrity is in fact a constructed part of his/the viewer's television universe: television, not life, is natural.

The depth to which *Monty Python's Flying Circus* took its demystification of the authority of television and the ways in which that became significant to an American audience become clearer in a close examination of a specific episode. The first show in the third season of *Monty Python* (the twenty-seventh of the forty-five produced) begins with a camera pan of a rocky, wind-blasted heath; a sudden loud chord is accompanied by the caption, in old Norse lettering, "Njorl's Saga." As the music fades, the camera continues to pan to a bearded Viking, who attempts to stammer out an introduction. However, the camera keeps on panning past him, stopping finally at a naked man who plays a fanfare on an electric organ. Cut to a newscaster sitting at a desk, who says, "And now"; a second cut introduces a haggard hermit, who says, "it's . . ."; and the *Monty Python* theme music (Sousa's "Liberty Bell") and opening animation sequence begin.[86] In the first minute of the show, then, Monty Python lays bare for ridicule not just the film/television epic itself but the conventions defining that epic, through the deliberate failure to stop the camera where it is "naturally" supposed to stop (on the Viking) and instead bringing it to rest on a figure—a naked organist—who not only has nothing to do with the "story" at hand but who is completely out of place for the medium in which he appears.[87] The denaturalization continues as the naked man plays a triumphant closing chord, before the story has begun, and is immediately followed by a newscaster, for whom "Njorl's Saga" appears to be but one more event in the progressive narrative of the day.

"Njorl's Saga" becomes a recurring sketch throughout the episode, in each instance mocking the conventions of the television historical epic by revealing and then shattering those conventions. The hero, who initially has trouble getting on his horse, soon finds himself in a twentieth-century commercial for the town of North Malden, as the BBC head of drama (John Cleese) continually interrupts the story to correct the narrator's mistakes, ask for help, and remand the head of the North Malden Icelandic Society for the inclusion of elements that "don't ring quite true to the spirit of the original text." In each manifestation of "Njorl's Saga," the norm—the televisual production of a fictional story—gives rise to comic *peripeteia* that reveal and attack that norm. On one level, Monty Python ridicules the conventions of the fiction itself through devices such as the corrected narration, the arrival of Njorl in North Malden, and his ensuing battle against the knights of Malden—who throughout the battle brandish signs and banners reading "Malden: Gateway to Industry" and "Invest in Malden." On a second level, the troupe addresses the televisual production of the story: the continuing pan opening the show; frightening music accompanying each appearance of the "Njorl's Saga" logo; quick zooms, fast cutting, and flash-frame intrusions of the battle scene. Most telling in this regard are sudden comic shifts in both Njorl's meeting with the mayor of North Malden and the battle sequence from a representational mode, in which the camera records the action "realistically" for the audience's later pleasure, to a presentational mode, in which the camera and its audience are addressed directly—shifts that uncover the construction of all television "fiction" and hold it up on ludic display.[88] Finally, the Python sketch(es) attack the industrial and institutional forces behind all the "Njorl's Sagas" by involving on air the "BBC head of drama" in its proper presentation and the commercial-minded citizens of North Malden, who simply want to use the saga to promote their town.

The ridicule of television established in "Njorl's Saga" continues throughout the episode, as the saga becomes something of a "metasketch," enveloping and/or referencing almost every other element in the show. Njorl appears, with theme music and logo, immediately after the apparent conclusion of what has turned out to be the "Malden Saga" as the bandaged defendant in a courtroom sketch, in which he is charged with conspiring to publicize a North London borough in a BBC saga and "to do things not normally considered illegal." When that sketch turns into the continuation of an earlier Terry Gilliam animation, the saga appears to be over, only to resume, with logo and music, as the rubric under which two old women decide to settle a laudromat argument about the philosophy of Jean-Paul Sartre by going to Paris—via Iceland—to visit him. Throughout, the mocking of television narrative, production technique, and institutional structures continues apace, with the referencing and cross-referencing between sketches deliberately making *Monty Python's Flying Circus* simply another television text to be mocked: when Sartre settles the old women's argument, the end of "Njorl's Saga" and, evidently, the *Monty Python* episode is noted with the on-screen graphic, "The End"—which is immediately followed by another sketch.

Each of the levels of comic intent present in both the initial installments of "Njorl's Saga" and its transmogrification throughout the episode includes references that have meaning only to a British audience: the significance of "Malden"—if any—for example, is lost on an American audience for whom "Malden" meant *Streets of San Francisco* star and American Express pitchman Karl. And each level of comic intent contains surprises that can be enjoyed on their own regardless of any connection to television: the slapstick of Njorl attempting to get on his horse, the subliminal insertion of "Invest in Malden" frames, the utterly ineffectual authority of the BBC head of drama. But in making the conventions of television as a whole the target of their humor, Monty Python succeeded in creating a comedy that not only could travel to the United States but could thrive there.

The final sketch in the "Njorl's Saga" episode provides a final example of the way in which Python comedy could be assimilated into American culture. One of two parodies of specific television forms in the episode, "Whicker's World" uses the name of the travelogue show that it targets.[89] The comic surprise fueling the narrative is that the tropical paradise of the week is Whicker's Island, a beautiful Caribbean resort that is home to countless hosts of travelogue shows who have no place else to go. Having immediately denaturalized the show and its genre, the troupe then addresses the presentational nature of its production by having each member dress up as and adopt the nasal, herky-jerky intonation of Alan Whicker, the host of the "real" *Whicker's World,* and trade off the lines of Whicker's monologue one after the other while crossing through the camera frame at dizzying angles. Their poly/monologue directly addresses the literary conventions of the script ("Well, there you have it, a crumbling / empire in the sun-drenched / Caribbean, where the clichés sparkle on the waters / like the music of repeat fees"), the conventions of its presentation ("... where gin and tonic jingle in a gyroscopic jubilee of something beginning with 'j' "), and the institutional conventions of the travelogue as a whole ("The practiced voice of the seasoned campaigner / cannot hide the basic tragedy here. / There just aren't enough rich people left to interview").[90] These forms of *peripeteia,* although specifically born out of the norms of *Whicker's World* and Alan Whicker, also explicitly address the norms of the medium through which Whicker and his world seem to come to natural life. There is comedy in the sketch that has nothing necessarily to do with the norms of television — the physical movements of the Whickers, or a fully clothed Whicker reporting from the middle of the swimming pool. There is also comedy to a knowing audience in seeing the specifics of *Whicker's World* being mocked. But, finally, there is comedy for audiences who would not know Alan Whicker from Alan Thicke in seeing the norms defining the construction of Whickers and their *Worlds* wherever being unmasked and ridiculed.

All these utterances concerning the mechanisms of television helped shape the response that *Monty Python* received in an American audience familiar with the medium from birth, as did other comic utterances of a slapstick variety that did not require specific knowledge of the culture from which they came. Other knowledge, however, also helped shape that response for an audience that had already acquired or was in the process of acquiring educational capital. As previously noted, the sketch concerning Sartre is meaningless without some basic knowledge of who Sartre is and what he produced; the sketch includes several references to Sartre's work in French and bases one of its jokes on the difference between Marxism and revisionism. The names of the two old women — Mrs.

Premise and Mrs. Conclusion—also set up the final joke of the sketch: when Sartre confirms Mrs. Premise's premise that *"Rues a Liberté* is an allegory of man's search for commitment," Mrs. Conclusion concludes the sketch, "Oh, coitus." "Njorl's Saga" itself, in addition to its mocking of its medium, also mocks the literary style of Icelandic sagas: "Erik Njorl, son of Frothgar, leaves his home to seek Hangar the Elder at the home of Thorvald Nlodvisson, the son of Gudlief, half brother of Thorgier, the priest of Ljosa water, who took to wife Thurunn, the mother of Thorkel Braggart. . . ." As is the case throughout the episode, the absurdity of the names used and the relations described ("Gudreed, daughter of Thorkel Long, son of Kettle-Trout, the half-son of Harviyoun Half-Troll") function as comic surprises independent of the norm being addressed. Recognizing the norm of the Icelandic saga, however, as well as the norm of Sartrean existentialism, requires knowledge obtained only by a discriminating few and contributes to the "snob merit" Peter Cook cited in the appreciation of an American audience for British humor a decade earlier.

Jolly British holiday picnics are about to meet blood-soaked American Westerns in "Sam Peckinpah's *Salad Days,*" one of many "overgraduate" sketches from *Monty Python's Flying Circus* that found a ready audience waiting in the United States. Photograph courtesy of Python (Monty) Pictures and BFI Films.

This "snob merit" and the education brandished by the troupe did not go unnoticed by those in the United States who were critical of the enterprise. Cleveland Amory, in a rare pan of British programming, commented in *TV Guide* on the show's presentation by the Eastern Educational Network of public broadcasters: "Exactly how it comes under the head of education we don't know, except that it has been described as containing overgraduate humor. . . . one thing is certain: Nothing is done over lightly here. Everything is done at least twice— and heavily."[91] Meanwhile, popular journals that were aimed at an audience rich in cultural capital were praising the troupe: the *New Yorker,* in its "Talk of the Town" blurb on the popularity of the show, described how a viewer of *And Now for Something Completely Different* fell out of his seat and then rolled to the front of the theater laughing.[92] Humorist Thomas Meehan presented a three-page appreciation for the *New York Times Magazine* that turned Amory's criticism upside down: " 'Undergraduate humor,' scornfully say the Pythons' critics, but there is such off-the-wall originality and intelligence in most of what they do that it might better be called 'overgraduate humor.' "[93] *Time* presented the success of the comedy group and its show as "bordering on a cult, that is now sweeping the U.S."; in an accompanying sidebar review of *Monty Python and the Holy Grail,* critic Richard Schickel wrote, "as funny as a movie can get, but also a toughminded picture—as outraged about the human propensity for violence as it is outrageous in its attack on that propensity."[94]

This clear division in the critical commentary on *Monty Python's Flying Circus,* as well as the measured demographic support it and later shows created by its individual members received in the United States, speaks again to the dichotomy of comedy addressed earlier.[95] The program's comic deconstruction of the norms of institutional authority, most particularly television, made it accessible on one level to an American audience who had grown up with those norms— and who had, in the end of the Vietnam conflict and the Watergate scandal, witnessed an anything-but-comic deconstruction of the ideals, if not the norms, of American policy and politics. The many levels of humor and the diverse types of *peripeteia* employed by the comedians, as exemplified in "Njorl's Saga," added to both the width (in terms of accessibility) and the depth of their relationship with that American audience. To characterize that relationship in terms of the "absorption and domestication" Gitlin associates with hegemony and assimilation willfully erases the anti-institutional utterances, both American and British, defining the dialogue; indeed, ABC's failed efforts in 1975 to bring *Monty Python* to an American audience defined by the constructs of commercial network broadcasting demonstrate how "domestication" can be directly resisted.[96]

Laughter engendered through all those utterances, however, was liberatory only in that it came at the sense of seeing the authority it addressed exposed; it could do nothing to change the nature of that authority. The very audience, in fact, that could laugh at the recognition of the emperor disrobed was precisely the audience gaining the training and the resources to sew the emperor's new raiment. For those, meanwhile, who found themselves embodied in the norms addressed by *Monty Python's Flying Circus*—women in particular—the Oxbridge-trained comics established themselves as but another elite authority continuing a tradition of hierarchical (or patriarchal) disrespect.[97] Once again, an opened ideological seam was sewn back up as the limits of comic subversion exerted themselves in the American reception of a British text.

Still, the reception of *Monty Python* in the United States, like that of *The Forsyte Saga* and *Upstairs, Downstairs,* transcended that of a passive audience absorbing whatever comic messages might be found in the program. Indeed, the participatory involvement of live audiences at Monty Python's stage performances in New York in 1976 and Los Angeles in 1980 represent both the ritual aspect of communication as defined by James Carey and the ritual aspect of carnival as defined by Bakhtin and Stam.[98] However ritualistic the responses of those audiences might have been, and however desirable their demographics were to public broadcasting and local independent stations, the fact remained that British programming per se had not since *The Avengers* successfully found its way to the mass American audience shared by the three major commercial networks. But just as *Monty Python* was becoming a critical and popular success in Britain, and just as *The Forsyte Saga* and *Masterpiece Theatre* were beginning to attract viewers well-off in both education and finance in the United States, another small but most influential American audience was paying a great deal of attention to British programming. It would be American television producers themselves who would provide the ultimate assimilation of British television into American culture.

6. All in the Anglo-American Family
Hollywood Reproductions of British Originals

They're all bleedin' foreigners anyway...there's not an Englishman in sight except for the poor devils that work for 'em. Go anywhere in London and ask your way today, they won't know what you're talkin' about. "Me no speaka the English, me wog." Well, I don't like wogs!

—Albert Steptoe, "Crossed Swords," *Steptoe and Son*[1]

Ain't nothin' on earth uglier than a 90-year-old white woman.

—Fred Sanford, "Crossed Swords," *Sanford and Son*[2]

One set of utterances assuming primary significance in the relationship between British television and American culture in the 1970s has yet to be explored: the "our-own-ness" provided by producers of American programming as they encountered and worked with the "otherness" of imported British shows and genres. As Horace Newcomb and Paul Hirsch observe, the television producer, in constructing a representation of social reality, is "seeking and creating new meaning in the combination of cultural elements with embedded significance...respond[ing] to real events, changes in social structure and organization, and to shifts in attitude and value." That meaning, they continue, is sought and created within an economic framework impelling those producers "to build on audience familiarity with generic patterns and instill novelty into those generically based presentations."[3] With the critical, popular, and/or demographic success of British programs, American producers had just such a source of novelty to reconstitute the conventions of the genres within which they worked and a new set of "cultural elements with embedded significance" with which to work. Although the import of British programs per se throughout the 1970s was limited either to the demographically desirable greenbelt of public television or the hardscrabble backstreets of syndication, British television became an important constituting element, thanks to the efforts of American producers, in each of the genres considered thus far: adventure, serialized literary/historical drama, and sketch comedy. More significantly, through the work of Norman Lear and his production company, British programming was translated and reconstituted for American audiences in the most basic genre of network television, a genre not previously addressed by British imports: situation comedy.

Sitcomic Visions

That American television would begin to adapt successful British shows and formats to its own audiences might have been predicted, given the experience of less developed nations producing their own versions of imported American programming once funding and technology became available.[4] That the situation comedy, a genre that defined American television in the way the Western defined American film, would be the locus of the most significant adaptations of British programming was not something that could have been foreseen: no British situation comedy had been broadcast in series form on American television by 1970. Some of the reason for that lack of trade was economically determined—the supply of and demand for domestically produced situation comedies was, if anything, heavier on the supply side than the demand, given the relatively low production costs. Meanwhile, British broadcasters, particularly the BBC, had just begun to investigate the American market as a source of revenue as major as that available through geographic (Europe) and cultural (Commonwealth) proximity.[5]

As important, however, in the refusal of American networks to import British situation comedies in the 1960s is the cultural nature of comedy, as discussed in Chapter 5. Comic utterances are dependent upon norms of a given culture that give rise to the surprises defining the comedy. The sketch comedy of the British *That Was the Week That Was* could be adapted to an American format because the specificity of its jokes and short sketches was easily translated from the norms of one "web of meaning" to those of another. The situation comedy, however, demands that jokes be placed into a narrative format involving continuing characters, adding depth and breadth to the normative function of the genre. The sitcom, as Barry Curtis explains it, is a text based on a social construction of "reality." Disruptions and/or exaggerations of that "reality," whether they come out of narrative (the "situation") or character, provide the comedy.[6] This realism, and the order and disorder it contains, is further encoded by such signifiers as dress, speech, and physical surroundings, which serve either as naturalized reinforcers of the norm or as comic exceptions revealing and, within the discourse of the show, legitimating that norm. Given that depth of coding and ideological structuring, the presence of a situation comedy based on a very different set of signifiers is always a dicey proposition, even when, as Neale and Krutnik present the case with American and British sitcoms, the norm in question—the importance of family—is a shared norm.[7]

There was no small irony, then, in the fact that at the end of the decade, it would be the notion of "realism" that would give the British situation comedy entrée into American culture. That understanding of "realism," however, was shaped by three significant vectors external to the sitcom form itself: a new understanding by American television networks about the makeup of their audience according to demographics; social changes that, although evident in demographic numbers, went far beyond what those numbers themselves might indicate; and an individual producer who sought both to address those developments and to give birth to a new form of television author.

Norman, Is That Us?

An article in the January 24, 1968, issue of *Variety* described a public outcry in Britain over the top-rated BBC situation comedy *Till Death Us Do Part*. The series, which made its debut in 1966 and featured verbal battles between Cockney working-class bigot Alf Garnett and the rest of his family, had previously occasioned public and parliamentary criticism. The left deplored Alf's no-slur-barred assaults on immigrants and British minorities, and the right fumed over his profanity, his irreverent attitude toward the clergy and the royal family, and his attacks on Conservative political "twits."[8] *Variety*'s coverage of the series piqued the interest of American producer Norman Lear.[9] A gagwriter for Dean Martin and Jerry Lewis who had gone on to some considerable success, with partner Bud Yorkin, as a movie producer and writer (*Come Blow Your Horn, Divorce American Style, The Night They Raided Minsky's*), Lear had been profiled in a 1967 *Variety* article as a filmmaker who "sees no good reason why the screen should not further its own dramatic literature, and inventiveness."[10] An inventive cinema notwithstanding, Lear obtained the rights to *Till Death Us Do Part* in 1968 so that his and Yorkin's Tandem Productions could adapt it for an American audience. At the time, Lear told *Variety* that the purchase was motivated by the social and political ferment of the day: "I became convinced that the American public is in the mood to have its social problems and shortcomings analyzed and in comedy such probing comes over less harshly than in other TV ways."[11] Later, however, he would say that the family conflicts at the heart of the British show were the elements that most appealed to him: "What inspired me was simply reading that somebody had done a show in which a father and son-in-law were arguing, were totally apart—not just a generation gap, but were divided on every issue.... That was all I needed to excite me, because I had lived that with my father."[12]

Evident in Lear's comments is the potential for multiple meanings in the text of *Till Death Us Do Part*—meanings that drew from political and social issues on the one hand and "family values" on the other. Indeed, the family structure, the ideological center of American situation comedy, would provide a layer of meaning in Lear's adaptation of *Till Death* that would make perceived political meanings palatable, at least to some degree, among Americans unused to such "messages" in a sitcom. More significant, however, is the reliance placed by Lear in each of his constructions of meaning on the relationship of the show to the "real world." The source of comic disruptions in *Till Death*, as Lear perceived them, was not the equivalent of Endora turning Darrin Stephens into a child on *Bewitched*, nor was it the absurdity of life in a world defined by television as portrayed by *Monty Python*. Instead, the richness of the British show lay in the reactions of its protagonist to contemporary social events, political figures, and cultural trends he encountered in the course of his day. As such, in Lear's apprehension of it, the comedy of *Till Death Us Do Part* veered closer to the satiric turf occupied previously by *That Was the Week That Was* than American situation comedies had dared; indeed, when *All in the Family* went on the air in 1971, *TV Guide* described the show as an "adult social satire."[13] At the same time, however, with the program locating Alf Garnett and his foils—wife Else, daughter Rita, son-in-law Michael—in a domestic family unit that argued about those events, figures, and trends, Lear could construct the show as one that, while maintaining the family structure central to the American sitcom, made that structure much more "real"—so real, in fact, that he could say he had lived it himself.[14]

With utterances born out of his own family conflict and social conscience guiding him, Norman Lear in 1968 undertook the task of turning the most-watched British situation comedy of its day into something somehow different for American audiences. His first two efforts, called *Justice for All* and *Those Were the Days*, failed to impress ABC, where programmers were concerned about the aggressiveness of protagonist Archie Justice and the disastrous experience the network had already had with "relevant" programming.[15] Lear's agents quickly took the show across the street to CBS, where president Robert Wood was beginning a plan to redefine the network and its audiences along demographic lines. Throughout the 1960s, CBS, which had the largest number of affiliate stations of the three networks, had retained its position as greatest among equals by featuring programs appealing to a spectrum of viewers as broad as the net itself: rural situation comedies (*The Andy Griffith Show, The Beverly Hillbillies, Green Acres*), formulaic sitcoms with known stars (Lucille Ball, Doris Day, Fred MacMurray), formulaic comedy-variety shows with known stars (Jackie Gleason, Red Skelton, Ed Sullivan), and Westerns (*Gunsmoke*). This strategy of farm, family, and familiarity had kept CBS at the top of the ratings during the 1960s, but what Robert Wood saw on his network in 1970 were shows with aging stars, aging story lines, and aging audiences that were losing their value to advertisers, particularly as the baby boom generation was becoming a major market force.[16]

When the ABC pilot for *Those Were the Days,* with its attention to social issues and its fractured family, crossed his desk in March 1970, Wood took notice. He ordered a third pilot for the series, with new actors Rob Reiner and Sally Struthers as the "kids" joining original cast members Carroll O'Connor and Jean Stapleton. The reaction in the CBS programming suite was close to ecstatic.[17] Audience tests showed that potential viewers still found the Archie character too abrasive, bigoted, and cruel, but the results on the whole were more positive than those for ABC had been, according to Les Brown, as the ideological arguments loudly voiced in the show had become, by the spring of Richard Nixon's bombing of Cambodia and the Kent State and Jackson State shootings, commonplace utterances.[18] With the final approval of network owner William Paley, Wood and his programmers scheduled Lear's version of *Till Death Us Do Part* to go on the air in January 1971—the same week in which PBS and Mobil would introduce *Masterpiece Theatre* in their own use of British programming for demographic purposes.

The show broadcast by CBS on January 12, 1971, however, was called *All in the Family,* recasting the marital and familial connections suggested by *Till Death Us Do Part* in a far sunnier, more advertiser-friendly way and situating the comedy exactly within genre and ideological conventions of American commercial television. Whatever conflict and controversy the show might engender, it was still, after all, to be contained within the familiar confines of a home occupied by a father, a mother, and two children. For CBS, the title both reflected its own traditions and served as damage control before the fact; for Lear, it restated his own construction of the British show as something that came out of his childhood experience; for the viewer, it was an assurance that what followed was not going to be something too terribly different from what had come before.[19] Similarly, Lear changed the last name of Archie and wife Edith from "Justice" to "Bunker," a revision that stripped one layer of meaning and added several others: Was it "Bunker" connoting the ur-American Battle of Bunker Hill (won, of course, by the British)? Or "Bunker" connoting the place where one takes cover while under/making an attack? Or "Bunker" connoting one who spews a load of bunk? The choice was left up to the viewer.[20]

The final formal change effected between the first pilot and the CBS version of the show, however, was a more radical one that again spoke to the relationship between American and British television. Following the established technical standards of the day, Lear had shot the ABC pilots for the series on film. When it came time to put down a final product for CBS, however, Lear decided to shoot the show using several cameras as a live continuous performance on videotape. The tape medium was cheaper by half than using film, which gave Lear a bargaining chip in dealing with the network; it also recalled the producer's early days working in variety shows, which used videotape and were shot "live."[21] But although soap operas, news broadcasts, and some variety series on American television used videotape, the notion that a prime-time representational comedy or drama program could or would be shot on videotape had faded with the decline of the anthology dramas of the 1950s, as ABC's demands of *The Avengers* had demonstrated. Because of cost, however, most BBC programs, including *Till Death Us Do Part, The Forsyte Saga,* and the serials that would soon be presented in the United States as *Masterpiece Theatre,* were recorded on videotape.[22] With his production of *All in the Family,* Norman Lear had, in essence, reclaimed British video technology standards as viable for American prime-time productions.

These final formal adaptations of *Till Death Us Do Part* merely reflected those in content that Norman Lear had made in his treatments of the show. Lear, in articles and publicity about the series, downplayed the role of the BBC series in the creation of *All in the Family* and instead attempted to establish the American version as an intensely personal remembrance of things past, citing individual lines spoken by Archie ("You're the laziest white man I've ever seen"; "Stifle yourself!") as having issued from his father's own lips.[23] Yet a close comparison of the two programs reveals the degree to which the British show shaped Lear's vision of an American family situation comedy and the degree to which utterances from American culture outside the Lear household played a role in the assimilation of *Till Death Us Do Part.*

Those inflections become immediately evident in an examination of the families at the heart of both series. The Garnetts in Johnny Speight's series were aitch-dropping Cockneys who lived in the rough working-class neighborhoods of London's East End; the opening credit sequence of the show aerially took the viewer over London into the neighborhood, a visual device copied (using New York) in *All in the Family.*[24] In Lear's version, the Bunkers were loud New Yawkers residing in the working-class borough of Queens, allowing the producer/writer the ability to create the same comic equation of class and dialect in the United States that was visible and audible in the British show. As the opening sequences indicated, however, the classes being considered were considerably different: the Garnetts lived, apparently, in an industrial backwater, with warehouses and dock cranes as much a part of the landscape as any dwelling; the Bunkers, however, resided in a single-family household surrounded by other single-family households. The closeness of the residences, and their evident lack of lawn space, signified that this was not upper-middle-class suburbia, but still, the Bunkers lived in a fashion that, as David Marc points out, was enviable to a good number of Americans whom they were supposed to represent, to say nothing of the Britons on whom they were modeled.[25]

Class, however, could not and would not be defined quite so rigidly in the American version, as the character of the son-in-law made clear. Michael in *Till Death Us Do Part,* while every bit the mod young Labourite, was also a mad young laborer whose confinement in the working class was as frustrating to him as the decline of the Empire and all it stood for was to Alf. Michael Stivic in Lear's show, however, was a college student, working his way through school as the first step in his, and his wife's, upward mobility. Given the autobiographical connection he found with *Till Death Us Do Part,* Lear's adaptation of the British character to address both an American cultural norm and his own rise in the world can again be read as both an ideological and a personal decision. Such was not the case, however, with the other change in the character: the addition of ethnicity. Merely another Cockney in *Till Death,* Michael of *All in the Family* was Polish, a perfect foil for Archie's indecorous ethnic jokes and slurs.[26] On one level, the decision created a level of tension between the characters of the father and son-in-law that was not present in the British version. On another level, however, the presence of Michael's ethnic heritage revealed the absence of same in the Bunkers. Lear was himself Jewish, and the childhood memories that so spurred his interest in *Till Death* were those of a Jewish household. In his reconstruction of that background, however, for an American commercial television audience in 1970, Archie, Edith, and Gloria became white Anglo-Saxon Protestants. Here again, an ideological concession to the naturalized norm of the American sitcom family served to open up the comedic possibilities of the show, as Archie was left with a clear field of differences to attack.[27]

Those attacks were foregrounded much more directly in the first episode of *All in the Family* than they were in Johnny Speight's first script for *Till Death Us Do Part.* Despite Lear's declarations of independence from the British show and assertive authorship of the first season's episodes for CBS, his first script

Alf Garnett (Warren Mitchell, left) regales wife Else (Dandy Nichols), son-in-law
Michael (Anthony Booth), and daughter Rita (Una Stubbs) in a typical *Till Death Us Do
Part* living room political commentary...

for *All in the Family,* "Meet the Bunkers," borrowed its central plotline directly
from Speight's first *Till Death,* "A House with Love in It": when Archie/Alf for-
gets his wedding anniversary, the children attempt to make amends by purchasing a card and gift for Edith/Else as if they were from her husband and plan a
dinner at which the moment of good feeling collapses into insult and argument.[28]
In the British original, although Alf does disparage Prime Minister Harold Wilson
in a drunken rant, the insults are kept largely within the family. When the kids
come down for dinner wearing hopelessly groovy Carnaby Street knockoffs and
shades, Alf tells his son-in-law that he looks like "a fake Peruvian ponce" and
his daughter that her outfit is "disgusting—you can see right through to your
bellybutton!" The appearance of his wife—a "silly moo," a phrase that in Britain
achieved the noxious ubiquity of Archie's "dingbat" reference to Edith in the
United States—occasions Alf's comment that she looks like "mutton dressed
up as lamb." The most direct slurs from Alf come at the posh West End French
restaurant to which Michael and Rita take her parents, consisting of relatively

... while the Bunkers of Norman Lear's *All in the Family* gather around their electronic hearth in Queens (from left: Jean Stapleton, Sally Struthers, Rob Reiner, Carroll O'Connor). Photographs courtesy of Photofest.

mild comments about the menu being "all in foreign" to his having "served in Froggyland for four years" during World War II.

In Lear's version, the French are virtually the only nationality or ethnic group left unscathed in Archie's diatribes: "If your spics and your spades want their rightful piece of the American dream, let them get out there and hustle for it, just like I did"; "Feinstein, Feinberg—it all comes to the same thing, and I know that tribe"; "What do you know about it, you dumb Polack?" As that line indicates, the children are also drawn into Archie's line of fire—"I didn't think you was gonna go to college and learn how to be a subversive"; "I knew we had a couple of pinkos in this house, but I didn't know we had atheists!"—but the father's rants, as opposed to the personal direction taken in *Till Death,* address Mike and Gloria primarily as representatives of social causes (and, in Mike's case, an ethnic group) of which he does not approve. This adaptive strategy allowed Lear to augment the controversial "adult social satire" he hoped to create and sell while reinforcing the naturalized assumption that the American family, whatever trials and problems it might endure, is, in its function as the basic social organization of American life, a good thing. The ending of "Meet the Bunkers," in which Edith is moved to tears by Archie's "gift"—lace handkerchiefs—and the greeting card, exemplifies the degree to which Lear was able to retain the stability of the cultural (and televisual) norm of the family while developing what seemed to be a radical new form of sitcomic political discourse.

Such, however, cannot be said of the "House with Love in It" episode of *Till Death Us Do Part*; indeed, what is truly radical by American standards in Speight's show is not the violent political or social commentary voiced by Alf but the violence it does to a commonsense norm of the nuclear family. Part of that dislocation is evident in the settings used for the two shows. In "Meet the Bunkers," Lear limits the action to the downstairs of the Bunker household, a decision mandated by the economic and production benefits of using a single set as well as by dramatic and ideological concerns.[29] No such form of domestic containment, however, is present in "A House with Love in It." Although the downstairs area of the Garnetts' row house provides the setting for much of the action, Speight also takes the audience up to the bedrooms, out to the neighborhood pub, and over to the fancy West End restaurant. The episode, then, visually reveals the irony of its title by getting the characters out of the house as much as possible.[30]

Much more significant in defining the radical nature of *Till Death Us Do Part,* however, and the key point of departure for Norman Lear's adaptation of the series, is the character of Alf's wife, Else. In Lear's reconstruction of the series's central family, Edith Bunker is a genteel household saint devoted to her husband and her children, forever trying to be the peacemaker between the two. The first image the viewer has of Edith in "Meet the Bunkers" is her arrival home from church wearing her Sunday best; the last image of her is of her rushing from the living room with her lace hankie to cry over the beauty of Archie's anniversary card. The first image the viewer has of Else Garnett in "A House with Love in It" is of a frowzy woman smoking a cigarette, sitting in a chair with curlers in her hair. She immediately launches into an accusatory yawp at her husband for forgetting their anniversary; when he responds in kind, she calls him "nothing but an ill-mannered drunken pig." She recants a bit when Alf gives her a brooch (again purchased by the children) as an anniversary present, but when Alf makes his displeasure known about the celebratory dinner, she shouts, "We're better off without you, you miserable old git, you!" A closet gambler, she places bets with the neighborhood milkman, and in the restaurant, it is she, not Alf, who makes the rudest comments about the French. In the closing scene, when she discovers that Michael had purchased Alf's gift—a plot turn the Lear show scrupulously avoids—instead of running from the room weeping in gratitude, she bursts out bawling, "You didn't buy it—you didn't remember me anniversary at all . . . and I give you me breakfast!"

The character of Else Garnett, familiar to 1960s British audiences from the post-D. H. Lawrence stereotype employed in "kitchen sink" drama and films, would not have been a complete stranger to an American television culture that was home to Alice Kramden and Wilma Flintstone.[31] Yet in Lear's adaptation of *Till Death Us Do Part,* whereas at least vestigial elements remained of Alf, Michael, and Rita, Else's character virtually disappeared, to be replaced by a kind but somewhat befuddled representative of the era of domestic containment, a woman who tended to her husband's every need while tolerating endlessly his verbal abuse. In Edith Bunker, Norman Lear acknowledged that the American domestic situation comedy, no matter how topically relevant or formally radical, could not countenance the "unruliness" of a housewife giving as good as she got from her husband, particularly at the class level of the Bunkers.[32] The notion that the Noble American Housewife could call the breadwinner "an ill-mannered drunken pig" or a "miserable old git" was unthinkable, which is why Lear's script for the first episode of *All in the Family* eliminated the plot moment—the revelation that Archie had nothing to do with the hankies and card—in which such an outburst would be plausible. This clear ideological reframing of *Till Death Us Do Part* was made to seem the natural order of things by those involved with the show through the discourse of "realism"; as Jean Stapleton herself would say of her character in 1974: "We can't hide the kind of woman who is restricted by her domestic life. She exists. And I think that by showing Edith *as she really is,* we are doing more good than an instant out-of-character liberationist would accomplish."[33] This despite the fact that Else Garnett, the character out-of-which Edith was created, was anything but a liberationist and, within Johnny Speight's British comedy, was anything but out of character.

Lear had, in *All in the Family,* skillfully cloaked the most traditional generic and ideological elements of the American situation comedy in a political topicality that seemed completely different from what the genre had previously provided. Having successfully decoded and recoded *Till Death Us Do Part* into an American series deep enough in potential meanings yet accessible enough in form to top the annual Nielsen ratings for five years (1971–76), Lear turned his attention to another British situation comedy that had been just as controversial—and revered—as the weekly diatribes of Alf Garnett. *Steptoe and Son* made its debut in 1962 as part of a series of one-off comedy playlets by former sketch comedy writers Ray Galton and Alan Simpson.[34] The first *Steptoe,* "The Offer," introduced Britain to nasty, whiny junk dealer Albert Steptoe and his son Harry, who desperately wants to leave home to start a life of his own but who is, through his father's scheming and his own weakness, unable to do so. Shot on a single cluttered, grimy set, which included an outhouse, and relying as much on the pathetic relationship between father and son as it did on jokes and visual gags (Albert cleaning the outhouse privy and then blowing his nose on the rag), "The Offer" led to a series of five episodes of *Steptoe and Son* later in the year, which were hailed as a "breakthrough" for British television comedy.[35]

Steptoe and Son made the transatlantic crossing well before Norman Lear decided to adapt it for an American audience: Jack Paar presented an episode of the show on his NBC prime-time show in 1964, proclaiming it "the greatest comedy series I have ever seen." With Paar's endorsement, Embassy Pictures purchased the American rights to *Steptoe* for some $250,000, arranging for Galton and Simpson to adapt their own scripts for an American cast and setting up a broadcast deal with NBC for the new series.[36] The deal, however, died with only a pilot episode having been produced. Alan Simpson blamed the failure of the venture on his perception that Americans only liked television shows "to be about affluent people living in nice homes."[37] With nothing but a failed pilot to show for its investment, Embassy sold the rights to Screen Gems, where *Steptoe and Son* languished on the shelf while still sparking controversy as one of the most watched programs in Britain. Lear and Bud Yorkin obtained the rights to the series from Screen Gems; their first pilot, however, unlike *All in the Family,* attempted to make *Steptoe* an overtly ethnic comedy by casting the father as Irish and the son as Italian. The networks rejected that hoary premise, forcing Lear and Yorkin to try another direction in their adaptation of *Steptoe and Son.*

One of the liberties Lear had taken with the adaptation of *All in the Family* from *Till Death Us Do Part* was the addition of an African American family — George, Louise, and Lionel Jefferson — living next door to the Bunkers, providing another target for Archie within the story and speaking "realistically" to the divide between the races outside. *All in the Family* as a result stood as an example of the limited way in which the civil rights movement of the 1960s, like the women's movement, had come to shape representational television comedy and drama. Seen regularly only in servant roles since the early 1950s, African Americans began to return to American television in the mid- to late 1960s. Almost without exception, however, black characters were constructed either as underlings (often with criminal backgrounds) to white bosses, as inconveniently colored residents of an otherwise totally white, middle-class suburbia, or, in the case of popular comedian Flip Wilson, as a complex combination of signifiers that allowed him to be read as a "coon show" stereotype mocking black society and culture as easily as he could be read as performing and celebrating that society and culture.[38] The Jeffersons in *All in the Family,* however, differed from other black characters in prime time in that they recognized and commented on what W. E. B. Du Bois referred to as the African American's "twoness — an American, a Negro; two souls, two thoughts; two unreconciled strivings." In "Meet the Bunkers," Lionel tells Mike and Gloria about Archie's asking him about his college career: "He likes to hear me say, 'Ahm gwiner be a 'lec-tical in-gineer!'" When Mike asks if he actually says that, Lionel responds, "Give the people what they want, man — how else do I get to become an electrical engineer?"[39]

As Lear had used *Till Death Us Do Part* to revive and reconstruct the long-dormant contemporary blue-collar American sitcom along lines he imagined to be his own, so *Steptoe and Son* would allow him to create a black family sitcom, again with the theme of a generational father-son conflict.[40] Redd Foxx, whose X-rated stand-up routines and record albums had made him a top draw on both black and white comedy circuits, was signed to play the father; Demond Wilson, whose most notable national exposure had been in a guest shot on *All in the Family,* got the part of the son, Lamont. Foxx, whose sense of self was almost as strong as Lear's, decided to give his character the name of his brother, Fred Sanford; so it was, then, that the British *Steptoe and Son* became the American *Sanford and Son* — at least in title.[41] As in Lear's previous adaptation, however, it would be necessary to make other changes in *Steptoe and Son* to engage an Amer-

Harold Steptoe (Harry J. Corbett) warns his dad Albert (Wilfrid Brambell) away from a priceless porcelain piece in the British *Steptoe and Son...*

ican audience. The junkyard was set in the Watts neighborhood of Los Angeles, an important move not only ideologically, in placing the show in an actual black neighborhood—and a neighborhood that signified blackness to audience members with memories of its 1965 riots—but technically, in that the Southern California setting allowed for brighter lighting and a less visually depressing background for the action than that of *Steptoe*.[42] The set itself was cleaner, with open spaces in the living room and a staircase to an unseen part of the house, which helped limit the downstairs clutter; the plumbing facilities were also contained inside. Instead of the Steptoes' flatulent old horse Hercules living in a stable outside the house, the Sanfords kept their pickup truck—not a pretty new pickup truck by any means, but a motorized vehicle far more "realistic" than an equine-drawn junk wagon—in the driveway. As the Bunker household in Queens was a notable step up from both the Garnett household in London and the means of many "middle Americans," so the sunny single-family dwelling and business of the Sanfords was a step up from the status of their British progenitors and many of the urban black families they seemed to signify.

. . . and Fred Sanford (Redd Foxx) makes a less-than-fatherly gesture toward his son Lamont (Demond Wilson) in the American *Sanford and Son*. Left-hand image captured by Donovan DeJong; right-hand photograph courtesy of Photofest.

These shifts in production technique and the visual style of the show were representative of what Newcomb and Hirsch refer to as "seeking and creating new meaning in the combination of cultural elements with embedded significance" as producers respond to social, political and technological changes— and, in the case of the Lear sitcoms, changes in cultural norms occasioned by the transfer of texts from Britain to the United States.[43] Those changes become particularly evident in a comparison of the first episode of *Sanford and Son* and the 1965 episode of *Steptoe* on which it was based. One difference in Lear's adaptations of British shows is quickly evident: although Lear may have borrowed plot elements from *Till Death Us Do Part*, his scripts, particularly for the early episodes, followed his personal vision for the show more than they did the original. For *Sanford and Son*, however, Lear, Yorkin, and writer/producer Aaron Ruben used the actual scripts written by Galton and Simpson for *Steptoe and Son*. As a result, *Sanford* was much closer (at least in its early episodes) in plot, setting, and dialogue to its British progenitor than *All in the Family* was to its.[44]

The first episode of *Sanford*, "Crossed Swords," like the 1965 "Crossed Swords" episode of *Steptoe*, involves a valuable piece of porcelain, identified by the "crossed swords" mark on the bottom, that Lamont/Harry obtains by chance from a wealthy household. The two men take the porcelain to an antique dealer, who offers them a fair amount of money for the piece; Lamont/Harry, however, envisioning his freedom from his father and the junk business, decides to take it to auction, figuring that he can get a higher price there. In attempting to up the price, the Sanfords/Steptoes get stuck with the high bid, more than twice what they had been offered by the antique dealer. When they return home, Fred/Albert attacks Lamont/Harry for auctioning the piece; the son responds by blaming his father for ruining his life; the father then accuses the son of wanting him dead. The guilty silence that follows ends with Fred/Albert picking up the porcelain piece in admiration, only to drop and shatter it, blaming his arthritis for the accident.

The only significant difference between the two episodes in terms of plot structure is the first scene of *Sanford and Son*, an initial encounter between the two lead characters drawn from the first scene of the *Steptoe* pilot: Lamont voices both his frustration at his father and their lot in life and his desire to "go on to something bigger," and Fred responds by announcing that he's going to be dying soon and then faking a heart attack. In terms of dialogue and character, however, Albert's political diatribes about the good old days—"If that had happened to me in my day it would have been worth a kick up the Khyber at least. That's the trouble with this country today. Nobody takes offense no more. In my day an Englishman's word was his bond"—are gone, as is his ridicule of "bleedin' foreigners" and "wogs," replaced by the relatively tame comment that there's "nothin' on earth uglier than a 90-year-old white woman." The closing father-son quarrel and the tragicomic breaking of the figurine is similar in intensity and dialogue ("You can't wait to hear the first shovelful of dirt hit the coffin, can you? I won't be mourned, I know that—you'll be dancin' on me grave") in the British and American versions. *Sanford and Son*, however, does not include the final *Steptoe* tag: as Albert assumes his usual perch on the loo, Harry rams old swords through the door and walls of the outhouse at his wailing father.

For all the similarities between the shows, what becomes clear in the British and American versions of "Crossed Swords" is the degree to which Lear and his cohort focused on the lead character in making the show speak to an American audience. Albert Steptoe was no less a Tory reactionary in *Steptoe and Son* than Alf Garnett was in *Till Death Us Do Part*, and was no less oblique in his slurs and criticism of the "wogs" and other foreigners who had turned London into a "vast stinkin' metropolis." *Sanford* writer/producer Ruben said of the character,

"In the English version, the father is very caustic, almost vicious. For a lot of reasons, we didn't feel that attitude was right for Redd, so we made him gentler."[45] But making Fred Sanford a kinder, gentler, American Albert Steptoe was facilitated as much by the initial decision to cast the character as a black man as it was any overt script changes made by Lear, Yorkin, or Ruben. Indeed, many of Steptoe's most annoying characteristics remained in Redd Foxx's portrayal of Sanford—phony heart attacks, convenient bouts with arthritis, blaming his son for everything that went wrong with the business.

The politics of the character, however, necessarily changed dramatically. Steptoe's paeans to the glorious days of Churchill, king, and empire issuing from the lips of an elderly black man in Watts would have in no way addressed the social realism central to Lear's vision of the sitcom. And although Fred Sanford retained elements of the racism voiced by Albert Steptoe, referring readily to "honkies" and ugly white women, and telling son Lamont to keep his Latino friend from "gettin' Puerto Rican all over our truck," it was the response both of a querulous old man and of a character who could not be presented on American television until 1972 because of his own race and class background.[46] Bud Yorkin's facile assertion that Fred Sanford "isn't bigoted—he's just honest" could be and was debated, just as the Sanford character, like Flip Wilson before him, could be seen as both a stereotyped putdown of black American culture and a realistic recognition, if not a celebration, of that culture.[47] What Lear, Yorkin, and Ruben accomplished, however, in their assimilation of Albert Steptoe was the creation of a character embodying a number of meanings and built from cultural elements with embedded significance specific to the United States. Herman Gray argues that *Sanford and Son* is one of several 1970s black sitcoms that "idealize and quietly reinforce a normative white middle-class construction of family, love, and happiness," whereas David Marc suggests that the show's progressive racial comedy makes a joke of standard white racism; both ignore the show's British origin.[48] Those arguments reveal, however, the way in which Lear and his company brought forth meanings from the historical experience of blacks and whites in the United States and placed them into Newcomb and Hirsch's "cultural forum," in which those meanings and questions about them are brought into public discussion.[49]

The American success of *All in the Family* and *Sanford and Son* provides a clear look at the complex ways in which cultural utterances shape the assimilation of transnational televisual texts. Norman Lear's personal interest in shows about a father-son conflict, based on his childhood experience in New York, guided *Till Death Us Do Part* and *Steptoe and Son* to American audiences. Without a growing recognition and discussion of the "generation gap" those shows represented to him, as well as an increased public dialogue on issues of racism, ethnicity, religion, and other social concerns that dug the chasm, however, Lear's personal vision might never have seen the light of millions of Zeniths and RCAs across America. And even with those utterances shaping the production and reception of his shows, had Lear not been able to adapt the British programs into the familiar conventions of American situation comedy, and had the networks distributing those shows not decided to redefine their economic base along demographic lines, *All in the Family* and *Sanford and Son* might today be a few reels of videotape fading away in a Hollywood studio warehouse. The popularity of Lear's sitcoms in the United States exemplifies the inextricable connections among personal, political, social, aesthetic, and economic utterances as they worked in the assimilation of the British texts of *Till Death Us Do Part* and *Steptoe and Son* into American culture. With their presence in the American cultural forum, and the growing space in that forum being occupied by British programs airing on PBS stations, the influence of British television on American culture was set to expand exponentially.

From Lear to Leer

The work of the American television producer on a cultural level, Newcomb and Hirsch argue, is to create new meaning out of combinations of familiar signifiers. On an economic level, both they and Todd Gitlin argue that familiarity has to be augmented by something novel in order to assure a program's success in attracting advertisers and viewer—in Gitlin's tripartite scheme, by placing familiar characters in new settings (the spin-off), by placing new characters in familiar settings (the copy/clone), or by recombining signifiers that have proven successful/become familiar elsewhere into a new show (the recombinant).[50] Norman Lear, in his translation of British situation comedies into top-rated American shows, achieved his success by combining some of the novelties—utterances of otherness—with the utterances of "our-own-ness" represented in the most basic form of American television: the domestic family comedy. With the acclaim afforded this combination by the American viewing public, producers could continue the assimilation of *Till Death Us Do Part* and *Steptoe and Son* into American culture.

Lear led the way, re-creating the conflicts of *All in the Family* and *Sanford and Son* in two spin-offs from the former. *Maude* played out its generational and social conflicts in a limousine liberal household governed by Edith Bunker's cousin, a loud Friedanesque feminist, and *The Jeffersons* moved Archie's bigoted and entrepreneurial black neighbor and his family up to a deluxe apartment on Manhattan's Upper East Side. A second-generation *All in the Family* spin-off owed as much to *Sanford and Son* as it did to its direct progenitors. *Good Times* took Maude's maid Florida Evans out of Long Island to the projects of Chicago's South Side. For the first time in a Lear series, the Archie character was placed on the young side of the generation gap, in the form of her loud, jive-talking son J.J.; the comedy was in turn based more on generational than social differences. It retained, however, its domestic base and, like *Sanford and Son,* represented that base in an African American community.

Each of those programs was a ratings success, demonstrating both the perspicacity of Lear's own tele-vision and the generative power of *Till Death Us Do Part* and *Steptoe and Son.* As Lear continued recombining his first hits—*One Day at Time,* which set the generational and working-class conflict in a single-mother family in Indianapolis—other producers and shows followed. Garry Marshall, whose sitcoms tended structurally to re-create the organic-genteel tensions of his first hit, *The Odd Couple,* borrowed the working-class element of *All in the Family* to make *Happy Days* and *Laverne & Shirley* top-rated successes in the mid-1970s. The generational, racial, and class issues of *Sanford and Son* were re-created by producer James Komack in his *Chico and the Man,* in which Albert/Fred became an old white garage owner and Harry/Lamont became his young Latino partner; there were even a sour old black garbageman and a battered truck to make the connection complete. Meanwhile, other British shows that featured the same kind of conflict as *Till Death* and *Steptoe* began to interest American producers. A popular BBC multiethnic comedy set in a British prison, *Porridge,* became the ABC 1975 sitcom *On the Rocks.* Don Taffner, a New York-based producer with ties to the British commercial television industry, adapted two other shows—*Love Thy Neighbor,* a British version of the Bunker-Jefferson relationship, and *For the Love of Ada,* which closely resembled *Maude*—for ABC, as *Love Thy Neighbor* and *A Touch of Grace.* Both, however, were pale copies of Lear's work, and lasted only half a season.

While the issues of race, generation, and class introduced in *Steptoe* and *Till Death* percolated their way through the American television industry, a separate controversial facet of the Lear sitcoms led to another American adaptation of a successful sitcom. Sex, as much as generational feuding or working-class bigotry, had been treated openly as the subject of comedy in *All in the Family,* just as it had in its British progenitor. The viewer actually meets Archie and Edith in the first scene of "Meet the Bunkers" when they walk in on Michael and Gloria passionately making out on their way up to their bedroom.[51] Episodes dealing with the themes of impotence, homosexuality, infidelity, miscarriage, and rape would follow; a number of episodes made reference, visually and verbally, to Gloria's tight blouses and miniskirts or tight jeans; Mike's allegedly insatiable sex drive was a frequent target for Archie's insults. With *All in the Family* again in the vanguard, sex and sexuality became central elements of American television in the early 1970s.

This new openness about sexuality was, as Lear's visual treatment of Gloria exemplifies, part of a continuing retrograde shift in the presentation of women on American television similar to the one that Tony Bennett and Janet Woollacott found working in the "Bond girl" at roughly the same time.[52] Every genre of American television had, in the decade since Emma Peel first kicked off her shoes and took down a karate master, made some effort to represent women outside the parameters of the ideology of domestic containment—even if it meant, as Bonnie Dow argues, re-creating the workplace as a contained scene of patriarchal domestic life.[53] What those programs seemed to lose, as they evidently addressed an audience of maturing women for whom a life outside the home was now much more a reality—or a necessity—than a fantasy, was something to address the male audience as well: a renewed hail to the patriarchy and the power of the male gaze. That hail would begin in the police and detective series inflected by the success of *The Avengers* in the 1960s. The female characters included in the corporate crimefighting units of *Mission: Impossible, Ironside,* and *The Mod Squad,* while clearly work partners whose social and sexual lives played little if any role in the cases they were supposed to help solve, were also attractive blonde women whose presence was designed to be as pleasing to the male eye as it was empowering to the "modern woman of today."

The beautiful blonde crimefighter was elevated to lead status in the Lear-era 1974 crime show hit *Police Woman.*[54] Played by Angie Dickinson, title character Pepper Anderson was sent into "undercover" action each week, almost always in a guise—stripper, prostitute, cocktail waitress—that required she use the lure of sex as part of the way to catch her man, and that not accidentally allowed for maximal use of minimal costumes. Whatever skill Pepper might have exhibited as a cop was mitigated by the fact that most episodes ended with her being rescued by male detectives—usually the ones who ordered her into the situation to begin with. And, as Susan Douglas notes, the crimes she was asked to solve often involved rape or some other form of violence against women—violence that seemed naturally and even rightfully visited upon those women and to which she herself was about to be subjected before her rescue.[55]

The delicate balance between a feminist representation of women as having escaped domestic containment and what Douglas calls an "antifeminist" representation of women as being defined both physically and in their work by male desire (and being punished when they fail to meet the expectations of that desire) reached its post-*Avengers* apotheosis in the 1976 ABC show *Charlie's Angels*. Producer Aaron Spelling recombined his *Honey West* and *Mod Squad* with *Police Woman* to give audiences three young, unattached females using their attractive and well-displayed bodies to fight crime for a private agency headed by the unseen patriarchal "Charlie." As both Douglas and John Fiske point out, *Charlie's Angels* was nothing if not multivocal, as a young middle-class female audience to whom Emma Peel would have appealed a decade before was equally taken with the strength, courage, wiles, and styles of the Angels (who, unlike Pepper Anderson, usually worked their own way out of various scrapes).[56] However, as was the case with the "Bond girl" in the 1970s, that power was beneficial only when exercised on behalf of patriarchal authority and presented in a form—the "jiggle"—directly addressing the male gaze.

This emphasis on the female body to signify a heterosexual male-defined construction of sex reached a similar apotheosis in the sitcom genre in another American adaptation of a British show, first presented by ABC in the 1976–77 season. The producers and writers of *Three's Company*—Don Nicholl, Michael Ross, and Bernie West—had served as story editors and writers for the first four seasons of *All in the Family*.[57] Unlike Lear, however, they took the text for their first production from commercial British television, not the BBC. Those commercial producers and distributors, looking with some envy upon the success BBC imports were having in the United States, whether on PBS or in their adapted commercial forms, began to search for ways into the American market that did not involve the "mid-Atlantic" effect sought by Lew Grade. One of those producer-distributors, Thames Television, employing utterances concerning the "special relationship" between Britain and the United States that were rampant in the latter's national bicentennial celebration, arranged a unique deal with New York independent station WOR-TV for September 1976. For one week, the American station's prime-time and late-night schedules consisted of nothing but Thames shows.[58] By almost every standard, the programming gimmick was a success: ratings for the week met Thames's hopes and exceeded WOR's norm; more important, American producers and distributors began purchasing the shows they had seen for presentation in the United States.[59]

Among those programs was a situation comedy called *Man about the House,* written by the team of Johnnie Mortimer and Brian Cooke. The show presented the misadventures of a heterosexual single man in need of a place to live and two young single women who decide to offer him the third room in their London flat. The sexual tension of that situation is compounded by the women's landlord, who doesn't approve of sex outside of marriage (and who, according to his wife, doesn't approve of it in marriage as well) and refuses to allow unmarried men and women to live together under his roof—until the women convince him that their potential new roommate is gay. Also built into the situation is a further apparent gender role reversal: the women both work outside the home, whereas the man is, at the start of the series, an unemployed chef; his skill in the kitchen is part of the persona concocted to fool the landlord. Don Taffner, previously responsible for the adaptations of *Love Thy Neighbor* and *A Touch of Grace,* bought the format and syndication rights to *Man about the House* and brought in the Lear veterans to craft it into an American hit.[60] What crafting Nicholl, Ross, and West may have done early in their creation of *Three's Company* out of *Man about the House,* however, had little to do with either the verbal or visual element of the program, as even the titles of the two series' first episodes suggest: *Man about the House* made its premiere with "Three's a Crowd," whereas *Three's Company* offered "A Man about the House."[61] A comparison of those episodes reveals that the American version, with minor exceptions, is almost a line-by-line remake of the British version.[62] And although the sets are slightly different—the American version seems more suburban than the British—lighting, camera angles, and editing are remarkably similar, aided by the videotaping technique used with each.

As was the case with *All in the Family,* the primary change the producers/ writers brought to the American adaptation from the British original lay in their presentation of the women in the episode. Although Chrissy (the brunette) and Jo (the blonde) in *Man about the House* were both attractive, neither was a glamour queen on the order of Pepper Anderson or Charlie's "angels"; and although neither was particularly bright, both were certainly competent enough to hold down jobs and run a household—and quick enough to think of a way to fool their nosy landlord when he threatened their household stability. That, however, changed when Chrissy and Jo became Janet (the brunette) and Chrissy (the blonde) of *Three's Company.* Instead of two women of moderate talent and beauty, the American series presented female leads that, in the terms used in the *Variety* review of the show, were "childish" and unfortunately notable for their "naivete."[63] This was particularly true of the Chrissy character, who embodied the comic "dumb blonde" stereotype employed by American television and film industries from Sally Struthers back to Thelma Todd. Moreover, the American women of *Three's Company* had much more amply endowed figures than their predecessors and were dressed to accent and reveal that amplitude, both fore and aft. The correlation could hardly be more clear: the bigger the "tits and ass," to use the colloquialism given shows such as *Three's Company* and *Charlie's Angels,* the smaller the brains—an inflection of the original British show made possible again by the mid-1970s effort to recontain women, if not in the patriarchal home and castle, then at least in the purview of the male gaze.[64] Indeed, that gaze, in the exaggerated leering performed by new roommate Jack Tripper—what connotations were available in *that* name!—at Chrissy's cleavage, became an integral part of the comic construction of *Three's Company.*[65]

By visually representing the male gaze, of course, Nicholl, Ross, and West made it available for comment and denaturalization, particularly as Jack's ogling often led to some comic deflation of his attitude (if nothing else) in a pratfall. There is little evidence, however, that audiences did either. Sex on *Three's Company* was not an issue to be placed under Norman Lear's apparently avant-garde lens of social realism; sex—or the concupiscent promise thereof—as defined by Tex Averyesque cartoon stereotypes of a drooling Priapus and a busty, dimwitted blonde, was the *only* issue for the characters in what David Marc refers to as the *"derrière garde"* American adaptation of *Man about the House.*[66] Whereas *All in the Family* remained a primary text of sitcom social realism, *Three's Company* veered much closer to the fantastic exaggerations Terry Lovell defines as farcical nonrealist comedy.[67] As Marc suggests, however, *Three's Company* as a comedy of "lifestyle" was still rooted in the realist tradition of comedy that Lear had exploited so well. No other "American" show, even by 1977, had dared to introduce the mainstream plausibility of homosexuality or couples' living together without being married, even if those topics were used as sources of comic exaggeration instead of dramatic conflict.[68] Indeed, *Three's Company* was as clearly a child of Lear's vision as his own creations were. Without the comic treatment of sex and sexuality in *All in the Family,* including the focus on the female physique as source and butt (in both senses) of the humor—Chrissy was hardly less developed intellectually or more developed physically than Gloria Bunker Stivic was—any adaptation of *Man about the House,* much less the one produced by Nicholl, Ross, and West, would have been unlikely. And without Lear's attention to British television as a source for American programming and his skill in assimilating the differences it offered into the most sturdy conventions of the American situation comedy (skills learned by Nicholl, Ross, and West), *Three's Company* would have been inconceivable. The prurience of *Three's Company* would be exceeded by the end of the decade by a truly farcical syndicated import from Thames Television, *The Benny Hill Show.*[69] By that time, the social consciousness that had informed the most notable of Lear's programs was gone. Those connec-

er, had been picked up and employed nearly as profitably — in every
t term — by American producers working in genres very different
presented by Lear.

Blow, Winds, Blow

Although the situation comedy retained its dominance as the central genre of
prime-time television into the 1970s, the topical satire of *That Was the Week That
Was* left its own tiny but distinct legacy to American culture. First with CBS's
The Smothers Brothers Comedy Hour in 1967 and then with NBC's *Rowan &
Martin's Laugh-In* the following year, the controversial sketch-based humor of
TW3 found new homes in the variety show format. The Smothers Brothers show
initially seemed to adopt the irreverence of its British predecessor to a greater
degree, with "anti-Establishment" skits that eventually led to enough "Estab-
lishment" complaints that CBS suddenly canceled the program in 1969.[70] The
TW3 influence on the Rowan and Martin-hosted show, however, was more directly
visible. Although less political than *The Smothers Brothers Comedy Hour, Laugh-
In* employed the short topical sketches, blackouts, and one-liners that marked
the *TW3* style of humor. A weekly collection of gags, "*Laugh-In* Looks at the
News," seemed almost lifted from the British format.[71]

However much *TW3* shaped the work of Lorne Michaels, an early writer for
Laugh-In who had returned to his homeland to star in his own Canadian Broadcasting Corporation sketch comedy series, the 1970 arrival in Canada of *Monty
Python's Flying Circus* proved to be a defining influence. "It was miraculous to me,
a revelation," Michaels would later say of *Monty Python*. "It seemed that once
again the winds of change were blowing from England."[72] Using clips from the
British show to define what he wanted to do with the medium, and even going so
far as to put a phony *Monty Python* writing credit on his résumé, Michaels in 1975
accepted an offer from NBC for a job as producer of a new late-night comedy-
variety program, "a show for the generation that grew up on television."[73] When
Saturday Night Live went on the air in fall 1975, however, the Python influence
was at best muted. The show's opening stand-up monologue (by a celebrity "guest
host") and parodic sketches barely went beyond standard prime-time offerings;
the show's repertory company, drawn from similar groups in the United States
and Canada, played only a minor role in the first few episodes; and the "Weekend
Update" feature owed more to *TW3* topicality than to Python absurdity. Perhaps
most important, the fact that *Saturday Night* was truly live, seen in Cedar Rapids
as it was being performed in New York, meant that the televisual production elements so central to the Python attack on the medium could not be used.[74]

Slowly but surely, however, Lorne Michaels's model for what television should be became more and more visible as the show progressed. The repertory group became the core of the program, performing in sketches that took film, television, and other forms of popular culture beyond simple parody into ridicule of the ways in which those forms were produced and received. Dan Aykroyd, whose performances as absurd media hucksters were among the show's sharpest and naughtiest bits, would explain the Python influence some years later: "A lot of American humor in television is based on real social situations and real relationships, and Python just takes that humor and explodes it."[75] Eventually, Eric Idle and Michael Palin would serve as "guest hosts" of *Saturday Night Live* on several occasions; Michaels also instigated and coproduced Idle's Beatles documentary parody *All You Need Is Cash* for NBC.[76]

Although American producers of both situation and topical sketch comedy series, as well as crime and detective shows, were able to "instill novelty into their generically based presentations" by turning to British models in the early 1970s, another genre remained untouched for several years. Even with the success of *The Forsyte Saga,* American producers shied away from serial dramas. The cost of mounting a weekly hour-long program requiring both period details and a large cast was excessive, especially given the requirement of shooting on film instead of video. Previous network experience with serial dramas of a more contemporary nature, with the brief exception in 1965–67 of ABC's *Peyton Place,* had not been good. Finally, the historical content of the British serial imports was a cause of concern in and of itself. America's historical drama in film and on television had always been the Western, which represented, in photogenic surroundings with plenty of action, debates about nature and culture, individual and society, race, and family that were central to the development of the republic. The Western, however, had faded throughout the 1960s, becoming part of the "old TV" that the emphasis on young demographics would not forbear.[77] And if Americans were no longer willing to revisit their own history in an episodic form, then it seemed highly unlikely that they would do so in a form requiring them to keep up with an ongoing story week after week.

Two producers nonetheless tried to repeat the narrow demographic success of *The Forsyte Saga* and *Masterpiece Theatre* in prime-time serials for American networks. CBS's *Beacon Hill* was produced by Briton Beryl Vertue, who had acted as go-between for the BBC and Norman Lear in Lear's acquisition of rights to *Till Death Us Do Part* and *Steptoe and Son.* In her reframing of *Upstairs, Downstairs,* Edwardian London became 1920s Boston, the Bellamys became the Lassiters, and the downstairs workers, instead of symbolizing the lower classes of Scotland, the Midlands, and Cockney London, represented the lower classes of American immigrants—blacks, Italians, Irish. Lavish period costumes and sets were built; expensive props were purchased. Little was left to chance in the re-creation of both Boston society and the British serial—Vertue even dared to use the videotape technique of her show's predecessor. The premiere episode of *Beacon Hill,* broadcast the week before the official network premiere week in September 1975, attracted 42 percent of the national audience. That figure dropped swiftly, however, and CBS announced the show's cancellation at the end of October.[78]

The failure of *Beacon Hill,* which probably owed as much to bad writing and acting as it did to any institutional utterances affecting its assimilation of a British text, did not keep PBS from going forward with its own serial historical drama, *The Adams Chronicles.*[79] Produced by Virginia Kassel, who had purchased *The Forsyte Saga* for WNET, and funded by Atlantic Richfield Oil (which followed the Mobil example in promoting the series), *The Adams Chronicles* traced the story of the first American dynastic family from founding parents John and Abigail to the education of Henry and the bankruptcy of Charles. By all viewership measures, the thirteen-episode series was a success: PBS's bicentennial broadcast drew the network's highest ratings ever in major markets, with ratings in New York, Boston, and San Francisco equaling those of the commercial networks.[80] By all economic measures, however, the *Chronicles,* which required 240 sets, thousands of costumes, and hundreds of extras, was a fiasco. At a cost of $5.2 million, *The Adams Chronicles* was $1.5 million over budget, even using the cheap medium of videotape, which forced producing station WNET to suspend production of several of its local programs.[81]

The financial fate of *The Adams Chronicles*—precisely the type of show that the original producers of *Masterpiece Theatre* hoped to create under its auspices—demonstrated once and for all to PBS and its corporate sponsors the economic wisdom of importing lengthy historical serialized dramas.[82] And the fate of *Beacon Hill* seemed to indicate that adaptations of the British model were doomed to failure on the commercial networks as well. Some signs, however, that serial productions based on literary works might attract a significant American audience, in both raw numbers and demographics, had appeared by the time *Beacon Hill* and *The Adams Chronicles* were broadcast. A production of Leon Uris's novel *QB VII,* made as a two-part "movie of the week" for ABC in 1974, drew a 38 percent share of the audience and led to the network's production in 1975 of a similar two-part "movie" based on Joseph Lash's Roosevelt biography *Eleanor and Franklin.*

ABC followed those successes with its television adaptation of Irwin Shaw's novel *Rich Man, Poor Man*. Published in 1970, Shaw's book was centered on a family, had historical sweep (from the 1940s to the 1960s), and dealt with cultural delineations of class. In short, it contained every element, except the Nobel Prize, that had made *The Forsyte Saga* a public broadcasting cause célèbre—except that in this case, the signifiers represented American life and culture. To deal with the projected twelve-hour length of its adaptation, ABC programming head Fred Silverman in 1975 mandated that *Rich Man, Poor Man* be presented in the same fashion that *The Forsyte Saga* and the newly popular *Upstairs, Downstairs* had been: as a serial, with ten installments. Silverman's rationalization of his decision reveals his debt to British television: "What we really want to prove is . . . that in the long run there is an audience for this kind of drama. . . . The big, novelistic kind that breaks down all walls and sets new standards. I think the show is a TV landmark. It will be what *Beacon Hill* should have been."[83]

With Silverman's programming idea aided by producer Harve Bennett's decision to cast the serial with familiar faces from American film and television—although it might follow a British model, it was assuredly not a British show—*Rich Man, Poor Man* became an extraordinary popular and critical success. For the 1975–76 season, ABC's Jordache saga finished second in the Nielsen ratings for all series, behind only Norman Lear's adaptation of *Till Death Us Do Part*.[84] Its three Emmy awards were among the eleven won in dramatic categories by programs that were either British in origin or adaptations of the British serial drama.[85] In the bicentennial year of the United States' declaration of independence from Great Britain, the most popular and the most honored programs on American television were shows that were direct imports from England or that owed their existence to British predecessors.

Although the Bicentennial itself and its reminders of the "special relationship" between the United States and Great Britain in some ways shaped Americans' acceptance of British programming, the most significant new utterance in that dialogue was the position successful producers had gained in the television industry over the course of the decade.[86] On one hand, those producers had developed a self-awareness of their role as, to borrow Marshall Sahlins's characterization of the "huckster of the symbol," those putting together "latent correspondences in the cultural order whose conjunction in a product-symbol may spell mercantile success."[87] As Horace Newcomb and Robert Alley suggest, producers' self-awareness foregrounded individual vision in finding and (re)constructing those "latent correspondences."[88] On the other hand, endowed with cultural (and financial) capital as a result of their place in the American "culture industry," those producers were socially positioned as part of an American elite that would engage with British television imports. As such, those British programs became part of a "cultural order," defined and organized by the principles of corporate capitalism, from which producers could create thirty- or sixty-minute product-symbols for an audience embodying much more than their own elite.

In this precarious balance between the legitimated exercise of their authority and their prescribed role in the profit-making system of American media, television producers could accomplish two things they might not otherwise. First, in making British constructions the novel element in an American genre (*All in the Family*) or in reconstructing a British genre as an American form (*Rich Man, Poor Man*), they might imbue American television as a whole with significations of "quality" previously associated only with the imports themselves. Second, they might each similarly use British television to establish an individual status as an author in a medium that had been loath to consider any such possibility. In essence, those producers wished to reorganize that "principle of thrift in the proliferation of meaning" in television out of commercial notions of advertiser-supported, network-distributed commodities and into personal aesthetic expressions that happened to be projected into the space of the marketplace.[89] The texts and genres of British television provided the means for Lear, Michaels, and others to do both, and no genre served that purpose better than the serialized historical drama.

That point would be made most effectively in 1977, when ABC presented David Wolper's production of Alex Haley's family history *Roots*. After hearing of Haley's ongoing research into the African origins of his slave ancestors in 1972, Wolper, with a lengthy and much-honored background in film and television documentary, acquired the forthcoming book two years later and sold ABC on the work as a two-part TV movie. Following the success of *Rich Man, Poor Man*, the network quickly turned the movie into a twelve-part miniseries. Although Haley's was perhaps the quintessential American story of family and class — and race — the miniseries *Roots* relied structurally on a British form and genre that, until recently, had been eschewed by prime-time commercial American television.[90] Broadcast over eight consecutive nights in January 1977, *Roots* averaged a 66 percent share of the audience and attracted an estimated 140 million viewers.[91] The success of *Roots* demonstrated both Wolper's skill in creating a controversial text that could speak to virtually every demographic group in the country and the significance of the serial form in the apprehension of that text.[92] And although David Wolper, in part to deflect criticism of the miniseries as being black history told from a white point of view, publicly represented Alex Haley as the person who "controlled totally" the television production, it was Wolper himself, along with African American poet Quincy Troupe, who would offer those viewers *The Inside Story of TV's* Roots, a mass-market paperback book that was as much a hagiography of the producer as it was chronicle of the production. The miniseries had made David Wolper a star—"the man who persuaded everyone to risk six million dollars and eight nights of television on a black slave story," as his own book noted—and had at the same time made its genre an essential element of commercial American broadcasting.[93]

With *Rich Man, Poor Man* and *Roots* establishing the British-based serialized drama in both its historical and literary forms in the United States, other producers, many with long-standing reputations in television and film, brought their own sensibilities to the genre—and the genre further into the workings of the American television industry.[94] Even James Michener, who a decade earlier had praised *The Forsyte Saga* to millions of Americans in the pages of *TV Guide,* found his own *Centennial* the subject of a miniseries adaptation.[95] It was, however, a specific British text—Shakespeare's *Romeo and Juliet*—that provided the coda to the influence of British serial drama on American television in the 1970s. Production executive Lee Rich found in the miniseries form a way to reshape the compassionate gentility of a rural Virginia family, represented in his program *The Waltons,* into the passionate hurly-burly of contemporary urban business society.[96] Also shaped by utterances representing the national fascination with and loathing of the petroleum industry, Rich's new program borrowed Shakespeare's Montagues and Capulets and moved them from the villas and plazas of Verona to the skyscrapers and oil fields of northern Texas. CBS purchased the show for a brief spring run in 1978 and promoted it as the story of "[a] family ruthless in its quest for power and passion. Ready to destroy two people who dared defy their own blood for the right to love."[97] Although the five episodes broadcast in that run, like the early episodes of *Upstairs, Downstairs,* featured self-contained plotlines, the network promoted the program as "a five-part miniseries," with the Romeo-and-Juliet story line of Bobby Ewing and Pam Barnes as the overarching narrative.[98]

Dallas, however, unlike other miniseries, would return as a regular series in the fall of 1978, meaning that the closure of a final episode, central to the form, was gone. The Romeo-Juliet story would fade, as the show turned to its Iago, Bobby's brother J.R., as the main source of its continuing dramatic tension. The British serialized historical drama had worked its way through the American commercial television system to emerge at the end of the 1970s as a soap opera of the rich and famous: *The Forsyte Saga* and *Elizabeth R* had finally become the saga of Southfork and J.R. This is not to denigrate *Dallas* or the clones and recombinations that followed: the show represented a remarkable confluence of utterances speaking to a remarkable number of audiences, as its popularity during the first half of the 1980s would attest. Not least among those utterances was that provided by the British serial "masterpieces" seen on PBS; indeed, one plausible reading of *Dallas* is that of a "thick description" of the industry responsible for the arrival and success of the genre on American public television. What it did mean, however, was that the British influence had become such a commonplace in American television that it was no longer a novelty, no longer an element that producers could draw on to create new meaning. What once seemed completely different was, by 1980, as American as cowboy hats, bourbon and branch, and a roll in the hay with the head of an international oil cartel.

7. British Television and American Culture
Something Completely Different?

They say, they say, they say. Ah, my child, how long are you going to continue to use those dreadful words? Those two little words have done more harm than all others. Never use them, my dear, never use them.

— **William Carlos Williams**[1]

Transatlantic Cables

Although it was J.R. Ewing who was shot in the 1980 cliffhanger episode of *Dallas,* it was prime-time network television that was mortally wounded. At the beginning of that season, ABC, CBS, and NBC had 92 percent of the viewing population. By the end of the 1980–81 season, that figure had dropped to 81 percent; by 1988, only 67 percent of prime-time viewers were watching network programming.[2] Reasons for the decline included greater numbers of local independent stations and the growth in popularity of VCR technology, but the most visible and plausible cause was the availability of new viewing options made possible by the spread of pay cable television. Used in only 5 percent of American households in the late 1960s, primarily to aid reception in rural areas, by 1981 cable had made its way into 26 percent of viewing households.[3] Cable offered those households not just clearer reception of local network affiliates (including the PBS stations stuck in the hard-to-receive UHF portion of the dial) but a plethora of new programming options — uninterrupted movies; around-the-clock news, sports, and public affairs; children's shows; religious programs; and much much more. As Kirsten Beck and J. Fred MacDonald suggest, the truism that cable television represented the triumph of narrow demographic specialization over the appeal to a mass audience that had defined network television throughout much of its existence is an oversimplification. The fact that a number of cable channels relied heavily upon off-network reruns, as well as the need for subscription channels like Home Box Office and Showtime to attract as many subscribers as possible, indicated that the search for the greatest number of viewers with the least objectionable programming had not yet ended.[4] But the existence of cable as a service for which consumers had to pay a monthly fee meant that the medium as a whole was pitched demographically to an audience wealthy in financial and educational capital, an audience quite similar to that which PBS had sought throughout the previous decade.

The British programs that found an American home on PBS quickly found an equally compatible environment on cable. As early as 1979, the English Channel was presenting repeats of programs from the library of Granada Television, a British commercial producer.[5] But it was, ironically, American commercial networks that would play a significant role in cultivating cable for (and, its proponents would argue, through) British television. ABC and CBS, as well as NBC's parent company RCA, saw the onrush of cable and were not going to let the new technology pass them by. ABC, with the Hearst Corporation as a partner, was the first to venture into cable programming with the ARTS network in April 1981. The reasons ABC chose to offer a cable service devoted to "quality" were achingly reminiscent of the PBS experience with British programs: ARTS could be run cheaply by using preproduced imported programming; it could attract corporate sponsors like Mobil; its audience would be "prestigious" and different from that of the ABC broadcast network, which would not offend affiliate stations. Mobil and its brethren in the petroleum industry also strongly supported CBS Cable, which became available in October 1981. Less reliant on imported series than ARTS, CBS Cable nonetheless called upon Britain for its television stagings of noted plays: John Osborne's *A Gift of Friendship, Hedda Gabler* starring Diana Rigg, *Macbeth* as performed by the Royal Shakespeare Company, among many others.[6] The Entertainment Channel, launched by RCA in summer 1982, was fundamentally different from its predecessors in that it was funded by subscribers, not advertisers or sponsors. As such, it needed to attract a broader audience than the clearly defined "culture channels." As Kirsten Beck notes, however, the new network's exclusive deal with the BBC for programs, while saving money, "telegraphed a cultural programming message to the rest of the world, a message the channel worked hard to overcome."[7]

With a programming mix that was, as one industry expert put it, "something between CBS and PBS," including BBC imports that were hardly the class productions presented on *Masterpiece Theatre,* the effort proved too difficult: the Entertainment Channel went out of business nine months after it began.[8] By that time, however, CBS Cable was already gone and ARTS was fading. In her analysis of CBS Cable's failure, Beck cites production costs and animosity from broadcast executives toward both cable and a "highbrow" audience. As significant, however, was the fact that the urban areas upon which much of the British programming offered by PBS built its popularity were the last places to be wired for cable.[9] Without that core audience, it was highly unlikely that three new cable outlets offering programming similar to that of public broadcasting would succeed. One, however, might. In December 1983, ARTS executives announced that the network would merge with what had been the Entertainment Channel, creating as of February 1984 the Arts and Entertainment Network (A&E). The new service would present twenty hours of programming a day, with 60 percent coming from the BBC.[10] Again, as had been the case with PBS fifteen years earlier, the savings provided by using imported shows combined with the long-standing cultural cachet of British programming gave the new network connotations of "quality" valuable to both its audience and potential advertisers. A&E attracted enough of each with such fare as the serial dramas *The Barrets of Wimpole Street, The Citadel,* and *The Life and Loves of a She-Devil* and the comedies *Blackadder* (in all four of its versions), *'Allo, 'Allo,* and *Yes, (Prime) Minister* in its first five years that it was able to cut its direct BBC imports by a third and begin both its own domestic productions and coproductions with overseas companies located in Britain and beyond.[11] As A&E has evolved in the 1990s, BBC and British productions have become secondary to the channel's own *Biography* series and reruns of American detective shows. Nonetheless, the channel has presented, with Jean Marsh as its Alistair Cooke, the BBC serial drama *The House of Eliott,* created by Marsh and Eileen Atkins in much the same fashion that they created *Upstairs, Downstairs,* as well as coproduced with Granada the influential detective series *Cracker.* It also continues to present British mystery series, many of which have already run on PBS, on a nightly basis. And, having run *The Avengers* in repeats early in the decade, A&E began marketing the video collection of the series in the summer of 1998, coinciding with the release of the big-screen feature film based on the series.

Whereas A&E used British television purposively to create a "narrative image," other cable channels have also employed British shows to increase their visibility to viewers and advertisers. Comedy Central, for example, included in its initial 1991 offering repeats of *Monty Python's Flying Circus* and *Saturday Night Live,* as well two Canadian offspring of *Python, SCTV* and *The Kids in the Hall.* The British improvisatory game show *Whose Line Is It Anyway?* has been a part of the channel's schedule since August 1991, joined in 1994 by its most notorious and notable British import, the scabrous situation comedy *Absolutely Fabulous.* The Sci-Fi Channel has shown repeats of *The Prisoner* and Lew Grade's *Space: 1999;* Romance Classics has run Mobil Showcase productions including *Edward and Mrs. Simpson;* British films, frequently funded in part by the commercial Channel 4, are a significant part of the programming on Bravo and the Independent Film Channel; British documentaries are a regular feature of Discovery, the Learning Channel, the History Channel, and other cable services. American cable has also, beginning with MTV, popularized and reshaped in its own image another British television entertainment form: the music video. As was the case with more traditional genres in the 1960s and 1970s, American producers and performers were quick to reshape the form once it found a domestic audience, as the careers of Michael Jackson and Madonna amply demonstrate.[12] Finally, the BBC itself entered the American cable universe in spring 1998, with its launch of BBC America, a cable channel offering news and documentary programming in addition to both current and archived entertainment series.[13]

The British presence on American cable television speaks to many of the same issues as its earlier presence on broadcast television. For services working in a new (for television) twenty-four-hour programming day, imported shows were a cheap way to fill time and build up ad revenues. British programs, coming from a familiar linguistic and cultural base, were the most likely candidates to fill that role; their reputation for "quality" superior to that of American series allowed several cable channels to structure their images around that quality. As those cable channels featured a specific type of programming and/or were designed to attract a specific audience, the shaping of the relationship between British imports and the viewer changed somewhat from its formation with commercial television. Product differentiation and narrative image in cable function on the channel or network level, not on the level of the individual show. In the case of A&E, British television defined the narrative image of the network, at least in its early years; in the case of Comedy Central, it was significant that *Absolutely Fabulous* and *Whose Line Is It Anyway?* were funny, not that they were British; in the case of MTV, national origin was of little importance as long as the music had a beat, the bands had big hair, and the women were next to naked. Commercial, social, and aesthetic properties of given programs are locked into place on cable in a way that they never were on the relatively open airwaves of commercial broadcasting. Viewers of British television on cable, as a result, find themselves even more tightly bound in the political and ideological programs of the medium than did viewers of *Masterpiece Theatre* on the Nixon-shaped and petroleum-bought PBS of the 1970s. What alternate meanings those viewers can derive of shows from the ones mandated by the cable channels through which they are sent is a subject ripe for examination by media ethnographers.

British television's relationship with American culture in the past twenty years has not been confined to cable, however. Public television for its part continued its equation of quality with British television—and its equation of both with corporate sponsoring. In 1979, Mobil's Herb Schmertz contacted WGBH with an idea for an anthology series consisting solely of British mysteries. Given the popularity of Dorothy Sayers's Lord Peter Wimsey mysteries that had been shown on *Masterpiece Theatre,* the broadcaster and the oil company developed *Mystery!,* which first aired in February 1980. Designed to showcase British serializations of novels by mystery writers ranging from Agatha Christie and Arthur Conan Doyle to Dick Francis and P. D. James, the anthology would also make room, following the example of *Upstairs, Downstairs,* for original television creations such as *Rumpole of the Bailey* and, later, *Prime Suspect.* To further the *Masterpiece Theatre* connection, Mobil and WGBH decided to employ a host to set up and comment on the dramas being presented. NBC film critic Gene Shalit served in that capacity for the first season, but as Shalit connoted Bronx chutzpah far more than he did British quality, orotund horror movie icon Vincent Price became the anthology's Alistair Cooke in its second season (Price began his theatrical career in England and was married to British actress Coral Browne). It was not until 1989, however, that *Mystery!* found a host that could connect the series's British quality to the key twenty-five to forty-nine age demographic sought by Mobil: the erstwhile Emma Peel, Diana Rigg.[14]

Local public broadcasters, meanwhile, followed the pattern established by the success of *Monty Python's Flying Circus* and began to purchase syndicated British series for broadcast after the conclusion of national PBS programming. With *Python* and John Cleese's series *Fawlty Towers* acting as comedic signifiers, and with the British origins of popular network shows such as *All in the Family* and *Sanford and Son* in popular currency, British situation comedies occupied increasing amounts of airtime on PBS stations around the country beginning in the mid-1970s. Britcoms including *The Fall and Rise of Reginald Perrin, Butterflies, To the Manor Born, Mr. Bean,* and *Are You Being Served?* have since then gained devoted American audiences. Local public stations in various markets have also presented the British cult science fiction series *Doctor Who* and *Blake's 7,* in addition to reruns of *The Prisoner.*

Network television itself, redefined by its assimilation of British productions and genres in the 1970s, seemed content to let British programming find its evidently natural home on PBS and cable during the 1980s and early 1990s. *Amanda's,* a 1983 attempt by ABC to re-create *Fawlty Towers,* and the *Three's Company* sequel *Three's a Crowd,* a 1984–85 ABC remake of the *Man about the House* sequel *Robin's Nest,* represented the only direct American commercial interest in British programming during the Reagan years. As cable continued to eat away commercial network market share, however, programmers at ABC, CBS, and NBC began in the mid-1990s to pay attention to critically acclaimed British series coming into American homes through other channels. The 1994 ABC detective series *Under Suspicion* bore a strong visual and thematic resemblance to *Prime Suspect*, a British series starring Helen Mirren that had already won two Emmys for the PBS/Mobil *Mystery!* franchise; both series owed a debt to the strong female crimefighter introduced to American audiences in *The Avengers*. While rumors abounded in the industry about an American version of *Absolutely Fabulous* to be produced by sitcom star Roseanne, the 1995–98 CBS sitcom *Cybill* rapidly developed the British show's central characterizations of two bibulous, foul-mouthed female friends into its own core attraction. A 1997 CBS replacement series *High Society*, was even more clearly patterned on the Comedy Central hit. ABC in 1997 offered its version of the critically acclaimed Granada/A&E detective series *Cracker*; in summer 1998, the network presented an American edition of the Comedy Central import *Whose Line Is It Anyway?*

While borrowing from and remaking known British commodities, networks and producers also, for the first time in twenty years, turned to British hits that had never been imported to the United States. Bill Cosby, whose *The Cosby Show* had reestablished the family sitcom as a significant element in American television in the 1980s, used *One Foot in the Grave*, a British show dealing with the comic predicaments of an older victim of downsizing, as the basis for his 1996 CBS return to situation comedy, *Cosby*. That same year, NBC presented *Men Behaving Badly*, an American version of a British sitcom of the same title as offensively hilarious in its treatment of gender as *Absolutely Fabulous* was in its. In summer 1998, following showings of the Oscar-winning claymation Wallace and Gromit films on various PBS and cable outlets and Comedy Central's import of the British animated sitcom *Bob and Margaret*, NBC presented the British cartoon *Stressed Eric* in prime time—the first time a British show had been given such a slot on network television since the Lew Grade summer variety series of the early 1970s.[15]

As had been the case in the late 1960s and early 1970s, American commercial television producers found themselves in the 1990s looking at British programs that had been acclaimed, either in their homeland or on the demographically charted channels of American public broadcasting and cable, as sources that might reinvigorate tiring forms and genres. The primacy of economics in their efforts is undeniable. The major networks, which had regained a substantial amount of the control of production and distribution they lost in the 1970s, were desperate to find ways to stop the exodus of viewers and advertisers to new network competition (Fox, WB, UPN), cable, the pleasures of the VCR, and computer-based entertainment that didn't even require the television to be on. At the same time, those networks were equally desperate to find forms—cartoons and game shows, for instance—that were cheap and would act as a counterweight against the exponentially escalating production costs of entertainment series. British television could serve as a source for the ideas, genres, and programs needed to reconstruct network television.

Again, however, this reinstitution of the dialogue between British television and American culture in its representation on network television cannot be defined simply by the economics of the matter. The voices of otherness and our-own-ness that shaped the reception of British television twenty to thirty years earlier were again audible in the reshapings of British series for American audiences—Bill Cosby's addition of race to the signifying elements of *One Foot in the Grave*; the toning down of the raucous humor of *Absolutely Fabulous* and *Men Behaving Badly* in their American assimilations, for example. Political and social vectors also clearly shape the renewed relationship, with the United States and Britain first working closely as allies in the Gulf War and its aftermath and then removing from power the conservatives who led them through the 1980s and early 1990s in favor of younger, more active, and more politically ambiguous figures who summoned (deliberately, in the case of Bill Clinton) images of Kennedy's Camelot. Finally, the intertextuality of television itself as visible in the publicity for the new British presence on American television—the familiarity of Bill Cosby from his previous sitcom and the importance of the success of *The Simpsons* (and cable's *Beavis and Butthead* and *South Park*) in the acceptance of any prime-time cartoon, for instance—again plays a distinct role in the ways in which Americans construct meaning from British imports. However different the circumstances might be, the transnational connection between British and American television requires the same breadth and depth of inspection in the 1990s as it did in the 1960s and 1970s.

Whose Line Is It Anyway?

While the expansion of the television universe in the 1980s and 1990s has meant an expansion of the British presence on the medium, the relationship of American viewers to British programming since 1980 merely amplifies the one established in the 1960s and 1970s—a relationship that in some ways can be defined by the myth of cultural imperialism. A major political and economic power exports media artifacts to a younger, less stable culture; those artifacts, which make their audiences complicitous in their ideological program, reshape the culture to which they have been sent. And along with the artifacts comes a system of broadcasting that further opens the market for the exporter's media products and their attendant industries. Although perhaps not the equivalent of the engulfing and devouring entity envisioned by Herbert Schiller in his 1969 text, the British influence more and more visible on American programming of the period and the creation of an American public broadcasting system in the image of an earlier British model demonstrate the power an exporting media producer can bring to bear on another culture.[16]

Adherents to the cultural imperialism theory would of course attack any suggestion that the British Empire may have found a new dominion over the New World through the medium of television as foolish sophistry—and they would be right. They would also, however, reveal key flaws of the theory: its failure to consider the dynamics of domestic cultures as they receive and work with imported programming and its assumption of mass effects on mass populations. Indeed, the relationship between Britain and the United States presented here resembles not so much the imperial one that Schiller argues the United States has imposed on the rest of the world as it does the one Joseph Straubhaar and Gloria Viscasillas have found between the United States and the Dominican Republic. In a 1987 survey of Dominican viewers, Straubhaar and Viscasillas discovered that although many of their respondents watched American television imports, their habits were circumscribed by several factors, including class, age, and genre. Upper-class audiences and younger, university-educated audiences tended to watch more American programming and to enjoy it more than did middle- or lower-class audiences; both groups preferred American feature films, cartoons, and action-adventure series and watched their own news, variety, and comedy programs. Those possessing a surfeit of cultural and educational capital, however, had a much lower opinion of both national and other regional programming (in particular the serialized *telenovelas* attracting primarily female audiences) than did other upper- or middle-class respondents. Finally, Straubhaar and Viscasillas point out, native programming that attracted Dominican viewers was frequently programming that had been adapted by domestic producers from foreign sources, including the United States, Mexico, and Brazil.[17]

The similarities between the relationship documented by Straubhaar and Viscasillas and the one between Britain and the United States during the 1960s and 1970s suggest that adherents to the theory of cultural imperialism may have themselves created a model of American exceptionalism that mirrors the Pax Americana exceptionalism of the 1950s and 1960s against which they responded.

Although the quantity of American cultural exports (and the apparent paucity of imports) appears to make the United States a unique case, the direct effects of those artifacts on a mass audience in Straubhaar and Viscasillas's research are no greater than those of British television on the mass American audience, and effects on domestic production are similar in breadth and depth. More important, both examples call into question Schiller's key assertion that media exports are the way in which "life styles and value systems can be imposed on poor and vulnerable societies."[18] Audiences for media imports in each society were drawn largely from a cultural and educational elite who (presumably) knew more about and were better able to choose foreign programming, and members of that elite who were in positions to produce media artifacts adapted those imports to address their own cultural norms. The "imposition" of alien values in either case allows for far more activity and choice by those imposed upon than most definitions of the term would.

As I noted at the beginning of this volume, it would be a mistake to equate the relationship in media and culture between Britain and the United States with others such as the one between the United States and the Dominican Republic. Issues of domination and control central to cultural imperialism do not carry the weight in the examination of transnational communication and culture involving two major media powers that they do in a consideration of relationships between First World exporters and Third or Fourth World importers. What Straubhaar and Viscasillas's research does reveal, however, is that processes similar to those they discovered in the Dominican Republic were at work in the relationship between Britain and the United States in the 1960s and 1970s—processes that were masked by the power of the myth of cultural imperialism. To address that myth most directly, in each case examined here, American audiences responded to British programming according to their own cultural values and accents, not those of the exporter. With *The Avengers,* it was a character speaking to the changing roles for women in American society that reached an audience unconcerned with the deliberately placed British elements of the show. With *Upstairs, Downstairs,* it was the centrality of family to American television culture and the power of serialized fiction that addressed an audience unfamiliar with the specific class codes presented in the program's weekly installments. And with *Monty Python's Flying Circus,* it was the centrality of television and its absurdities in the midst of comic sketches referencing minutiae of British society and culture that drew an audience whose own society and culture were equally defined by "the boob tube and its boobery." In each of these cases, the fact that the texts in question *were* in some way different from artifacts available in domestic culture at the time also played a visible role in their reception by American audiences—a role ignored and/or elided by the myth of cultural imperialism. Indeed, the belief, criticized in 1856 by Walt Whitman but reinforced by media a century and more later, that British cultural artifacts are better than American ones was a significant element in the American reception of British television programming throughout the period in question.

At the same time that reception provides an example that argues against the imposition of values on a passive domestic culture upon which the myth of cultural imperialism is based, it also demonstrates the problems inherent in theories based on notions of polysemic texts and audience activity. In the first case, the audience inclined to accept the equation of British programming with quality unavailable in American television was one either endowed with cultural, educational, and financial capital or in the process of earning it. The appeal of the difference available in British programming to this audience served its own interests by distinguishing it, as Bourdieu argues, from other elements of society and affirming its place as a cultural elite.[19] With that distinction made, none of the readings made by that audience, however many meanings might be available in British programs, can be construed as "oppositional" or "resistant" to the institutional sources responsible for them and their appearance in the United States. Emma Peel may have been constructed as a role model for young middle-class women searching for a way out of an ideology of domestic containment, and as such represented a resistance to that ideology; she was not, however, constructed as resistant to the technology or the commercial commodification central to both that ideology and the world she represented in *The Avengers*. And an appreciation of PBS's presentation of *Upstairs, Downstairs* based on the show's soap opera form and not Mobil's politics of commerce still did not actively resist or oppose either Mobil's plans for the series or the Nixon administration's construction of public television as a whole.

More significant than the activity (or lack thereof) of the audience itself, however, is the overriding role that utterances developed within American culture played in the shaping of meaning, whether those utterances, for example, voiced the political and commercial intent of the Nixon administration and Mobil Oil or spoke of the ideological centrality of family guiding the audience response to those programs. As noted previously, those accents and values have a liberatory function as part of specific reading formations, insofar as they mediate and mitigate the presumed effects arising from the intent of the producers of imported media artifacts. They also, however, serve to circumscribe potential meaning as they contain the readings of a given text within the ideological strands of an already existing cultural web. Emma Peel became a role model of a powerful independent woman for an audience of young middle-class female Americans, but she was also, for an audience of males, still contained within the parameters of "to-be-looked-at-ness" defining the controlling patriarchal gaze. This other form of domestic containment can be seen even more clearly in the work of American producers such as Norman Lear, who reconfigured British television programs for American audiences. Even as those producers exhibited a very direct effect of the import of British programs, their restructuring of class, gender, and racial norms presented in British models as they developed programs ranging from *All in the Family* to *Roots* demonstrated the primary significance of American utterances in the creation of meaning out of transnational communication.

The reception of British television in the United States, then, serves to support Celeste Condit's assertion that both the activity of audiences and the availability of meaning have finite limits, defined by the social, ideological, and historical situations of both texts and readers.[20] The importance of the American elements of those situations also at first glance seems to represent Todd Gitlin's definition of hegemony as a "historical process in which one picture of the world is systematically preferred over others, usually through practical routines and at times through extraordinary measures." His description, which further characterizes that process as the already discussed one of "absorbing and domesticating conflicting values," is of particular interest when applied to transnational communication and culture.[21] What Gitlin refers to as "hegemony" can also be seen as the means by which a "vulnerable" indigenous culture might protect itself from the potential effects of outside media and cultural artifacts; indeed, such a process typifies what Barthes refers to as "inoculation" — the use of a small part of a potentially disruptive ideological text to ward off its more threatening elements.[22] That process, in both its emancipatory and its repressive phases, can be witnessed most vividly in the adaptations and transmogrifications of the Emma Peel female action hero made by the American television industry in the decade following the success of *The Avengers:* women could be tough and resourceful on the job, but the resource they had to work with most was their bodies, as seen and used by men.

The history of Emma Peel and her descendants also demonstrates, however, that the limits Gitlin places on meaning in his definition of hegemony reduce the polyvalence of meaning presented by Condit to a univocal construct — "one pic-

ture of the world" — that allows for no response, no dialogue. Much of the reason for the popularity of *The Avengers* was the tension between two clearly different gender-based readings available from the character of Emma Peel, just as
much of the popularity of *The Forsyte Saga* and *Upstairs, Downstairs* came from
the tension between the series' "snob" appeal to an educated and established audience and their hailing of the lower-class pleasures of soap opera. The open-ended
quality of both *The Prisoner* and the television-based absurdity of *Monty Python's
Flying Circus* also invited, if not demanded, a multiplicity of responses from
viewers. The reduction of many to one that Gitlin makes in his discussion of
hegemony leaves no room for this sort of variance, as it simply inverts the linear
sender-receiver paradigm of communication: in this case, a powerful receiver ap-
prehends a message sent through a text and puts that message to use for its own
purposes, rather than the sender transmitting a message that organizes and controls distant audiences for its own purposes.

And as it simply inverts the linear sender-receiver paradigm, so does Gitlin's
presentation of hegemony simply invert, rather than challenge, the myth of cultural imperialism as an explanation of transnational communication and culture.
An all-powerful, monolithic receiving culture, in Gitlin's construction, makes the
messages presented and represented in imported media texts conform to and ultimately uphold its values and norms. Like Schiller's theory, Gitlin's notion of
hegemony fails to take into consideration the dynamics of a culture in its consideration of texts from any source — including the importance played by utterances outside the content of a text in shaping how readers create meaning from
that text. Indeed, the reception of British television by American viewers during
the 1960s and 1970s is defined as much, if not more, by matters external to the
shows themselves: the cultural significance of John Kennedy, the social movement of women's liberation, the political machinations of the Nixon administration, the economic goals of the petroleum industry, demographic shifts in the
American population, and the changes necessary in the television industry itself
to respond to those shifts. In working with that intertextuality, the audiences
considered here successfully read around the efforts of numerous institutional
sources — the publicists and critics responsible for narrative image, the government, commercial sponsors, American networks, and British producers — to make
the meaning associated with a given program more than a single specific construct. Even in the most clearcut cases of what can be called absorption and domestication of British television — the American remakes produced by Lear et
al. — audience responses were anything but univocal, as the national debates

over the political and social significance (or correctness) of *All in the Family* and *Sanford and Son* demonstrated.[23]

If the American reception of British television is to be contained within a discussion of hegemony, "hegemony" then needs to be considered as Raymond Williams defines and discusses it. Williams stresses in his treatment of the term its ultimate inability to absorb or domesticate completely. "The hegemonic," he argues, is always faced with "alternative political and cultural emphases ... [that] are important not only in themselves but in what the hegemonic process has in practice had to work to control." Such control, however, can never be total; the most difficult and important part of the study of culture, Williams says, is the examination not of the moments in which the hegemonic can be found to be "active and formative" but of the moments when alternatives to the process can be found at work. Those alternatives, frequently found in works of art (or television, Schiller's injunctions to the contrary), may indeed be found to be tied to the dominant culture—or absorbed and domesticated by it—but they may also serve as authentic and original breaks, oppositional or otherwise, from those dominant constructs. "And we are better able to see this," Williams concludes, "if we develop modes of analysis which instead of reducing works to finished products, and activities to fixed positions, are capable of discerning, in good faith, the finite but significant openness of many actual initiatives and contributions."[24]

Williams' language—his use of *alternative* instead of and in addition to *resistance* and *opposition*—and the centrality of openness and variability to his concept of "the hegemonic" breaks through the linearity of both the cultural imperialism paradigm and the plausible use of Gitlin's definition of hegemony in the discussion of transnational communication. It also, and just as significantly, creates a needed bridge between "hegemony" and the Bakhtinian concept of "assimilation" that has informed this work from the start. Bakhtin's refusal to see human communication as defined by direct lines from senders to receivers located in "fixed positions," and his emphasis on the *varying* voices of otherness and *varying* voices of our-own-ness in the creation of meaning from the act of communicating, presents precisely the mode of analysis Williams is looking for in his examination of "the hegemonic." Is the understanding of Emma Peel as a role model by high school girls in Wilmette or Edina or Shaker Heights something free of the hegemonic ideological structure of American corporate capitalism? No. But is that creation of meaning from *The Avengers* a moment in which a genuine break occurs, in which an alternative to an ideology of domestic containment is both visible and audible? Assuredly yes—and it is a moment that is created from the varying utterances of one culture meeting, acting on, and being acted on by the varying utterances of a separate culture.

Unlike totalizing concepts of imperialism, hegemony, or assimilation, Bakhtin's theory also allows for the desirability of difference evident in every example of American reception of British television presented here. As might be expected from that theory, the significance of that difference varied—or was mobile, to return to Bennett and Woollacott's phrase[25]—from instance to instance: it offered cohesion during a period of national trauma; it made a strong British female character a viable role model to American women; it affirmed the elite status of public broadcasting viewers; it provided American producers with a new means of entering the commercial marketplace. In each case, however, the fact that the shows being watched were from a source outside the United States acted as an important utterance guiding their reception by American audiences—just as it was an important element in the intertextuality surrounding those shows. Even as the American television industry seemed during the 1970s to grade over the British differences so significant at the beginning of the decade, those differences still retained their power through the period, as the deliberate referencing of *Romeo and Juliet* that framed the narrative image of *Dallas* indicates.

Bakhtin's theory of assimilation, in conclusion, grants communication in general and transnational communication in specific the complexity—and, perhaps, the mystery—they deserve. The American reception of British programming in the 1960s and 1970s, as I have shown, represents an instance in which transnational communication is defined by neither linear nor totalizing processes, but instead by what Raymond Williams calls "the finite but significant openness of many actual initiatives and contributions."[26] The British television programs imported then were never finished products, despite the best efforts of institutional authorities to so fix them, as those voices of otherness and our-own-ness in and around those shows continually met at play in fields of meaning. And the American audiences viewing those programs were themselves never fixed, as they refracted and reflected the utterances of history, culture, and ideology they encountered as they moved through those fields.

The story of British television and American culture, then, is a story of assimilation without final control, a story in which difference matters as it helps de- and reconstruct the familiar. It is a story in which the reception of artifacts from one nation by another shifts from moments of dominance to moments of liberation and back again in an unpredictable ebb and flow. It is a story in which the "dreadful" words "They say, they say, they say" are met and addressed in dialogue by "We say"—whether the "they" in question were the utterances of a British text or the domestic ideological constraints realized by American audiences in their understandings of that text. It is, finally, a story in which meanings constructed "here" speak about, with, and to meanings from "there"—and vice versa—and in which nothing, inevitably, is completely different.

Notes

Introduction

1. William Carlos Williams, *In the American Grain* (New York: New Directions, 1956), 74.

2. David Marc, *Demographic Vistas* (Philadelphia: University of Pennsylvania Press, 1984), 31–32.

3. For a full discussion of polysemy and television, see John Fiske, *Television Culture* (London: Routledge, 1989), 62–83.

4. Todd Gitlin, *The Whole World Is Watching: Mass Media in the Making and Unmaking of the New Left* (Berkeley: University of California Press, 1980), 256.

5. Herbert I. Schiller, *Mass Communications and American Empire* (New York: Augustus M. Kelley, 1969). For analyses of the influence of Schiller and his theory, see Daniël Biltereyst, "Qualitative Audience Research and Transnational Media Effects," *European Journal of Communication* 10, no. 2 (1995): 245–70; Colleen Roach, "Cultural Imperialism and Resistance in Media Theory and Literary Theory," *Media, Culture & Society* 19 (1997): 47–66.

6. Mikhail Bakhtin, "Discourse in the Novel," in *The Dialogic Imagination: Four Essays by Mikhail Bakhtin*, ed. Michael Holquist, trans. Caryl Emerson and Michael Holquist (Austin: University of Texas Press, 1981), 281.

7. Tony Bennett and Janet Woollacott, *Bond and Beyond: The Political Career of a Popular Hero* (London: Methuen, 1987), 64.

8. Horace Newcomb and Paul Hirsch, "Television as Cultural Forum," in *Television: The Critical View*, 4th ed., ed. Horace Newcomb (New York: Oxford University Press, 1987), 457.

9. Clifford Geertz, *The Interpretation of Cultures* (New York: Basic, 1973), 3–30.

10. Armand Mattelart, *Mapping World Communication: War, Progress, Culture* (Minneapolis: University of Minnesota Press, 1994), quoted in Roach, "Cultural Imperialism," 56.

1. Here Not There

1. Herbert I. Schiller, *Mass Communications and American Empire* (New York: Augustus M. Kelley, 1969), 147–48.

2. Walt Whitman, "Prefatory Letter to Ralph Waldo Emerson, 1856," in *Leaves of Grass: The Norton Critical Edition*, ed. Scully Bradley and Harold Blodgett (New York: W. W. Norton, 1973), 734.

3. My use of the term *culture* throughout follows the definition established by Clifford Geertz in *The Interpretation of Cultures* (New York: Basic, 1973): "Believing, with Max Weber, that man is an animal suspended in webs of significance he himself has spun, I take culture to be those webs, and the analysis of it to be... an interpretive one in search of meaning" (5). See also James Carey, "Mass Communication and Cultural Studies," in *Communication as Culture: Essays on Media and Society* (Boston: Unwin Hyman, 1989), 37–68.

4. Ed Folsom, "Talking Back to Walt Whitman: An Introduction," in *Walt Whitman: The Measure of His Song*, ed. Jim Perlman, Ed Folsom, and Dan Campion (Minneapolis: Holy Cow! 1981), xxii.

5. Michael Schudson, *The Power of News* (Cambridge: Harvard University Press, 1997), 163, 164.

6. Schudson's definition here merely reconfigures Roland Barthes's dictum: "Myth is a type of speech chosen by history: it cannot possibly evolve from the 'nature' of things." See Roland Barthes, *Mythologies* (New York: Noonday, 1973), 110.

7. As Schudson points out, myths are "polysemous" (*The Power of News*). Just as the myth of the press in Watergate could be read as one demonstrating the validity of investigative reporting or the danger of biased and uncontrolled reporting, so each of these central American myths could be read to support either Bernstein and Woodward et al. or Nixon.

8. See Daniël Biltereyst, "Qualitative Audience Research and Transnational Media Effects: A New Paradigm?" *European Journal of Communication* 10, no. 2 (1995): 245–70; Colleen Roach, "Cultural Imperialism and Resistance in Media Theory and Literary Theory," *Media, Culture & Society* 19 (1997): 47–66.

9. Schiller, *Mass Communications,* 3.

10. Ibid., 8–9.

11. Ibid., 100.

12. Ibid., 112.

13. Ibid., 3. See also John Tomlinson, *Cultural Imperialism* (Baltimore: Johns Hopkins University Press, 1991), 37–41.

14. Fred Fejes, "Media Imperialism: An Assessment," *Media, Culture & Society* 3 (1981): 281–89.

15. Schiller, *Mass Communications,* 14. The official was Charles Frankel, assistant secretary of state for education and cultural affairs.

16. In her discussion of the development of the cultural imperialism thesis, Roach points out the popularity of the idea among scholars and officials in Latin America, where the heavy hand of U.S. hemispheric imperialism had been felt from the digging of the Panama Canal to the Allende coup in Chile ("Cultural Imperialism," 47–48). The term *dumping* is taken from Jeremy Tunstall, *The Media Are American* (New York: Columbia

University Press, 1977). Tunstall defines cultural imperialism as "[the argument that] authentic, traditional and local culture in many parts of the world is being battered out of existence by the indiscriminate dumping of large quantities of slick commercial and media products, mainly from the United States" (57).

17. Schiller, *Mass Communications,* 156–59. Dallas Smythe, in his introduction to *Mass Communications and American Empire,* directly points to these political and social concerns: "The point of view which permeates the book makes it relevant to the concerns which a Black Power-shocked and Vietnam-shocked American electorate is facing" (viii).

18. Adorno and Horkheimer's 1947 book *The Dialectic of Enlightenment* (Amsterdam: Querido) established the tone of the 1950s debate over mass culture, with its condemnation of the "culture industry" at work in the popular arts and media as replacing the transcendent qualities of great art with an artificial and mechanical style. Adorno's 1954 essay "Television and the Patterns of Mass Culture" made the attack specific: television programs reinforced rigidly conservative values through "hidden messages" that eliminated questions about social norms and led audiences to conform to a thoughtless, unfeeling status quo. Adorno's essay was included in what might be considered the bible of the attack on American film, broadcast, and popular print media, *Mass Culture: The Popular Arts in America,* which was edited by Bernard Rosenberg and David Manning White (Glencoe, Ill.: Free Press, 1957), 474–88. Rosenberg's introduction to that volume struck the tone followed by Schiller, among many others: "The mass media present a major threat to man's autonomy. To know that they might also contain some small seeds of freedom only makes a bad situation nearly desperate" (5). Equally influential in Schiller's book was the work of C. Wright Mills, whose concept of an interlocking directorate of corporate, government, and military interests controlling power in the United States, as presented in *The Power Elite* (New York: Oxford University Press, 1956), guided the political and economic thrusts of Schiller's argument.

19. Schiller, *Mass Communications,* 153. Minow's comment, delivered at the 1961 convention of the National Association of Broadcasters, provided a governmental imprimatur on the stance taken by critics of American popular culture in the 1950s. See also Erik Barnouw, *Tube of Plenty,* 2d ed. (New York: Oxford University Press, 1990), 299–303.

20. Biltereyst, "Qualitative Audience Research," 247–53.

21. See Kaaren Nordenstreng and Tapio Varis, *Television Traffic: A One-Way Street?* (New York: UNESCO, 1974); see also Tapio Varis, "The International Flow of Television Programs," *Journal of Communication* 34 (1984): 142–52.

22. Colin Hoskins and Rolf Mirus, "Reasons for the U.S. Dominance of the International Trade in Television Programs," *Media, Culture & Society* 10 (1988): 500. Hoskins and Mirus's work has been influential in the work of Joseph Straubhaar, whose studies of transnational communication I consider at greater length in the final chapter of this book.

23. Ien Ang, *Watching Dallas: Soap Opera and the Melodramatic Imagination* (London: Methuen, 1985); Tamar Liebes and Elihu Katz, *The Export of Meaning: Cross-Cultural Readings of Dallas* (Oxford: Oxford University Press, 1990). On British cultural studies

in practice and theory, see in particular Stuart Hall, "Encoding, Decoding," in *The Cultural Studies Reader,* ed. Simon During (London: Routledge, 1993), 90–103; Charlotte Brunsdon and David Morley, *Everyday Television:* Nationwide (London: British Film Institute, 1978); David Morley, *The* Nationwide *Audience: Structure and Decoding* (London: British Film Institute, 1980); John Fiske, "British Cultural Studies," in *Channels of Discourse,* ed. Robert C. Allen (Chapel Hill: University of North Carolina Press, 1987), 254–90; Graeme Turner, *British Cultural Studies* (London: Routledge, 1992). On "wall-to-wall *Dallas,*" see Richard Collins, *Television: Policy and Culture* (Boston: Unwin Hyman, 1990), 151–52.

24. The problem of limitless meaning is addressed most productively by Celeste Condit in her essay "The Rhetorical Limits of Polysemy," in *Television: The Critical View,* 5th ed., ed. Horace Newcomb (New York: Oxford University Press, 1994), 426–47. Condit, who tracked male and female responses to an episode of *Cagney & Lacey,* suggests that the term *polyvalence,* not *polysemy,* best defines the way in which individuals make meaning out of a given text: "Polyvalence . . . is not a multiplicity or instability of textual meanings but rather a difference of audience evaluations of shared denotations that best accounts for the two viewers' discrepant interpretations" (430). Roach also criticizes the use and misuse of "resistance" in the study of transnational communication ("Cultural Imperialism," 50–60).

25. Herbert I. Schiller, "Not Yet the Post-Imperialist Era," *Critical Studies in Mass Communication* 8 (1991): 25. See also Roach, "Cultural Imperialism," 52–57.

26. Mikhail Bakhtin, "Discourse in the Novel," in *The Dialogic Imagination: Four Essays by Mikhail Bakhtin,* ed. Michael Holquist, trans. Caryl Emerson and Michael Holquist (Austin: University of Texas Press, 1981), 263.

27. Mikhail Bakhtin, "The Problem of Speech Genres," in *Speech Genres and Other Late Essays,* ed. Caryl Emerson and Michael Holquist, trans. Vern W. McGee (Austin: University of Texas Press, 1986), 68.

28. Ibid., 71.

29. Ibid., 69.

30. Ibid., 94.

31. Bakhtin, "Discourse in the Novel," 276.

32. Bakhtin, "The Problem of Speech Genres," 80.

33. As such, Bakhtin's definition lends some credence to Hoskins and Mirus's "cultural discount" concept: linguistic similarity constitutes one degree of "our-own-ness" involved in one culture's apprehension of artifacts introduced by another culture ("Reasons for the U.S. Dominance").

34. Todd Gitlin, *The Whole World Is Watching: Mass Media and the Making and Unmaking of the New Left* (Berkeley: University of California Press, 1980), 256, emphasis added.

35. E. San Juan, *Hegemony and Strategies of Transgression* (Albany: State University of New York Press, 1995), 35–50.

36. Raymond Williams, *Marxism and Literature* (Oxford: Oxford University Press, 1977), 113.

37. Tony Bennett and Janet Woollacott, *Bond and Beyond: The Political Career of a Popular Hero* (London: Methuen, 1987), 64, emphasis added.

38. Ibid., 262.

39. Ibid., 42.

40. Ibid., 32–33.

41. Christopher Booker, *The Neophiliacs* (Boston: Gambit, 1970), xiii.

42. See, for example, Tunstall, *The Media Are American,* 129; Hunter Davies, *The Beatles* (New York: W. W. Norton, 1996), 20–21, 30–31; Dick Hebdige, *Hiding in the Light* (London: Routledge, 1988), 54–56. The growing financial interest of American movie studios in British film production during the 1960s is one of the major themes of Alexander Walker's *Hollywood U.K.: The British Film Industry in the Sixties* (New York: Stein & Day, 1974). In addition, George Melly's encyclopedic chronicle of 1960s British popular culture, *Revolt into Style* (New York: Anchor, 1971), takes 1950s "Americanization" as its starting point—although Melly's other characterization of the phenomenon/myth, "States Worship," suggests that Britons were active participants in the process, and that at least some American imports had significant intrinsic worth (1–19).

43. Bennett and Woollacott point out the important influence of British spy novelists such as John Buchan on the work of Ian Fleming (*Bond and Beyond,* 23). Davies, in his discussion of the importance of Elvis in the early career of the Beatles, also discusses the significance of the British skiffle movement during the 1950s, as well as the brass band background of Paul McCartney's father (*The Beatles,* 20–21, 29–32). Hebdige addresses the efforts of the BBC to keep rock and roll music off the British airwaves during the 1950s (*Hiding in the Light,* 54–55).

44. Hebdige, *Hiding in the Light,* 70–76; Dominic Strinati, "The Taste of America: Americanization and Popular Culture in Britain," in *Come on Down: Popular Media Culture in Post-war Britain,* ed. Dominic Strinati and Stephen Wagg (London: Routledge, 1992), 46–81. See also Denis McQuail's comments on Americanization in "Commercial Imperialism and Cultural Cost," in *Cultural Transfer or Electronic Imperialism? The Impact of America Television Programs on European Television,* ed. Christian Thomsen (Heidelburg: Carl Winter Universitätsverlag, 1989), 207–17.

45. Booker, *The Neophiliacs,* xii–xiii.

46. See David Anderson, "Post Office's Ban on 'Chatterley' Is Upset by Court," *New York Times,* July 22, 1959, 1; see also "Excerpts from Court's Ruling on 'Lady Chatterley,'" *New York Times,* July 22, 1959, 18. The complete legal history of the *Lady Chatterley* case can be found in Charles Rembar, *The End of Obscenity* (New York: Random House, 1968), 59–160.

47. This figure comes from sales charts in *Publishers Weekly,* June–October 1959.

48. Alfred Kazin, "Lady Chatterley in America," *Atlantic Monthly,* July 1959, 36; see also Sonya Rudikoff, "D. H. Lawrence and Our Life Today," *Commentary,* November 1959, 408–13.

49. Booker, *The Neophiliacs,* xiii.

50. As Rudikoff wrote: "The question of nature and civilization is widely discussed at the present time, in many different forms: it crops up in matters of private morality and public behavior, in relation to the angry young men and the beatniks, to juvenile delinquency, underdeveloped countries, child-rearing, urban life and so on" ("D. H. Lawrence," 411).

51. For background on the Angry Young Men, see Kenneth Allsop, *The Angry Decade* (London: Peter Owen, 1964), 15–50; John Hill, *Sex, Class and Realism: British Cinema 1956–1963* (London: British Film Institute, 1986), 20–27; Booker, *The Neophiliacs,* 114–19.

52. Richard Findlater, "The Angry Young Man," *New York Times,* September 29, 1957, II, 1; David Dempsey, "Most Angry Fella," *New York Times Magazine,* October 20, 1957, 22–27.

53. Brooks Atkinson, "Look Back in Anger," *New York Times,* October 13, 1957, II, 1.

54. "New Plays in Manhattan," *Time,* October 14, 1957, 85.

55. Harold Clurman, "Theatre," *The Nation,* October 19, 1957, 272.

56. Dempsey, "Most Angry Fella," 22; see also "New Plays in Manhattan," 85; Clurman, "Theatre," 272.

57. Review of *Room at the Top, Newsweek,* April 6, 1959, 113.

58. Walker, *Hollywood U.K.,* 51–52. See also Hill, *Sex, Class and Realism,* 157–64.

59. A. J. Weiler, review of *Room at the Top, New York Times,* March 30, 1959, 23.

60. Stanley Kauffmann, "Not Quite All Right, Jack," *New Republic,* April 17, 1961, 20.

61. Walker cites the involvement of United Artists, which provided all of the financing, in the making of *Tom Jones* as both a curse and a blessing—a curse in the way it set a precedent for American studios and finance to become dominant in the British film industry, and a blessing in the freedom it gave Richardson and Osborne to make the film they wanted to make (*Hollywood U.K.,* 138–39).

62. "The New Madness," *Time,* November 15, 1963, 64.

63. "The Unbarbershopped Quartet," *Time,* February 21, 1964, 46. Washington, D.C., disk jockey Carroll White, reputed to have introduced the Beatles to the American public in December 1963, said in a 1995 National Public Radio interview that he believed the sudden popularity of the Beatles was largely due to a desire on the part of Americans to put the shock and grief of the Kennedy assassination behind them. *Weekend Edition,* host Scott Simon, National Public Radio, September 9, 1995.

64. ABC, which participated only as a partner with CBC, was actually first by a split second to present the BBC kinescope of the coronation to the United States. See "Canada's Network First to Get Films," *New York Times,* June 3, 1953, 17. A full-page NBC ad in

the *New York Times* the same day, however, said that it had presented photos of the ceremonies only nine minutes after they were taken, and that its film coverage (also taken from CBC) presented the "spectacle first to *most* Americans" (12).

65. Tino Balio, "Retrenchment and Reorganization, 1948–," in *The American Film Industry,* ed. Tino Balio (Madison: University of Wisconsin Press, 1985), 423. See also Ernest Bornemann, "United States vs. Hollywood: The Case Study of an Antitrust Suit," also in *The American Film Industry,* 449–62. Initial contacts between the film and television industries came during the freeze on the licensing of individual stations imposed by the Federal Communications Commission from 1948 to 1952. The freeze, while entrenching the well-established networks—CBS and NBC—in a position of superiority, also allowed for experimentation in technology and programming; equally as important, it provided the 108 stations already licensed with a lot of time for ad sales. During the freeze, as much as 20 percent of the programming in many markets was devoted to B-studio films and serials—and the numerous commercials that were cut into them. See Balio, "Retrenchment and Reorganization," 422–36; Barnouw, *Tube of Plenty,* 112–16; William Boddy, *Fifties Television: The Industry and Its Critics* (Urbana: University of Illinois Press, 1993), 50–53.

66. Restrictive clauses in postbreakup contracts limited the major studios to releasing only films made prior to 1948; studios also wanted to hold on to their more valuable properties. See Sydney Head and Christopher Sterling, *Broadcasting in America,* 5th ed. (Boston: Houghton Mifflin, 1987), 93; Balio, "Retrenchment and Reorganization," 422–36.

67. During the week of February 1–7, 1952, for example, a quarter of the movies included in newspaper television listings in the multichannel cities of New York, Boston, Washington, Atlanta, Detroit, Chicago, and San Francisco were of British origin. This figure does not include American remakes of British originals, international films produced by Britons but released by Hollywood studios, or movies made by American companies with corporate ties to British filmmakers.

68. See Geoffrey Macnab, *J. Arthur Rank and the British Film Industry* (London: Routledge, 1993), 78; J. Fred MacDonald, *One Nation under Television* (New York: Pantheon, 1990), 121.

69. "A Cooke's Look at America," *Life,* August 25, 1952, 120–23.

70. "Only One Cooke," *Newsweek,* January 5, 1953, 38–39.

71. Bennett and Woollacott, *Bond and Beyond,* 45.

72. Jane Feuer, "The MTM Style," in *MTM: Quality Television,* ed. Jane Feuer, Paul Kerr, and Tise Vahimagi (London: British Film Institute, 1984), 56.

73. Matthew Arnold, "Culture and Anarchy," in *The Norton Anthology of English Literature,* 4th ed., ed. M. H. Abrams et al. (New York: W. W. Norton, 1979), 1430.

74. Glenn Altschuler and David Grossvogel, *Changing Channels: America in* TV Guide (Urbana: University of Illinois Press), 27. "Dialsmanship" was the 1950s equivalent of what today would be called "zapsmanship."

. Ibid., 25–30.

6. "As We See It," *TV Guide*, August 18, 1962, inside front cover. For more on the Pilkington Report and its influence on British broadcasting and society, see Asa Brooks, *The BBC: The First Fifty Years* (Oxford: Oxford University Press, 1985), 320–28; Burton Paulu, *Television and Radio in the United Kingdom* (Minneapolis: University of Minnesota Press, 1981), 82–83; Bernard Sendall, *Independent Television in Britain: Expansion and Change, 1958–1963* (London: Macmillan, 1983), 85–134.

77. The economic structure of the just-installed British commercial system mandated not only commercials but imports (including twelve American shows in 1955–56) to hold costs down and exports to earn production funds. See Paulu, *Television and Radio,* 46–87. *Robin Hood, The Adventures of Sir Lancelot,* and a third British costume drama import, *The Buccaneers,* were produced by Lew Grade for Sapphire Films, before he went on to his more notable success at ATV, which I discuss in Chapters 2–4. See Alain Carrazé and Hélène Oswald, *The Prisoner* (New York: Barnes & Noble, 1995), 204.

78. Review of *The Adventures of Robin Hood, TV Guide,* November 12, 1955, 21.

79. Review of *The Adventures of Sir Lancelot, TV Guide,* November 17, 1956, 23.

80. See "As We See It," *TV Guide,* March 19, 1966, 2.

81. "As We See It," *TV Guide,* August 9, 1969, 2.

82. See Nordenstreng and Varis, *Television Traffic,* 31. Although Tunstall argues that British commercial television would not have existed without an American presence (*The Media Are American,* 101), other historians are split on that interpretation. Barnouw suggests that the strategy for a commercial network came directly from an American advertising agency (*Tube of Plenty,* 229–30), and Burton Paulu and Bernard Sendall stress internal British political developments in their account of the creation of the Independent Broadcast Authority. See Paulu, *Television and Radio,* 58–60; Bernard Sendall, *Independent Television in Britain: Origin and Foundation, 1948–62* (London: Macmillan, 1982), 17–18.

83. Douglas Miller and Marion Nowak, *The Fifties: The Way We Really Were* (New York: Doubleday, 1977), 14–15.

84. See Barnouw, *Tube of Plenty,* 184–88.

2. Danger Men

1. Quoted in "Bond's Creator," *New Yorker,* April 21, 1962, 33–34.

2. Quoted in William Kirtz, "Out to Beat Bond," *New York Times,* January 23, 1966, II, 17.

3. Grade was also a pioneer in the use of technical elements—film instead of videotape, color—that aided the marketability of British exports in the United States. See Dick Richards, "Lew Grade Puts ATV's Film Series in Color, Ups Cost by $1.7 Mil.," *Variety,* June 2, 1965, 38; see also "Lew Grade's Example May Stir Brit. Vidfilmers to Pursue O'Seas Loot," *Variety,* July 28, 1965, 34.

4. Program description of *Danger Man, TV Guide* (Minnesota ed.), April 1, 1961, A-45.

5. See Alain Carrazé and Hélène Oswald, *The Prisoner* (New York: Barnes & Noble, 1995), 204–6.

6. Roger Marshall, then a production assistant for the show, had as a primary duty the job of culling Fleming's novels for potential story ideas and characters. Roger Marshall, interview, March 27, 1998. See also David Buxton, *From* The Avengers *to* Miami Vice: *Form and Ideology in Television Serials* (Manchester: Manchester University Press, 1990), 78; Carrazé and Oswald, *The Prisoner,* 204.

7. McGoohan's spoken introduction to each episode read: "Each government has its secret service. The United States has the CIA, France the Duexième Bureau, England MI5. NATO too has its secret service. A dirty job to be done? That's when they usually call on me. Or someone like me. By the way, my name is Drake, John Drake." All that was missing was the martini. See Carrazé and Oswald, *The Prisoner,* 206.

8. Lew Grade's rise to power and modus operandi are detailed in Jack Tinker, *The Television Barons* (London: Quartet, 1980), 37–78. *Danger Man* was actually the second "secret agent" series Grade managed to export to the United States: *The Invisible Man,* putatively based on the H. G. Wells novel and subsequent film, made its title character an affiliate of MI5, working to help British intelligence take down villainry around the world. The show ran in the 1958–59 season on CBS. See Carrazé and Oswald, *The Prisoner,* 204; Tim Brooks and Earle Marsh, *The Complete Directory to Prime Time Network TV Shows: 1946–Present,* 5th ed. (New York: Ballantine, 1992), 433.

9. *The Adventures of Sir Francis Drake,* a vestige of 1950s British costume dramas, was broadcast on NBC in summer 1962. Coincidentally, the series included a character named John Drake (the adventurer's son). Brooks and Marsh, *The Complete Directory,* 18.

10. " 'Saint' Suddenly No. 1 Summer Sub," *Variety,* August 16, 1967, 31; see also Brooks and Marsh, *The Complete Directory,* 567–68, 773.

11. See "Britain's Sale of Shows to Yank Nets Sparks a New Anglo-US Video Era," *Variety,* October 27, 1965, 1. For further information on the individual series, see Brooks and Marsh, *The Complete Directory,* 71, 154, 189, 547.

12. Jacqueline Kennedy was the first to use the term "Camelot," which she claimed was her husband's favorite song, in an interview with Theodore White, "For President Kennedy: An Epilogue," *Life,* December 1, 1963, 158–59. See also Theodore White, *In Search of History: A Personal Adventure* (New York: Harper & Row, 1978), 518–24. The Mailer quote comes from Norman Mailer, "Superman Comes to the Supermarket," *Esquire,* November 1960, 123.

13. Kennedy's experiences in Britain are fully discussed in David Nunnerly, *President Kennedy and Britain* (New York: St. Martin's, 1972), 15–23.

14. For discussion of the British and Irish elements of the "text of Kennedy," see Garry Wills, *The Kennedy Imprisonment* (Boston: Little, Brown, 1981), 61–83.

15. John Dickie, *Special No More: Anglo-American Relations, Rhetoric and Reality* (London: Weidenfeld & Nicholson, 1994), 105–32; see also Nunnerley, *President Kennedy and Britain,* 25–37, 225–36.

16. Mary Ann Watson, *The Expanding Vista: American Television in the Kennedy Years* (New York: Oxford University Press, 1990), 35–70.

17. Hugh Sidey, "The President's Voracious Reading Habits," *Life*, March 17, 1961, 59.

18. British sales figures for Bond novels are given in Tony Bennett and Janet Wool-lacott, *Bond and Beyond: The Political Career of a Popular Hero* (London: Methuen, 1987), 26–27. They show a marked increase in sales of all Bond books in 1961, the year of Kennedy's endorsement, and an exponential increase beginning in 1962, the year the film *Dr. No* was released in Britain. Yearly sales figures for the American market are harder to come by, largely because Fleming's novels sold almost exclusively in paperback. Bond novels with the greatest sales through 1975, however, were those that were made into the Sean Connery films: *Dr. No, From Russia with Love, Goldfinger, Thunderball.* For specific figures, see Alice Payne Hackett, *Eighty Years of Best Sellers, 1895–1975* (New York: R. R. Bowker, 1977).

19. For more on Kennedy's cultural sensibilities, see Wills, *The Kennedy Imprisonment,* 141–50.

20. Pierre Bourdieu, *Distinction: A Social Critique of the Judgement of Taste,* trans. Richard Nice (Cambridge: Harvard University Press, 1984), 86.

21. Watson, *The Expanding Vista,* 35–70.

22. Fleming returned to CBS later in the decade with thirty-two scripts, none of which the network bought. A script rejected by NBC became the plot outline for *Dr. No.* See Alexander Walker, *Hollywood U.K.: The British Film Industry in the Sixties* (New York: Stein & Day, 1974), 183; see also Brooks and Marsh, *The Complete Directory,* 171–72.

23. In a profile for the *New Yorker,* Fleming, over martinis fittingly made with American vermouth and Beefeater gin, turned Kennedy's endorsement into a story of his first meeting with "Jack and Jackie Kennedy" in Washington: " 'Not *the* Ian Fleming!' they said. What could be more gratifying than that?" See "Bond's Creator," 33–34.

24. Vincent Canby, "United Artists' Fort Knox — No Pic Ever Like Its 'Goldfinger,' " *Variety,* March 31, 1965, 3.

25. Bennett and Woollacott, *Bond and Beyond,* 22–37.

26. Michael Denning suggests that Bond, like *Lady Chatterley's Lover,* represents key moments in a new organization of sexuality in consumer capitalism that uses the word *liberation* to cloak fetishization and oppression of women. See Michael Denning, "Licensed to Look: James Bond and the Heroism of Consumption," in *Contemporary Marxist Literary Criticism,* ed. Francis Mulhern (London: Longman, 1992), 227.

27. Bennett and Woollacott argue that Leiter becomes a major inflection for American audiences in the way he links the power of American intelligence and military forces to the lone British agent (*Bond and Beyond,* 209–10). See also Lars Ole Sauerberg, *Secret Agents in Fiction: Ian Fleming, John Le Carre and Len Deighton* (New York: St. Martin's, 1984), 154–56.

28. Walker, *Hollywood U.K.,* 186–90.

29. Geoffrey Bocca, "The Spectacular Cult of Ian Fleming," *Saturday Evening Post,* June 22, 1963, 68.

30. See William O'Neill, *Coming Apart: America in the 1960s* (New York: Quadrangle, 1971), 94–103; Todd Gitlin, *The Sixties: Years of Hope, Days of Rage* (New York: Bantam, 1987), 312–13.

31. John Cawelti and Bruce Rosenberg, *The Spy Story* (Chicago: University of Chicago Press, 1987), 32.

32. Ibid., 11–32.

33. Ibid., 151–56.

34. Canby, "United Artists' Fort Knox," 3.

35. Bennett and Woollacott, *Bond and Beyond,* 208–9.

36. See Fredric Jameson, "Reification and Utopia in Mass Culture," *Social Text* 1 (1979): 130–48.

37. See Cawelti and Rosenberg, *The Spy Story.* Despite the similarities in the written language, the problem of the differences between spoken British and American English had been considered for some time to be a hindrance to the development of a cultural dialogue between the two nations. American critics, for example, found the Midlands British dialects of such films as *Saturday Night and Sunday Morning* and *This Sporting Life* to be "grotesque" and "peculiar... not always comprehensible." See Bosley Crowther, review of *Saturday Night and Sunday Morning, New York Times,* April 4, 1961, 44; review of *Saturday Night and Sunday Morning, Variety,* November 9, 1960, 6.

38. Bennett and Woollacott, *Bond and Beyond,* 35. As the title of his essay "Licensed to Look" indicates, Michael Denning also considers the connections between Bond and the development of consumerism in the 1960s. In his analysis, Bond is a neocolonialist for whom danger most profoundly exists in the revocation of his "license to look"—his pleasure in taking and using what he can of exotic cultures and women.

39. Cawelti and Rosenberg, *The Spy Story,* 138, 151–52.

40. Bennett and Woollacott, *Bond and Beyond,* 35.

41. See "Sexy Sleuth 007 Goes Way of All Box Office Hits," *Variety,* December 2, 1964, 13; "James Bond vs. Red-Nosed Rudolph," *Variety,* February 24, 1965, 2. Lawyers for United Artists were very careful about the marketing of Bond, forcing Prince Macaroni to quit advertising its product as "Goldnoodle" and Bond Bread to cancel its ads featuring "James Bread for Bond." Vincent Canby, "Climb on UA's Band Wagon," *Variety,* June 2, 1965, 5.

42. Erik Barnouw, *The Sponsor: Notes on a Modern Potentate* (New York: Oxford University Press, 1980), 41–55.

43. Ibid., 68–73.

44. As Christopher Anderson notes in *Hollywood TV: The Studio System in the Fifties* (Austin: University of Texas Press, 1994), the development of private eye "agencies" in the ABC programs was part of a Warner Bros. formula designed to ensure the continued production of those series should one of their stars suddenly leave in a contract dispute, as

Clint Walker (*Cheyenne*) had (239–46). See also David Marc, *Demographic Vistas* (Philadelphia: University of Pennsylvania Press, 1984), 82–84.

45. Horace Newcomb and Robert Alley, *The Producers' Medium* (New York: Oxford University Press, 1983), 32–33. I discuss the role of the American producer in the British-American cultural dialogue at much greater length in Chapter 6.

46. For the Felton-Fleming story, see Peter Bogdanovich, "With Gun in Hand and Tongue in Cheek," *TV Guide,* October 24, 1964, 10–13; Richard Meyers, *TV Detectives* (San Diego: A. S. Barnes, 1981), 96–97.

47. Bennett and Woollacott, *Bond and Beyond,* 33–34. See also Cawelti and Rosenberg, *The Spy Story,* 131–32; Meyers, *TV Detectives,* 100–101.

48. The balance between adventure and humor was a difficult one for Felton to maintain. During the show's second season, story lines began a noticeable swing away from adventure and toward campy spoofery. The increasingly silly plots and arch humor—encouraged, according to Richard Meyers, by the sudden success of ABC's deliberately hokey *Batman* series—began to alienate the show's fans and led directly to the show's demise in 1968. See Meyers, *TV Detectives,* 102.

49. Ibid., 100–101. See also Leslie Raddatz, "The People from U.N.C.L.E.," *TV Guide,* March 16, 1966, 15–18.

50. "The Toys from U.N.C.L.E.," *Variety,* June 30, 1965, 42.

51. Quoted in Raddatz, "The People from U.N.C.L.E.," 18.

52. See "Great TV Spy Scramble," *Life,* October 1, 1965, 118–20.

53. Roland Barthes, *Mythologies* (New York: Noonday, 1973), 138–43. See also John Fiske, *Television Culture* (New York: Routledge, 1989), 42–44.

54. Cawelti and Rosenberg, *The Spy Story,* 30–31.

55. "Lew Grade Sees Secret Agent Sale as Major Brake [*sic*] for Brit Shows," *Variety,* March 10, 1965, 42. There was some disingenuity in Grade's comments; what was truly important about the sale, as *Variety* noted, was the new marketability of British programs in the United States made possible by the use of film technology instead of videotape.

56. Program description for *Secret Agent, TV Guide* (Minnesota ed.), April 3, 1965, A-12.

57. The MI9 agent, identified simply as "105," was played by Patrick Newell, who would later join *The Avengers* as Mother, John Steed and Tara King's boss.

58. See "The Battle of the Cameras," *Secret Agent,* exec. prod. Ralph Smart; prod. Sidney Cole; perf. Patrick McGoohan, Dawn Addams, Niall MacGinnis; CBS, April 3, 1965.

59. Quotations from "Yesterday's Enemies," *Secret Agent,* exec. prod. Ralph Smart; prod. Sidney Cole; writ. Donald Jonson; dir. Charles Crichton; perf. Patrick McGoohan, Maureen Connell, Howard Aaron Crawford; CBS, May 1, 1965. Even this overt reference to the Communist enemy, however, is problematic: The former agent says that he thought of going over because "they were the only people who wanted to fight Hitler and Mussolini."

60. See Cawelti and Rosenberg, *The Spy Story.*

61. David Buxton cites the contretemps between Drake and his supervisors in this episode as proof of the state's control over the pleasures of consumption it apparently endorses: "[Drake's] freedom to consume in exotic places, to frequent the sites of pleasure, is no more than a 'compensation' for his enslavement to a government bureaucracy" (*From The Avengers to* Miami Vice, 82).

62. Bennett and Woollacott, *Bond and Beyond.*

63. John Ellis, *Visible Fictions: Cinema, Television, Video* (London: Routledge & Kegan Paul, 1982), 30. Ellis's discussion of narrative image is amplified throughout his Chapter 2, pp. 23–37.

64. At no time was this more the case than in the 1960s, when network domination of American television was at its peak. See Les Brown, *The Business Behind the Box* (New York: Harcourt Brace Jovanovich, 1971), 3–16.

65. Kirtz, "Out to Beat Bond," II, 17.

66. Ibid.

67. Robert Musel, "James Bond Is No Hero to Him," *TV Guide,* May 14, 1966, 12.

68. Letters, *TV Guide,* April 2, 1966, A-2.

69. Letters, *TV Guide,* July 16, 1966, A-2.

70. Les Brown, "Britain Makes It on US TV—O'Seas Influence Makes Its Mark," *Variety,* June 30, 1965, 1. Ratings figures for *Secret Agent* are taken from a syndication ad placed by ATV/ITC in *Variety,* July 27, 1966, 46.

71. Roger Watkins, "British Prepare US Invasion—Majors, Indies Pitching Shows," *Variety,* November 3, 1965, 25.

72. Brooks and Marsh, *The Complete Directory,* 1099.

73. ITC advertisement, *Variety,* July 27, 1966, 46.

74. Les Brown, "All TV Nets Give Mother England the Brush in Fall Season Shows," *Variety,* February 23, 1966, 35.

75. Cleveland Amory, "Second Thoughts," *TV Guide,* June 11, 1966, 12.

76. "ITC—the Rocking Redcoat: Biz Booming on All U.S. Fronts," *Variety,* May 4, 1966, 179.

77. As Tony Williams points out, the popular acceptance of Patrick McGoohan as auteur of *The Prisoner* elides the contributions of others, particularly script editor George Markstein, who left the series angrily after arguing that McGoohan had strayed too far from the original premise. This direct conflict in authorship, to say nothing of the multiple meanings available within the text and their activation by an audience, was resolved by the narrative image created for the series in the United States by publicity and press coverage, as will be seen. Tony Williams, "Authorship Conflict in *The Prisoner,*" in *Making Television: Authorship and the Production Process,* ed. Robert Thompson and Gary Burns (New York: Praeger, 1990), 65–66. See also Carrazé and Oswald, *The Prisoner,* 209–23.

78. That openness is visible in the press material quoted by Joan Barthel in *TV Guide:* " 'He has no idea who has abducted him,' says the publicity booklet for the series. 'They

could be his own people. They could be enemies. Perhaps both.'" Joan Barthel, "An Enigma Comes to American TV," *TV Guide*, May 25, 1968, 23–24. McGoohan himself some years later commented: "Explanation lessens what the piece was supposed to be: an allegorical conundrum for people to interpret for themselves. If one gives answers to a conundrum, it is no longer a conundrum." Quoted in Carrazé and Oswald, *The Prisoner*, 6.

79. Quotations from "Arrival," *The Prisoner*, prod. George Markstein, David Tomblin; writ. Patrick McGoohan; dir. Don Chaffey; perf. Patrick McGoohan; CBS, June 1, 1968.

80. To this statement, Number Two responds: "Six of one, half a dozen of the other." As it appeared in the remaining sixteen episodes, the line became "I am not a number! I am a free man!" See Meyers, *TV Detectives*, 112–13.

81. Barthel, "An Enigma," 22.

82. Robert Lewis Shayon, "Orwellian Necessities," *Saturday Review*, September 7, 1968, 54.

83. "The Private I," *Time*, June 21, 1968, 65.

84. Fiske, *Television Culture*, 123.

85. In their ongoing debate about Number Six and John Drake, viewers of the show who claim that at one point in the series Number Six is actually called "Drake" are countered by those who cite that as a mishearing of the word *break*. See Brooks and Marsh, *The Complete Directory*, 726.

86. On Grade's approach to *The Prisoner*, see Barthel, "An Enigma," 22. On the premodern "style" of the show's setting and costumes, see Carrazé and Oswald, *The Prisoner*, 212.

87. Buxton, *From* The Avengers *to* Miami Vice, 93. See also "CBS Pacts Carol Burnett Series, Buys British 'Prisoner' and Dickers Doris Day," *Variety*, October 12, 1966, 35. Buxton's account differs somewhat from that of Carrazé and Oswald, who suggest that the initial contract was for thirteen episodes, with the possibility of seventeen more if the first ones went well. Only four of the extra seventeen episodes would be made, because of production expenses and loud "creative differences" between McGoohan and others involved with the show. In both accounts, however, Grade plays the key role in determining the length of the series' run. See Carrazé and Oswald, *The Prisoner*, 210–28.

88. Quoted in Barthel, "An Enigma," 24.

89. Shayon, "Orwellian Necessities," 54. In the final episode of the series, "Fallout," Number Six does escape. After being offered leadership of the village, he storms "the Castle" in which the panopticians live and confronts the never-before-seen Number One— who turns out to be Number Six himself. Acting out of the shock of recognition, Number Six, with two other prisoners and his butler, destroys the castle and its repressive machinery and returns to London, where the final scene of the show replicates the opening scene of the introduction to "Arrival." The episode closes off no meanings whatsoever. "Fallout," *The Prisoner*, prod. David Tomblin; writ./dir. Patrick McGoohan; perf. Patrick McGoohan, Kenneth Griffith, Alexis Kanner, Leo McKern; CBS, September 11, 1968.

90. On the concept of "clawing back," see John Fiske and John Hartley, *Reading Television* (London: Methuen, 1978), 86–87.

91. "The Private I," 65, 67.

92. Shayon, "Orwellian Necessities," 54. See also "The Private I," 65; Jack Gould, "The Prisoner Opens," *New York Times,* June 17, 1968, 79.

93. Raymond Williams, *Marxism and Literature* (Oxford: Oxford University Press, 1977), 114.

94. In addition to printed letters citing the show as "one of the most exciting intriguing, suspenseful new shows ever to hit television" and "providing the intelligent public with an intelligent program," the magazine included a rare editorial synopsis of other letters it had received: "Readers called it 'refreshingly new... utterly fascinating... unusual... sophisticated... startling... ingenious... a thinking man's series at last... Kafka in pop clothing.' Said one: 'Tripe.'" Letters, *TV Guide,* June 29, 1968, A-2.

95. Shayon, "Orwellian Necessities," 54.

96. Barthel, "An Enigma," 22.

97. Cawelti and Rosenberg, *The Spy Story.*

98. Buxton, *From* The Avengers *to* Miami Vice, 95–96.

99. Ibid., 96.

100. Quotation from "Fallout."

101. For specific and skeptical discussions of the roles of—and the distinctions between—the New Left and the counterculture in the 1960s, see O'Neill, *Coming Apart,* 233–318; Gitlin, *The Sixties,* 195–221, 353–61.

102. Buxton, *From* The Avengers *to* Miami Vice, 96.

103. Denning, "Licensed to Look," 219–23.

104. For a thorough discussion of what he calls the "yin and yang of the same epochal transformation," see Gitlin, The *Sixties,* 195–221.

105. Buxton, *From* The Avengers *to* Miami Vice, 95.

106. Ibid., 96.

107. *Get Smart* was canceled by NBC in 1969; CBS, however, picked it up for its 1969–70 schedule and altered the program in significant ways. See Brooks and Marsh, *The Complete Directory,* 340.

108. For further discussion of the shifts in the crime genre during the late 1960s and early 1970s, see Marc, *Demographic Vistas,* 85–93.

3. Mrs. Peel Goes to Washington

1. Quoted in Adam Sweeting, "Back with a Vengeance," *Guardian* (London), October 19, 1993, 26.

2. In the *Secret Agent* episode "Yesterday's Enemies," for example, the Beirut bureau chief, explicitly the holder of a desk assignment, is a woman, whom Drake takes to task for mismanagement when she is unable to supply him with the backup agents he needs.

3. As such, those spies followed in the long-standing "Mata Hari" convention in spy fiction discussed at length by Julie Wheelwright in "Poisoned Honey: The Myth of Women in Espionage," *Queen's Quarterly* 100, no. 2 (1993): 291–309.

4. As Julie D'Acci notes in her appreciation of the series, *Honey West* scriptwriters Richard Levinson and William Link claim that ABC programmers who were nervous about public acceptance of a tough, independent woman detective insisted upon the inclusion of a male partner. D'Acci argues that the character was seen by many women as both tough and independent; she also, however, acknowledges the reliance on the strong and containing presence of Sam Bolt in many episodes. See Julie D'Acci, "Nobody's Woman? *Honey West* and the New Sexuality," *The Revolution Wasn't Televised: Sixties Television and Social Conflict*, ed. Lynn Spigel and Michael Curtin (New York: Routledge, 1997), 85–86.

5. For further discussion of the "Bond girl," see Tony Bennett and Janet Woollacott, *Bond and Beyond: The Political Career of a Popular Hero* (London: Methuen, 1987), 231–32, 241–47.

6. Ibid., 241.

7. A lengthy discussion of the gendered constructions of daytime and prime-time television genres can be found in John Fiske, *Television Culture* (New York: Routledge, 1989), 215–23. See also Nick Browne, "The Political Economy of the Television (Super)Text," in *Television: The Critical View*, 4th ed., ed. Horace Newcomb (New York: Oxford University Press, 1987), 585–99.

8. See Horace Newcomb, *TV: The Most Popular Art* (New York: Anchor, 1974), for complete discussions of sitcoms, Westerns, and detective and adventure series. See also Fiske, *Television Culture*, 144–45.

9. For the early history of *The Avengers*, see Dave Rogers, *The Complete Avengers* (New York: St. Martin's, 1989), 12–86. A further gloss on that history is presented by Toby Miller, *The Avengers* (London: British Film Institute, 1997), 7–17.

10. Anthony Carthew also noted that *The Avengers* "owes a lot to Ian Fleming's James Bond novels. But the writers of the series . . . have taken Bond to the ultimate, logical absurdity and made their hero aware of his posturings, a Bond played tongue in cheek." Anthony Carthew, "Tweedy Thriller," *New York Times*, December 15, 1963, II, 25.

11. Robert Musel, "Violence Can Be Fun," *TV Guide*, May 9, 1964, 12–14.

12. Rogers, *The Complete Avengers*, 86–87.

13. Les Brown, "Britain Makes It on US TV—O'Seas Influence Makes Its Mark," *Variety*, June 30, 1965, 1. Brown's article was the first industry herald of a British television "invasion," citing not only the arrival of *Secret Agent* and *The Saint* but the direct influence British programming and producers had already had on several American shows (all on ABC), including the pop music series *Shindig* and the prime-time soap opera adaptation of *Peyton Place*, in addition to *Honey West*. See also, for the literary genesis of *Honey West*, Michael Richardson, "Under the Influence of *The Avengers*," *Primetime* 15 (1989): 8; D'Acci, "Nobody's Woman?" 83.

14. Cleveland Amory, review of *Honey West, TV Guide,* October 23, 1965, 12; Rogers, *The Complete Avengers,* 56–59.

15. Toby Miller suggests that the "commodity aesthetics" of the fashion in *The Avengers,* which at the same time revealed and provided an ironic commentary on the social and class distinctions at the core of the series, were paramount in its export to the United States (*The Avengers,* 41–63). Thomas Andrae similarly cites the importance of fashion in the series as being a precursor to the "commodity feminism" of advertising in the 1980s and 1990s. Thomas Andrae, "Television's First Feminist: *The Avengers* and Female Spectatorship," *Discourse* 18, no. 3 (1996): 131–32.

16. On the origin of the "M appeal" story, which I first heard in 1970 while attending high school, see Rogers, *The Complete Avengers,* 87. Roger Marshall, however, who was head writer of the show at the time the name would have been coined, casts some doubt on the myth: "I can truly say that I never heard that until last year. . . . It's a good story but is—I suggest—just that. I think a publicist is credited with the idea. As they say, you couldn't prove it by me." Roger Marshall, letter to author, May 3, 1996.

17. Rogers, *The Complete Avengers,* 87–88; Patrick Macnee, *Blind in One Ear: The Avenger Returns* (San Francisco: Mercury House, 1988), 238.

18. Noted film producer Julian Wintle, responsible for the definitive British New Wave films *Tiger Bay* and *This Sporting Life,* was hired as executive producer to oversee the change to filming. See Rogers, *The Complete Avengers,* 87–88.

19. "Brit ABC-TV Poised with Two New Film Series, One with US Partner," *Variety,* December 1, 1965, 29.

20. Advertisement for *The Avengers, Variety,* January 26, 1966, 48. *Variety* had several months earlier taken note of *The Avengers* and Diana Rigg in its review of her first episode in Britain, using discourse similar to that in the ad and later journalistic copy: "Diana Rigg shaped as a more than adequate sparring partner. . . . A leggy girl, with a doll's face, she maintained the tradition of fighting prowess. . . . She had the necessary poise to work with Macnee, and was dressed in a fine offbeat wardrobe, parading, for instance, in well-above-the-knee skirts which exaggerated her rangy statistics." Review of *The Avengers, Variety,* October 5, 1965, 44.

21. Stanley Price, "From Lear to Leer," *New York Times,* March 13, 1966, II, 19.

22. "Good-Chap Sexuality," *Newsweek,* April 4, 1966, 94. The emphasis on "kinkiness" in the article is an element of the American narrative image that has its origins in British intertextuality: in 1964, *Avengers* stars Macnee and Blackman released what would later be called "the first Marxist novelty-number rap record," "Kinky Boots." The record stiffed in Britain on its release, although the "kinky" descriptive stuck all the way to America. In a final irony, the record was rereleased in 1991 and climbed to number five on the British pop charts. See Cynthia Rose, "Kinky," *New Musical Express,* April 23, 1983, 12; "Crib Sheet: *The Avengers,*" *Mail Magazine, Mail on Sunday* (London), October 24, 1993, 80.

23. Laura Mulvey, "Visual Pleasure and Narrative Cinema," in *Movies and Methods,* vol. 2, ed. Bill Nichols (Berkeley: University of California Press, 1985), 309. Andrae use-

fully employs an analysis of the male gaze in addressing an episode of the series itself ("Television's First Feminist," 120–21).

24. Cleveland Amory, review of *The Avengers, TV Guide,* May 14, 1966, 1.

25. Program description of *The Avengers, TV Guide* (Minnesota ed.), January 14, 1967, A-69.

26. Robert Musel, "En Garde!" *TV Guide,* January 14, 1967, 19.

27. Ibid., 20.

28. Elaine Tyler May, *Homeward Bound: American Families in the Cold War Era* (New York: Basic Books, 1988), 3–14.

29. William Chafe, *The American Woman* (New York: Oxford University Press, 1972), 218–19.

30. Sara Evans, *Personal Politics* (New York: Knopf, 1979), 8–9. See also Chafe, *The American Woman,* 219–24.

31. Betty Friedan, *The Feminine Mystique* (New York: W. W. Norton, 1963), 282–309.

32. Betty Friedan, "Television and the Feminine Mystique," *TV Guide,* February 1, 1964, 6.

33. Betty Friedan, "Television and the Feminine Mystique," *TV Guide,* February 8, 1964, 22, 24. Ironically, the first of these two quotes appeared on a page next to an ad for D-Con Mouseprufe showing a housewife standing on a chair and screaming, "Eek! A MOUSE!" On the next page, "Poor Deborah" and "Gay Deborah" demonstrated the ability of Midol to relieve menstrual cramps. On p. 24, Friedan's words were accompanied by an ad for Angel Face cosmetics. See also Glenn Altschuler and David Grossvogel, *Changing Channels: America in* TV Guide (Urbana: University of Illinois Press, 1992), 137–38.

34. For more on male industry perceptions of the female audience, see Lynn Spigel, *Make Room for TV: Television and the Family Ideal in Postwar America* (Chicago: University of Chicago Press, 1992), 73–98. On criticism of Friedan, see Alice Echols, *Daring to Be Bad: Radical Feminism in America, 1967–1975* (Minneapolis: University of Minnesota Press, 1989) 167–69; Chafe, *The American Woman,* 230–32; Evans, *Personal Politics,* 19.

35. Spigel, *Make Room for TV,* 82–83.

36. Christopher Schemering, *The Soap Opera Encyclopedia* (New York: Ballantine, 1985), 304–5.

37. For a more quantitative analysis of the portrayal of women on television in the early 1960s, see Diana Meehan, *Ladies of the Evening: Women Characters of Prime-Time Television* (Metuchen, NJ: Scarecrow, 1983), 109–14.

38. Tim Brooks and Earle Marsh, *The Complete Directory to Prime Time Network TV Shows: 1946–Present,* 5th ed. (New York: Ballantine, 1992), 655–56.

39. Mary Ann Watson, *The Expanding Vista: American Television in the Kennedy Years* (New York: Oxford University Press, 1990), 43–44.

40. Brooks and Marsh, *The Complete Directory,* 384–85.

41. Susan Douglas, *Where the Girls Are: Growing Up Female with the Mass Media* (New York: Times Books, 1994), 126–38; Meehan, *Ladies of the Evening,* 96–98.

42. Douglas, *Where the Girls Are*, 130–32. See also David Marc, *Comic Visions* (Boston: Unwin Hyman, 1989), 140–41.

43. William O'Neill, *Coming Apart: America in the 1960s* (New York: Quadrangle, 1971), 196; Chafe, *The American Woman*, 236–37; Evans, *Personal Politics*, 17–22; May, *Homeward Bound*, 219–20.

44. All dialogue quoted in this section is from "The Cybernauts," *The Avengers*, exec. prod. Julian Wintle; prod. Brian Clemens, Albert Fennell; writ. Philip Levene; dir. Sidney Hayers; perf. Patrick Macnee, Diana Rigg; ABC, March 28, 1966.

45. The character of Dr. Armstrong adds a level of intertextuality to the show in its resemblance to the insane title character of the film *Dr. Strangelove*.

46. Les Brown, "All TV Networks Give Mother England the Brush in Fall Season Shows," *Variety*, February 23, 1966, 35.

47. Quoted in Rogers, *The Complete Avengers*, 90.

48. David Buxton, *From* The Avengers *to* Miami Vice: *Form and Ideology in Television Serials* (Manchester: Manchester University Press, 1990), 101–4. Buxton's reading is echoed in some ways by Toby Miller, who finds the same dialectic of tradition and modernity at work in the characters of Steed and Peel themselves (*The Avengers*, 36, 58–61).

49. Buxton, *From* The Avengers *to* Miami Vice, 107.

50. See, for example, the episodes "Mission: Highly Improbable" and "Two's a Crowd," in which East-West conflict is a humorous counterpoint to the technology being fought for. See also Miller, *The Avengers*, 121. For comments on American fears of nuclear holocaust, see, among others, Godfrey Hodgson, *America in Our Time: From World War II to Nixon—What Happened and Why* (New York: Vintage, 1976), 315; Todd Gitlin, *The Sixties: Years of Hope, Days of Rage* (New York: Bantam, 1987), 20–24; May, *Homeward Bound*, 22–23.

51. Janice Radway, "Identifying Ideological Seams: Mass Culture, Analytic Method and Political Practice," *Communication* 9 (1986): 108–9. See also Bennett and Woollacott, *Bond and Beyond*, 64.

52. Roger Marshall speaks directly to the difference in the character as created in England and its reconstruction by young women in the United States: "By definition, everyone who worked on *The Avengers* . . . had lived through the '39–'45 war. Most of us had grown up during it and memories of it were vivid. Bear in mind the essential difference between us and our American counterparts. . . . For us, occupied France was 20 miles away. Apart from relatives going off to fight and some not returning, the impact of the war on most American families was, by comparison, slight. In the U.K. the war was vivid reality, from air raids to food rationing to total conscription. We all grew up in the midst of it. Most important, we all saw Women in Uniform, Women Doing Things. It was as much a part of our lives as the postman on the street. Women served in all three services, they formed the Women's Land Army and did practically all the farming. They built the tanks and airplanes. They drove all the buses and ambulances. A far cry from that period of

'domestic containment' you speak about. With this real experience behind us, it was a short step to creating a fictional Action Woman. I can't remember, but I don't imagine anybody involved thought that by creating Cathy Gale or Emma P. we were doing anything innovative or strange. 'Why not?' would have been the reaction." Marshall, letter to author.

53. Andrae, "Television's First Feminist," 131; Musel, "En Garde!"

54. "On the Scene: *The Avengers:* Jolly Good Show," *Playboy*, March 1967, 143. Publisher Hugh Hefner had told friends that *The Avengers* was one of his favorite shows. See Macnee, *Blind in One Ear*, 242.

55. Buxton, *From* The Avengers *to* Miami Vice, 75–76, 96–99.

56. The *Avengers* ad exemplifies Roland Barthes's discussion of the two "themes" of photography: the "studium," which represents cultural complicity between the photographer and the observer; and the "punctum," which reveals and punctures the ideological order represented in that complicity. The look back at the looker in this case breaks the two-dimensional containment of the image and thus also shatters the idologies of objectification and containment behind it. See Roland Barthes, *Camera Lucida* (New York: Hill & Wang, 1981), 25–28, 42–45. Toby Miller provides several examples of individual shows in which Emma returns the gaze (visually or verbally) of taunting male opponents (*The Avengers*, 77–78). The trope is nowhere more significant than in the final Peel episode, "The Forget-Me-Knot": As Steed peeps through his curtains to gaze at his ex-partner getting into a car with her long-lost husband, Emma's last act in *The Avengers* is to look back up at him—and the camera. "The Forget-Me-Knot," *The Avengers*, prod. Brian Clemens, Albert Fennell; writ. Brian Clemens; dir. James Hill; perf. Patrick Macnee, Diana Rigg, Linda Thorson; ABC, March 20, 1968. See also Miller, *The Avengers*, 143–44.

57. Letters, *TV Guide*, May 21, 1966, A-2.

58. Letters, *'Teen*, December 1966, 6.

59. "The Lethal Look," *Mademoiselle*, July 1966, 82–83.

60. During summer 1966, *The Avengers* received a 12.3 rating, compared with an industry average of 12.1, and an audience share of 28.3, a respectable showing made all the more impressive by the fact that the show was competing with a first-run American series, *The Dean Martin Summer Show*. Ratings chart, *Variety*, October 5, 1966, 43.

61. For the story of Rigg's resignation, see Rogers, *The Complete Avengers*, 124; Macnee, *Blind in One Ear*, 245.

62. Rogers, *The Complete Avengers*, 158.

63. "ABC Spots Don Boyle in Brit. to Ride Herd on Trio of Entries," *Variety*, June 5, 1968, 23. See also Rogers, *The Complete Avengers*, 158.

64. See Miller, *The Avengers*, 78–79.

65. Robert Musel, "Can She Make Them Forget Mrs. Peel?" *TV Guide*, March 2, 1968, 13.

66. Quoted in ibid., 14.

67. See also Andrae, "Television's First Feminist," 132–33.

68. Rogers, *The Complete Avengers*, 160; Miller, *The Avengers*, 103–7.

69. "Avengers Goes Spoof Happy on H'wood Classics," *Variety*, October 30, 1968, 35.

70. Review of *The Avengers*, *Variety*, March 27, 1968, 62.

71. Letters, *TV Guide*, April 13, 1968, A-2.

72. Letters, *TV Guide*, July 6, 1968, A-2.

73. Les Brown, "UK's 'Finest Aura' in US TV—Economy-Minded ABC Slots Three," *Variety*, March 13, 1968, 33; see also Les Brown, "ABC's Journey into Unknown," *Variety*, March 27, 1968, 37; " 'Avengers' as Yankee Boodle Dandy," *Variety*, April 3, 1968, 39. In the March 13 article, Brown reported that ABC was looking to use Thorson as a "certain exploitative lift" when she replaced Rigg. In the March 27 article, he reported that the cost to ABC for a single episode of *The Avengers* would be $110,000, compared with the $200,000 CBS had to pay for an episode of *Gunsmoke*.

74. Les Brown, "ABC '68: Cherchez Le Femme—Guns and Gore Yields to Girls," *Variety*, May 1, 1968, 31.

75. Quoted in Robert Musel, "She's Miss Rigg of St. John's Wood, Now," *TV Guide*, August 10, 1968, 17. Musel noted that Rigg, at the height of the series's popularity, "drove around with sacks of unopened mail in her car."

76. Program description of *The Avengers*, *TV Guide* (Minnesota ed.), September 21, 1968, A-27.

77. A spinoff of *The Man from U.N.C.L.E.*, *The Girl from U.N.C.L.E.* teamed the character of April Dancer, portrayed by Hollywood-born actress Stephanie Powers, affecting a British accent, with British agent Mark Slate (Noel Harrison). The Britification of the characters, along with the efforts at humor and fantastic plots, was lifted directly from *The Avengers*, as were Ms. Dancer's mod outfits and knowledge of martial arts and swordplay—one photo in the closing credits goes so far as to show Powers/Dancer wearing an Emma Peel jumpsuit and holding an épée. NBC canceled the program after only one year. I discuss later adaptations of *The Avengers* in Chapter 6. See also Andrae, "Television's First Feminist," 133.

78. Raymond Williams, *Marxism and Literature* (Oxford: Oxford University Press, 1977), 113.

79. Ibid.

4. Down the Up Staircase

1. E. B. White, in Carnegie Commission on the Future of Public Television, *Public Television: A Program for Action* (New York: Bantam, 1967), 13.

2. Tony Bennett and Janet Woollacott, *Bond and Beyond: The Political Career of a Popular Hero* (London: Methuen, 1987), 42–43.

3. For a critique of economic definitions of transnational success, see Michael Tracey, "Popular Culture and the Economics of Global Television," *InterMedia* 16 (1988): 9–25. Despite the 1969 demise of British secret agent series, Grade remained in the American market through his other stock-in-trade: mod mid-Atlantic variety series, starring British

singers with American guests. *This Is Tom Jones* became his greatest American success, receiving fall pickup orders from ABC in 1969 and 1970. Although *Variety* heralded his number of sales in the United States, however, none of his later network series, including ABC's *The Persuaders* (with Roger Moore and Tony Curtis) and *Shirley's World* (starring Shirley MacLaine), lasted longer than a season. See "Lew Grade Gives ATV an $8-Mil. Sales Wk. in U.S.," *Variety,* March 12, 1969, 35; "ITC's $30-Mil Gross for Fiscal Year Doubles Previous, Profits Up 130%," *Variety,* July 30, 1969, 46; Les Brown, "London's Bridges to U.S. Tele; Grade's ATV Now a H'wood Major," *Variety,* April 29, 1970, 197; Jack Tinker, *The Television Barons* (London: Quartet, 1980), 48–49; Les Brown, *The Business Behind the Box* (New York: Harcourt Brace Jovanovich, 1971), 130, 204–8, 232–36, 351–60.

4. For more on *The Muppet Show,* see Tim Brooks and Earle Marsh, *The Complete Directory to Prime Time Network TV Shows: 1946–Present,* 5th ed. (New York: Ballantine, 1992), 608–9.

5. In addition to Carnegie Commission, *Public Television,* see William Hoynes, *Public Television for Sale: Media, Market and the Public Sphere* (Boulder, Colo.: Westview, 1994), 47–52; James Ledbetter, *Made Possible By...: The Death of Public Broadcasting in the United States* (New York: Verso, 1998), 20–27; John Macy, *To Irrigate the Wasteland* (Berkeley: University of California Press, 1974), 21–27; David Stone, *Nixon and the Politics of Public Television* (New York: Garland, 1985), 8–16; Twentieth Century Fund, *Quality Time?* ed. Robert Somerset-Ward (New York: Twentieth Century Fund, 1993), 82–85. See also Les Brown, "PTV: Is Everybody Happy? Striking a Blow for Status Quo," "Carnegie & Ford Clash over Who Pays the Freight," and "NBC, ABC Mum on Carnegie Report; Stanton Vocal re CBS' Blessings," all in *Variety,* February 8, 1967, 35.

6. On the Public Broadcasting Act and its passage, see Erik Barnouw, *Tube of Plenty,* 2d ed. (New York: Oxford University Press, 1990), 398; Macy, *To Irrigate the Wasteland,* 25–26; Stone, *Nixon and the Politics,* 19–20; Twentieth Century Fund, *Quality Time?* 82–85. See also Larry Michie, "Hosannas for Public Television, but There's a Serpent in Paradise," *Variety,* April 19, 1967, 69; Larry Michie, " 'Fly Now, Worry Later' Themes DC Mood on Public TV Legislation," *Variety,* May 3, 1967, 68; "PTV Forces No Less Anxious Than Solons to Keep Gov't Hands Off," *Variety,* August 30, 1967, 32; "Happy Days for ETV Crowd," *Variety,* October 25, 1967, 37.

7. The full story of the machinations in the public television industry and government leading to incorporation of PBS can be found in Robert Pepper, *The Formation of the Public Broadcasting Service* (New York: Arno, 1979). Until 1969, national program distribution for educational stations was handled by the Ford Foundation-funded National Educational Television (NET), also a leading producer of educational programming. See Ledbetter, *Made Possible By...,* 42–57; Stone, *Nixon and the Politics,* 8–16.

8. Barnouw, *Tube of Plenty,* 436–37; Christopher Sterling and John Kittross, *Stay Tuned: A Concise History of American Broadcasting* (Belmont, Calif.: Wadsworth, 1978),

392–93. See also "Harris Poll Sez 33,000,000 Now View Public TV," *Variety,* October 27, 1971, 45.

9. American public broadcasting in the late 1960s resembled the broadcasting systems of the Third World described by Kaaren Nordenstreng and Tapio Varis in *Television Traffic: A One-Way Street?* (New York: UNESCO, 1974). Lacking in funds and experience, but possessing the needed technology and building a national system, public broadcasting in the United States was ripe for exploitation by experienced and wealthy foreign distributors.

10. The number of countries receiving *The Forsyte Saga* prior to its American broadcast varies from forty to eighty, depending upon the source. Its popularity, however, remains a constant: times for public events in the Netherlands were changed when they conflicted with showing of the *Saga*; sixty thousand people came out to see series star Susan Hampshire when she visited Oslo, Norway; even viewers in the Soviet Union were enthralled with the stories of the Forsyte family. See Fred Ferretti, " 'Forsyte Saga' Will Unfold on Channel 13," *New York Times,* October 4, 1969, 70; James Michener, "A Hit— in Any Language," *TV Guide,* May 30, 1970, 4–9; "Talk of the Town: Saga," *New Yorker,* January 10, 1970, 15–16.

11. Brown, *The Business Behind the Box,* 270.

12. Ferretti, " 'Forsyte Saga' Will Unfold," 70.

13. Richard Doan, "The Doan Report," *TV Guide,* July 26, 1969, A-1.

14. Ferretti, " 'Forsyte Saga' Will Unfold," 70.

15. Viewers of *The Forsyte Saga* also saw another contribution to assimilation in interviews conducted by NET president James Day with members of the show's cast. In his first interview with Kenneth More (Jolyon Forsyte), Day followed the line established by print critics in suggesting that both More's character and his nemesis Soames were "in some respects Galsworthy." He also directed viewers toward the reception of the program elsewhere through comments elicited from More: "I get letters from Rumania, Yugoslavia. . . . It's stopped the countries everywhere it's been—it was something that worked from the word go." James Day, interview with Kenneth More, following "A Family Scandal," *The Forsyte Saga,* NET, October 12, 1969.

16. Jack Gould, "Galsworthy's Social Trilogy, 'Forsyte Saga,' Here from Britain," *New York Times,* October 6, 1969, 94.

17. Anthony Burgess, "Seen Any Good Galsworthy Lately?" *New York Times Magazine,* November 16, 1969, 64.

18. Michener, "A Hit," 9.

19. For more on the visual technique of soap opera production, see Bernard Timberg, "The Rhetoric of the Camera in Television Soap Opera," in *Television: The Critical View,* 4th ed., ed. Horace Newcomb (New York: Oxford University Press, 1987), 164–78; Horace Newcomb, *TV: The Most Popular Art* (New York: Anchor, 1974), 161–82. Description of the visual aspect of *The Forsyte Saga* taken from "A Family Wedding" and "A Family

Scandal," *The Forsyte Saga,* prod.-writ. Donald Wilson; dir. David Giles; perf. Kenneth More, Eric Porter, Margaret Tyzack, et al.; NET, October 5 and 12, 1969.

20. In "A Family Wedding," the viewer can hear off-camera noises, including coughs and bangs.

21. See, for example, Dennis Porter, "Soap Time: Thoughts on a Commodity Art Form," in *Television: The Critical View,* 2d ed., ed. Horace Newcomb (New York: Oxford University Press, 1979), 87–96.

22. Michener, "A Hit," 9.

23. Burgess, "Seen Any Good Galsworthy Lately?" 64.

24. Margot Hentoff, "Vogue Spotlight: Television," *Vogue,* January 1, 1970, 78.

25. Michener, "A Hit," 6. The comments of Burgess, Hentoff, and Michener also are supported by Charlotte Brunsdon in her assessment of "quality" programming in Britain. In writing of the domestic popularity of the serialized television version of Evelyn Waugh's *Brideshead Revisited,* she notes the "legitimating force" of the novel: " 'Middle-brow' literature (to use an old-fashioned, but rather useful term) is not itself spoilt by the vulgar medium of television, and indeed enhances the upstart with a little culture." Charlotte Brunsdon, "Problems of Quality," *Screen* 31 (spring 1990): 85.

26. Roland Barthes, *Image, Music, Text* (New York: Hill & Wang, 1977), 147; Michel Foucault, "What Is an Author?" in *The Foucault Reader,* ed. Paul Rabinow (New York: Pantheon, 1984), 118–19.

27. Burgess, "Seen Any Good Galsworthy Lately?" 57.

28. Michener, "A Hit," 6.

29. John Fiske, *Television Culture* (New York: Routledge, 1989), 94. See also Roland Barthes, *S/Z* (New York: Farrar, Straus & Giroux, 1974), 3–7.

30. Hentoff, "Vogue Spotlight," 78. Although "realism" as discussed here has a specific literary connotation, it does not differ substantially from the "realist paradigm" Brunsdon identifies as one of the central discourses of "quality television": "anything . . . in which key criteria are those of adequacy, objectivity, immediacy. . . . although its philosophical home is with non-fiction programming, it is frequently the central critical criterion used in discussion of fiction programs, and is one of the dominant common-sense aesthetics of this culture" ("Problems of Quality," 78).

31. Hentoff, "Vogue Spotlight," 78.

32. John Caughie, "Playing at Being American: Games and Tactics," in *Television: The Critical View,* 5th ed., ed. Horace Newcomb (New York: Oxford University Press, 1994), 589.

33. "Talk of the Town," *New Yorker,* January 10, 1970, 16.

34. Quoted in Michener, "A Hit," 4.

35. John Caughie, "Before the Golden Age: Early Television Drama," in *Popular Television in Britain: Studies in Cultural History,* ed. John Corner (London: British Film Institute, 1991), 27. The first British serialized literary drama was *Jane Eyre,* broadcast in 1955.

36. James Carey, "A Cultural Approach to Communication," in *Communication as Culture: Essays on Media and Society* (Boston: Unwin Hyman, 1989), 18.

37. Janice Radway, "Identifying Ideological Seams: Mass Culture, Analytical Method and Political Practice," *Communication* 9 (1986): 93–123.

38. For the centrality of family to soap operas, see Robert Allen, *"The Guiding Light: Soap Opera as Economic Product and Cultural Document,"* in *Television: The Critical View*, 4th ed., ed. Horace Newcomb (New York: Oxford University Press, 1987), 141–63. Family in prime-time television is the subject of Ella Taylor's *Prime-Time Families: Television Culture in Postwar America* (Berkeley: University of California Press, 1989).

39. Twentieth Century Fund, *Quality Time?* 83–84; Stone, *Nixon and the Politics,* 9–11; Michie, "Hosannas for Public Television," 84; "Happy Days," 37.

40. Twentieth Century Fund, *Quality Time?* 84–85.

41. For more on Nixon's history with media, see William Porter, *Assault on the Media: The Nixon Years* (Ann Arbor: University of Michigan Press, 1976), 1–42. See also Ledbetter, *Made Possible By . . .* , 58–59; Stone, *Nixon and the Politics,* xiii–xiv, 42–54.

42. On the history of NET and its relationship to PBS, see Ledbetter, *Made Possible By . . .* , 42–57, 72–73. See also Brown, *The Business Behind the Box,* 318–22; Stone, *Nixon and the Politics,* 15–24; Twentieth Century Fund, *Quality Time?* 86–87; "NET's Dawn of a New 'Day' — but More Time Spent Up in Air Than on It," *Variety,* September 10, 1969, 68; "NET to Be Programmer, Not Web, under New Grants from Ford, CPB," *Variety,* November 5, 1969, 33; "Recent Moves by NET a Tipoff to Nervousness re White House," *Variety,* December 31, 1969, 21; Bill Greeley, "Public TV a Gov't Divided; NET's Day Scores Grassroots Trap," *Variety,* March 18, 1970, 35.

43. Larry Michie, "CPB's Macy Tells of Censorship Safeguards for Public TV Network," *Variety,* October 1, 1969, 34; Stone, *Nixon and the Politics,* 21–24, 33–41; Twentieth Century Fund, *Quality Time?* 87.

44. On Agnew's attacks on television, see Jules Witcover, *White Knight: The Rise of Spiro Agnew* (New York: Random House, 1972), 302–16; Theo Lippmann Jr., *Spiro Agnew's America* (New York: W. W. Norton, 1974), 191–96; Barnouw, *Tube of Plenty,* 443–46; Brown, *The Business Behind the Box,* 227–32; Porter, *Assault on the Media,* 45–49, 255–62; Stone, *Nixon and the Politics,* xiv–xv.

45. Critics within and outside of PBS criticized the network for programming cuts, including a Lawrence Ferlinghetti poetry reading and a documentary criticizing American involvement in Third World conflicts, and for additions such as a documentary on the White House Conference on Hunger. See Ledbetter, *Made Possible By . . .* , 63–65; Stone, *Nixon and the Politics,* 26–27; Bill Greeley, "PBS Cool on Controversy, So NET May Have to Save Its Heat for New York," *Variety,* November 18, 1970, 46; "Poet's Nixon Rap in Upcoming Seg Trimmed by NET," *Variety,* December 31, 1969, 1; "Recent Moves by NET," 21; "Five NET Affils Kill 'Who Invited,' Pressure Hinted," *Variety,* February 18, 1970, 35.

46. See Bill Greeley, "Budget Setback for ETV Web; Ford Fdn. Nixes $24-Mil Request," *Variety,* March 4, 1970, 35; Bill Greeley, "Public Television's Song and Dance;

Clips NET Role in 'Journal'-ism," *Variety,* April 14, 1970, 29; Bill Greeley, "PBS Keeps Tabs on Warning Flags; It's a Race between NET and WGBH," *Variety,* February 10, 1971, 26; "CPB's Big Gifter: Guess Who?" *Variety,* October 21, 1970, 27; "The Nixon Network," *Newsweek,* January 1, 1973, 58–59.

47. Ledbetter, *Made Possible By . . . ,* 70–74; Stone, *Nixon and the Politics,* 84–90, 210.

48. Ledbetter, *Made Possible By . . . ,* 70–74; Macy, *To Irrigate the Wasteland,* 98–107; Stone, *Nixon and the Politics,* 163–71. See also Larry Michie, "CPB Beats White House Lobby—House Bill OK's 2-Yr. $155-Mil," *Variety,* June 7, 1972, 29; Larry Michie, "Senate OK's 2-Yr. $155-Mil for CPB, But Nixon May Grant Only $45 Mil," *Variety,* June 28, 1972, 36.

49. Nixon's veto most upset local public television executives, who needed the funding whether it was routed through a central agency or not; meanwhile, PBS gavel-to-gavel coverage of the Senate Watergate hearings attracted viewer subscriptions and donations as nothing previously had. See Ledbetter, *Made Possible By . . . ,* 85–88; Stone, *Nixon and the Politics,* 163–65, 300–308.

50. Ledbetter, *Made Possible By . . . ,* 87–88; Porter, *Assault on the Media,* 153–54; Twentieth Century Fund, *Quality Time?* 88.

51. Ledbetter, *Made Possible By . . . ,* 59–60; Porter, *Assault on the Media,* 152–53; Stone, *Nixon and the Politics,* xvii–xix.

52. Quoted in "Nixon's BBC Salute," *Variety,* June 28, 1972, 34.

53. Tony Prosser, "Public Service Broadcasting and Deregulation in the United Kingdom," *European Journal of Communication* 7 (1992): 173–93.

54. Burton Paulu, *Television and Radio in the United Kingdom* (Minneapolis: University of Minnesota Press, 1981), 31; Prosser, "Public Service Broadcasting," 176.

55. Paulu, *Television and Radio,* 154.

56. For a full description of Reith's vision of the BBC, see Asa Brooks, *The BBC: The First Fifty Years* (Oxford: Oxford University Press, 1985), 53–56.

57. Caughie argues that the creation of the serialized literary drama genre allowed the BBC to bring the "quality" desired by Reith to the entertainment necessary for television broadcasting ("Before the Golden Age," 27–28). As Toby Miller points out in *The Avengers* (London: British Film Institute, 1997), Reith's "public service" ideal did not exclude the light entertainment and drama programming provided by the BBC, particularly during the war years, just as British commercial television did not completely eschew the more elite ideals of public service (31). With commercial interests so entrenched in American television at the time PBS was organized, however, it became much easier for those responsible for American public broadcasting to attend to Reith's loftier aspirations in thought and word, if not always in deed.

58. For further commentary on White, see Patricia Aufderheide, "Public Television and the Public Sphere," *Critical Studies in Mass Communication* 8 (1991): 173.

59. Macy, *To Irrigate the Wasteland,* 40.

60. C. T. Dornan, "Fear and Longing in the United Kingdom: Cultural Custody and the Expansion of Public Television," unpublished manuscript, 1992, 6–8.

61. Macy, *To Irrigate the Wasteland*, 40.

62. Victor Turner, "Process, System and Symbol: A New Anthropological Synthesis," *Daedalus* 106, no. 3 (1977): 73.

63. Macy, *To Irrigate the Wasteland*, 56.

64. Pierre Bourdieu, *Distinction: A Social Critique of the Judgement of Taste*, trans. Richard Nice (Cambridge: Harvard University Press, 1984), 26.

65. Les Brown points out that advertising for *The Forsyte Saga* and other PBS programs in 1970 appeared on a daily basis in the *New York Times*, whereas it showed up on only a "nominal" basis in the city's tabloid dailies, the *Daily News* and the *Post* (*The Business Behind the Box*, 317). Hoynes argues that the *Times* "symbolizes the abstract ideal of the realm in which public television seeks approval," as it is "the elite circles" the newspaper embodies that "public television pursues in both readers and supporters" (*Public Television for Sale*, 128).

66. Steve Millard, "Specialized Audiences: A Scaled-Down Dream?" in *The Future of Public Broadcasting*, ed. Douglass Cater and Michael Nyman (New York: Praeger, 1976), 191.

67. Millard, for example, argued that a specialized audience need not mean a small audience, in opposition to arguments made by public broadcasting benefactor Lloyd Morrisett, who wanted public television to appeal to "specific interests and specific tastes." See ibid., 192–94; Lloyd Morrisett, "Rx for Public Television," in *The Future of Public Broadcasting*, ed. Douglass Cater and Michael Nyman (New York: Praeger, 1976), 172–78.

68. For a full discussion of the "audience-as-market" and "audience-as-public" paradigms, see Ien Ang, *Desperately Seeking the Audience* (London: Routledge, 1991), 26–32.

69. See Aufderheide, "Public Television," 168–83; Hoynes, *Public Television for Sale*, 115–35.

70. Hoynes, *Public Televison for Sale*, 134.

71. Ang, *Desperately Seeking the Audience*, 32.

72. Newcomb, *TV*, 232–33. According to Les Brown, ABC's *Peyton Place* itself owed its existence in part to the success of evening serials on commercial British television. Les Brown, "Britain Makes It on US TV—O'Seas Influence Makes Its Mark," *Variety*, June 30, 1965, 1.

73. Taylor, *Prime-Time Families*, 17–42. See also Elaine Tyler May, *Homeward Bound: American Families in the Cold War Era* (New York: Basic Books, 1988).

74. "Streamlining," as Ang defines it, refers to the practice of using behavioral research techniques to define demographically specialized audiences whose individual variations in viewing habits can be smoothed over (streamlined) to present a usable profile to the networks (*Desperately Seeking the Audience*, 60–67).

75. "CPB Survey on Who Watches PTV Found 'Surprising,'" *Variety*, April 1, 1970, 27.

76. "CPB's Big Gifter," 27; Lawrence Jarvik, "PBS and the Politics of Quality: Mobil Oil's *Masterpiece Theatre,*" *Historical Journal of Film, Radio and Television* 12, no. 3 (1992): 253, 263. For further background on the creation of *Masterpiece Theatre,* see Terence O'Flaherty, Masterpiece Theatre: *A Celebration of 25 Years of Outstanding Television* (San Francisco: KQED, 1996), 7–8.

77. Macy, *To Irrigate the Wasteland,* 59.

78. Mobil was concerned internally about revamping its image of complacency and conservativeness that was increasingly out of step with market activity. Externally, the corporation wanted to address what it saw as a bias not only against the oil industry but against capitalistic industry as a whole given increasing voice during the 1960s, including the bombing of Mobil's corporate office in New York. See Jarvik, "PBS and the Politics of Quality," 254–57.

79. Hoynes, *Public Television for Sale,* 134.

80. Jarvik, "PBS and the Politics of Quality," 258.

81. Ang, *Desperately Seeking the Audience,* 32.

82. According to a 1982 poll, Mobil was named by 31 percent of "upscale" respondents as the gasoline most often purchased. Mobil chairman Rawleigh Warner interpreted the high figure as proof that Mobil's public relations campaign had won over the demographic segment it hoped to attract not merely to *Masterpiece Theatre* but to its product at point of sale. See Jarvik, "PBS and the Politics of Quality," 258.

83. *Marlborough* was one of the books, along with *From Russia with Love,* that John F. Kennedy had listed as his favorites in a 1961 *Life* interview. That fact was never exploited in Mobil's publicity for the show—a tacit acknowledgment of the mobility of the signification of "British television" in the United States after the years of Bond. See Hugh Sidey, "The President's Voracious Reading Habits," *Life,* March 17, 1961, 55–60.

84. Robert Musel, "How to Offend Everybody," *TV Guide,* February 7, 1970, 38.

85. Quoted in O'Flaherty, Masterpiece Theatre: *A Celebration,* 11.

86. Christopher Sarton, executive producer (for WGBH) of *Masterpiece Theatre,* acknowledged that the Churchill name and Hampshire's presence made *The First Churchills* an almost necessary choice, despite its weaknesses: "Anyone who thought we should open the series with *The First Churchills* was really out of his mind.... So why did we do it? Well, Susan Hampshire had just finished *The Forsyte Saga,* so everybody knew her. Then the name Churchill was in the title, and that was another reason they were going to watch." Quoted in O'Flaherty, Masterpiece Theatre: *A Celebration,* 9.

87. Photograph, *Los Angeles Times,* January 9, 1971, 2B.

88. Elizabeth Sullivan, "Fleur Returns," *Boston Globe TV Week,* January 10, 1971, 11; see also cover.

89. Rick DuBrow, "Susan Hampshire, Forsyte's Fleur, in New TV Series," *Chicago Tribune,* January 11, 1971, III, 13.

90. Cecil Smith, " 'Churchills' Opens Theatre," *Los Angeles Times,* January 11, 1971, IV, 18.

91. See, for example, Mary Ellen Brown, *Soap Opera and Women's Talk: The Pleasure of Resistance* (London: Sage, 1994), 42–48; Tanya Modleski, "The Rhythms of Reception: Daytime Television and Women's Work," in *Regarding Television — Critical Approaches: An Anthology*, ed. E. Ann Kaplan (Frederick, Md.: University Publications of America, 1983), 67–75.

92. Fred Ferretti, "TV: Bawdy 'First Churchills' Bows," *New York Times*, January 11, 1971, 91.

93. Stephanie Harrington, "Hate Thy Neighbor," *New York Times*, January 24, 1971, II, 18.

94. Richard Burgheim, "Viewable Alternatives: *The First Churchills*," *Time*, February 8, 1971, 66.

95. William Woods, "First Churchills," *Washington Post*, January 9, 1971, C1.

96. Molly Haskell, "Those Churchills: Another Man's Family," *Vogue*, April 1, 1971, 158.

97. "Push Ratings for PTV Masterpiece via Mobil," *Variety*, January 27, 1971, 28.

98. Mobil advertisement for *The First Churchills*, *New York Times*, January 31, 1971, II, 22.

99. If the first reviews of *The First Churchills* were any indication, Mobil had already succeeded with that part of its campaign, as both the *New York Times* and the *Los Angeles Times* columns about the program mentioned Mobil's sponsorship.

100. Quoted in O'Flaherty, Masterpiece Theatre: *A Celebration*, 2.

101. "CBS Buys Prestige Brit. Drama Series for Summer Play," *Variety*, March 24, 1971, 35; "6 Wives of Henry 8th Leads Brit TV Awards; BBC Sweeps ITV, 17–6," *Variety*, March 17, 1971, 60.

102. Richard Doan, "The Doan Report," *TV Guide*, July 17, 1971, A-1. *TV Guide* publicity also included a viewer letter from a transplanted Briton who told readers: "Just a few months ago . . . I watched this marvelous series on BBC. I'm sure American viewers will enjoy it as much as I did." Letters, *TV Guide*, May 1, 1971, A-2.

103. Quayle's Shakespearean background and roles in classical and historical epics had been well publicized earlier in 1971, when he starred on NBC in a short-lived Lew Grade import, *The Strange Report*. See Ross Drake, "Finally I Had Become a Man," *TV Guide*, April 3, 1971, 20–25.

104. Doan, "The Doan Report," July 17, 1971, A-1. At eight hundred thousand dollars for six episodes, the price of a single installment of *Six Wives* to CBS was just seven thousand dollars less than the cost of the entire twenty-six-episode *Forsyte Saga* to NET just two years earlier.

105. "Mobil Renews PBS 'Masterpiece,'" *Variety*, July 14, 1971, 40; "Mobil Oil Backs Public TV Series," *New York Times*, July 14, 1971, 71; "PBS Tudor Twin: '6 Wives,' 'Eliz. R' in 'Masterpiece,'" *Variety*, August 11, 1971, 37. CBS had also been negotiating with BBC to pick up *Elizabeth R*. See Katie Kelly, "Henry & Catherine & Anne & Jane & Anne, Etc.," *Time*, August 9, 1971, 51.

106. John Leonard, "Superb Series on Sexist King: *The Six Wives of Henry VIII*," *Life*, August 6, 1971, 14. For further comments on the role of television critics in defining "quality television," see Brunsdon, "Problems of Quality," 80–81.

107. "NBC Buys BBC 'Nile' Six-Parter for Tues. Nights," *Variety*, December 8, 1971, 25.

108. "TV Syndication: Alistair Cooke's 'America,' " *Variety*, December 22, 1971, 40; "Did NBC Make a Tactical Error with Tues. Slot?" *Variety*, March 29, 1972, 47.

109. For more on Mobil's strategy to use *Masterpiece Theatre* against commercial networks, see Jarvik, "PBS and the Politics of Quality," 261–62.

110. Bill Greeley, "Floppo Season for PTV Web — Dullness Tells in Ratings Fade," *Variety*, November 29, 1972, 41; "PTV Audience Drop Pointed Up in Early Rating Books for November," *Variety*, December 20, 1972, 36.

111. Greeley, "Floppo Season," 41.

112. Quoted in Jarvik, "PBS and the Politics of Quality," 265.

113. Review of *Upstairs, Downstairs*, *Variety*, December 20, 1972, 38.

114. Clive James, "Good Old Boring Best-in-the-World," *TV Guide*, March 10, 1973, 9. James also criticized several of the BBC's most recent serial dramas, including *Elizabeth R*, as "essentially unimaginative project[s] with bigness as [their] only reason for being."

115. Richard Price, "Programme Selling: Better Not Easier," *Televisual*, May 1986, 13.

116. The episodes purchased did not fall in any sort of order. In a restatement of a 1960s concern, WGBH did not purchase five episodes that had been produced in black and white due to a technician's strike during the first six weeks of British broadcast; indeed, the first episode of the series had to be reshot in color for LWT to put together an export package. Richard Price would later note, "Without that first episode in colour I doubt if it would ever have sold in the US." Ibid., 13.

117. Mobil advertisement for *Upstairs, Downstairs*, *New York Times*, January 6, 1974, II, 16.

118. Alistair Cooke, introduction to "On Trial," *Upstairs, Downstairs*, prod. John Hawkesworth; writ. Fay Weldon; dir. Raymond Menmuir; perf. Angela Baddeley, Pauline Collins, Gordon Jackson, Jean Marsh, et al.; *Masterpiece Theatre*, PBS, January 6, 1974.

119. Dialogue from "On Trial." Later shows in the season did revolve around an affair between James Bellamy and Sarah; intercourse between the classes, however, was far less a component of the series than Mobil's ad suggested.

120. "Rating Is 'Upstairs,' " *Variety*, January 16, 1974, 70.

121. Cleveland Amory, review of *Upstairs, Downstairs*, *TV Guide*, February 23, 1974, 20.

122. Helen Bohn Jordan, "Lady Marjorie Would Swoon," *TV Guide*, February 16, 1974, 16–17.

123. See, for example, John O'Connor, "A Top-Flight 'Upstairs, Downstairs' Begins New Series," *New York Times*, November 4, 1974, 30; Cecil Smith, "A New Cycle of Plays

to Begin on *Upstairs, Downstairs,*" *Los Angeles Times TV Week,* November 4, 1974, 2; Robert Musel, "The Man from Downstairs," *TV Guide,* December 28, 1974, 24–26; Roy Andreas de Groot, "Mrs. Bridges Surpasses Herself," *Esquire,* January 1975, 109.

124. See, for the first example, Mobil advertisement for *Upstairs, Downstairs, New York Times,* November 3, 1974, II, 30.

125. The oil embargo ended March 18, 1974; the first season of *Upstairs, Downstairs* concluded on March 29, 1974. See O'Flaherty, Masterpiece Theatre: *A Celebration,* 16.

126. Quoted in Jarvik, "PBS and the Politics of Quality," 265.

127. Quoted in O'Flaherty, Masterpiece Theater: *A Celebration,* 13.

128. The first words of Cooke's introduction to *Upstairs, Downstairs* were, "Tonight, *Masterpiece Theatre* makes a radical departure from its habit of taking a work of fiction and dramatizing it." Introduction to "On Trial."

129. Stuart Hall, "Culture, the Media and the 'Ideological Effect,' " in *Mass Communication and Society,* ed. James Curran, Michael Gurevitch, and Janet Woollacott (London: Sage, 1979), 315–48.

130. Nora Ephron, "Missing Hazel," *Esquire,* July 1976, 32.

131. Ephron's comment on Cooke: "I was sorry that Alistair Cooke had so much more to say about the plague than he did about the death of Hazel, but perhaps he has become wary of commenting on the show itself after everyone (including me) took offense at some of the things he had to say about George Sand." Ibid.

132. Ibid., 33.

133. See, for example, Richard Schickel, review of *Upstairs, Downstairs, Time,* February 4, 1974, 65; Sander Vanocur, "Class Tells," *Washington Post,* January 11, 1976, G1. Vanocur was coanchor, with Robert MacNeil, of the PBS news series that occasioned the wrath of Richard Nixon earlier in the decade; after his departure, the show evolved into *The MacNeil-Lehrer Report.*

134. Fiske, *Television Culture,* 117–26.

135. Judith Martin, *"Upstairs, Downstairs:* Outs, Ins," *Washington Post,* January 15, 1977, C6.

136. John O'Connor, "A Fond Cheerio to 165 Eaton Place," *New York Times,* May 1, 1977, II, 25.

137. Anthony Lewis, "Reality in Romance," *New York Times,* May 9, 1977, 31.

138. Jean Marsh, "A Touch of Class On Screen and Off," *Washington Post,* May 1, 1977, L1.

139. O'Connor described his mail in general as that in which "friends and total strangers offer their opinions on new characters and developing story lines" ("A Fond Cheerio," II, 25).

140. Jarvik, "PBS and the Politics of Quality," 269. Those opinion leaders included Nora Ephron and her "long, long love letter" to *Upstairs, Downstairs.*

141. Mobil advertisement for *Upstairs, Downstairs, New York Times,* January 16, 1977, II, 27. The ad featuring Rose ran on the preceding page.

142. PBS was mentioned twice in the ad as the network on which the program was shown, and once in connection with WGBH, in noting its role as *Masterpiece Theatre* producer.

143. Carey Winfrey, "Reunited Cast Bids Last Adieu to Eaton Place," *New York Times,* May 2, 1977, 35. Winfrey doesn't report which side won.

144. Lewis, "Reality in Romance," 31.

145. Judith Martin, " 'Forsyte Saga,' " *Washington Post,* January 3, 1977, B1.

146. Stone, *Nixon and the Politics,* 317.

147. The 1971 CPB budget was $141.4 million, out of which the federal government was responsible for 16.8 percent, or $23.7 million. By the time CPB's 1976 budget, for $361.4 million, was approved, the federal government was footing 27.1 percent of the bill, or $97.9 million. During the same period, however, although the total dollar values contributed by state and local governments increased, the percentage of funding they paid for decreased—in the case of state government, from 46.4 percent to 24.5 percent. Total government backing for CPB dropped from 64 percent to 59.7 percent in 1976—a difference only slightly less than the difference in the increase in corporate funding during those years: from 2.2 percent ($3 million) to 7.8 percent ($28.2 million). Mobil could rightfully argue that it had played a leading role in the increased attention corporations were giving public broadcasting. For 1971 data, see Macy, *To Irrigate the Wasteland,* 81; for 1976 data, see "Is Public TV Going Commercial?" *Media Decisions,* October 1976, 106.

148. Mobil had enlisted independent commercial stations as well as public broadcasting in its cold war against the networks: in 1974, the company began sponsoring a series of specials on independent stations under the rubric, "The Mobil Showcase Network." Among the shows seen were the *Masterpiece Theatre*–oriented *Edward the King* and *Edward and Mrs. Simpson.* See Jarvik, "PBS and the Politics of Quality," 267; Bill Greeley, "Schmertz Plots 'Mobil Network,' " *Variety,* April 7, 1976, 1.

149. Jarvik cites an internal Mobil document indicating that the synergy of *Masterpiece Theatre* and op-ed advocacy ads had resulted in "changed . . . perceptions of national needs" in each of the four groups of "opinion leaders" it tracked in politics, media, academics and business ("PBS and the Politics of Quality," 268–70).

150. Brennan argues that *Masterpiece Theatre* represents, through the commercialization of public television it embodies and the popularization of "high art" upon which it relies, a linkage of British and American "national myths" that "strengthen imperial attitudes in an era of European and North American decline." In his reading, enjoyment of the serialized form merely plays into the show's ultimate elitism: that the nations responsible for *Masterpiece Theatre* are "better than" all other nations. Strong as Brennan's argument is in many regards, his leap from industrial and aesthetic definitions of elitism to a geopolitical definition reads far beyond what the evidence will bear on the issue. See Timothy Brennan, "*Masterpiece Theatre* and the Uses of Tradition," in *American Media and Mass Culture,* ed. Donald Lazere (Berkeley: University of California Press, 1987), 373–83. See also Mike Budd, Robert Entman, and Clay Steinman, "The Affirmative Char-

acter of U.S. Cultural Studies," *Critical Studies in Mass Communication* 7 (1990): 169–84; William Seaman, "Active Audience Theory: Pointless Populism," *Media, Culture & Society* 14 (1992): 301–11.

5. (Naughty) Bits of Limey Eccentricity

1. Statement made in *Life of Python,* exec. prod., Charles Brand; prod.-dir. Mark Redhead; BBC/Devillier Donegan Enterprises, 1989.

2. Read also points out that those filmed sitcoms, representing American middle-class life, frequently entered cultures in which owning a television signified upper-class status. The reception, then, of *I Love Lucy* and *The Flintstones* in those cultures was similar to that of the PBS British imports a decade later in the United States, with meaning being shaped by utterances defining a small audience gifted in cultural, educational, and/or economic capital. See William Read, *America's Mass Media Merchants* (Baltimore: Johns Hopkins University Press, 1976), 76–95. See also Joseph Straubhaar, "Asymmetrical Interdependence and Cultural Proximity: A Critical Review on the International Flow of TV Programs," unpublished manuscript, 1992, 16–18.

3. Read, *America's Mass Media Merchants,* 91–92; Straubhaar, "Asymmetrical Interdependence," 17–18.

4. The relative popularity of the American action-adventure and soap opera can be seen as another example of Hoskins and Mirus's cultural discount. Colin Hoskins and Rolf Mirus, "Reasons for the U.S. Dominance of the International Trade in Television Programs," *Media, Culture & Society* 10: 500–501. See also Straubhaar, "Asymmetrical Interdependence," 13–18.

5. Jerry Palmer, *The Logic of the Absurd* (London: British Film Institute, 1987), 75–95.

6. Ibid., 115–40.

7. Todd Gitlin, *The Sixties: Years of Hope, Days of Rage* (New York: Bantam, 1987), 36.

8. David Marc, *Demographic Vistas* (Philadelphia: University of Pennsylvania Press, 1984), 141–48.

9. For the history and an analysis of *The Goon Show,* see Roger Wilmut and Jimmy Grafton, *The Goon Show Companion* (London: Eyre Methuen, 1976).

10. Quoted in Roger Wilmut, *From Fringe to Flying Circus* (London: Eyre Methuen, 1980), 18; for the complete story of the creation and production of *Beyond the Fringe,* see pp. 16–27.

11. Quoted in ibid., 11.

12. Quoted in ibid., 24.

13. Quoted in ibid., 25.

14. On Meader, see Mary Ann Watson, *The Expanding Vista: American Television in the Kennedy Years* (New York: Oxford University Press, 1990), 54–55.

15. Andrew Crisell argues that the creation of the BBC's *That Was the Week That Was* owed an immense debt to the independent commercial network's (ITN) news broadcasts,

which presented greater skepticism toward authority than could the BBC's own news programming. Andrew Crisell, "Filth, Sedition and Blasphemy: The Rise and Fall of Satire," in *Popular Television in Britain: Studies in Cultural History,* ed. John Corner (London: British Film Institute, 1991), 148–49.

16. The show's performers included singer Millicent Martin (who performed the title tune, with topically adjusted lyrics, each week), Timothy Birdsall, Kenneth Cope, David Kernan, Roy Kinnear, Al Mancini, Lance Percival, and William Rushton, a friend of Frost's from Cambridge and cofounder of the satirical monthly *Private Eye.* Another Cambridge friend and *Eye* founder, Christopher Booker, was hired as head writer (with Frost) for the television revue; critic Bernard Levin was signed as an essayist and as a querulous interviewer of people in the news. See Wilmut, *From Fringe to Flying Circus,* 59–66. For a collection of material, verbal and visual, from the British *TW3,* see David Frost and Ned Sherrin, eds., *That Was the Week That Was* (London: W. H. Allen, 1963).

17. Review of *That Was the Week That Was, Variety,* December 5, 1962, 28.

18. The show's regular lampooning of Prime Minister Macmillan led to protests from Conservative Party officials and, finally, a BBC edict forbidding the edited use of its news footage for anything other than documentary purposes. See Wilmut, *From Fringe to Flying Circus,* 64–71.

19. "The BBC's 'TWTWTW,'" *Variety,* December 19, 1962, 26.

20. The significance of American satirists and observational comics in establishing a narrative image for *TW3* is evident in *TV Guide*'s half-page "Closeup" feature on the premiere episode: "It's only a few years since people were complaining, 'What this country really needs is some good satire.' Well, we got it. Most of it started in the coffee houses and smaller nightclubs, and a good deal of it wound up on TV. Sahl, Newhart, Berman and Gregory are nationally known. . . . But it was in England, and on TV, that the most savage—and most popular—revue originated. *TWTWTW* carried irreverence to an extreme that shook the Government." "Closeup: *That Was the Week That Was,*" *TV Guide* (Michigan ed.), November 9, 1963, A-22.

21. Premiere episode, *That Was the Week That Was* (American version), prod. Leland Hayward; writ. Earl Doud, Robert Emmett, Gerald Gardner; dir. Hal Gurnee, Marshall Jamison; perf. Nancy Ames, Henry Fonda, Henry Morgan, et al.; NBC, November 10, 1963.

22. *Variety,* for instance, called the premiere "a 60-minute barb-tinged romp that, over most of the course, proved delightful in its freshness and impishness." Review of *That Was the Week That Was, Variety,* November 13, 1963, 35. *TV Guide* referred to the show in a quasi-editorial sidebar as "a refreshing blast of cool and invigorating impudence, " also noting that NBC had received almost two thousand calls and telegrams to the five stations it owned, of which 80 percent were favorable. Its own correspondence about the show, the magazine reported, ran seven to one in favor of *TW3.* "For the Record," *TV Guide,* November 23, 1963, A-3.

23. Quotations from *That Was the Week That Was* (British version), prod. Ned Sherrin; writ. Christopher Booker, Caryl Brahms, David Frost, Herbert Kretzmer, David Lee,

Bernard Levin; perf. David Frost, Roy Kinnear, Millicent Martin, et al.; NBC, November 24, 1963. See also Watson, *The Expanding Vista,* 221–24; David Frost, *David Frost—An Autobiography: From Congregations to Audiences* (London: HarperCollins, 1993), 104–9.

24. *New York Times* critic Jack Gould reported that the *TW3* broadcast had received the greatest response of any single network program on the assassination, with NBC callers praising "the vigor and compassion displayed in the imported presentation's incisive portrayal of President Kennedy and its estimate of the potential of President Johnson." Jack Gould, "Government Praises Network for TV Coverage of Tragedy," *New York Times,* November 27, 1963, 75. See also Frost, *David Frost,* 108–9; Watson, *The Expanding Vista,* 221–22.

25. It was a "special arrangement" in more ways than one, as the American Federation of Television and Radio Artists had tried to block Frost's work visa, charging that he was taking a job that could and should have been held by an American performer. Producer Leland Hayward and NBC argued that Frost's work as creator and host of the British version of *TW3* made his participation appropriate. The U.S. Immigration Service sided with Hayward and the network. See "David Frost OK'd for 'TW3,'" *Variety,* January 15, 1964, 38; Frost, *David Frost,* 114–15.

26. The British *TW3* fell afoul of the BBC in fall 1963, when the resignation of Prime Minister Macmillan and his controversial appointment of Sir Alec Douglas-Home to replace him led to the show's most scabrous attacks on the Tory hierarchy. The resultant outcry aggrieved members of the BBC's Board of Governors, who were responsible for maintaining the political balance mandated by the corporation's charter. With a general election due in 1964, the board decided in November to end the second series of *TW3* programs at the end of the 1963 calendar year—although, as those associated with the show pointed out, the BBC had known that the country would have an election before it began running the second series. See Frost, *David Frost,* 98–104; Wilmut, *From Fringe to Flying Circus,* 70–71; Paul Gardner, "Originator Here to Assist 'TW3,'" *New York Times,* January 3, 1964, 49.

27. Gould, "Government Praises Network," 75.

28. Steve Neale and Frank Krutnik, *Popular Film and Television Comedy* (London: Routledge, 1990), 93–94.

29. Ibid., 19–21.

30. That problem became a public one almost immediately: When executives at Brown & Williamson discovered that *TW3* was presenting a sketch borrowed from the British edition of the show on the health hazards of smoking, they told NBC that if the sketch went on as planned, the company would pull out its one-minute ad for the evening. Although *TW3* producers indicated that the sketch might be dropped, in the end it stayed and the commercial was replaced. "Smoke Gets in Your Eyes" became one of the program's most praised and popular pieces. See "'TW3' Smoking Spoof Gets in Sponsor's Eye," *New York Times,* January 24, 1964, 57; Jack Gould, "TV: Finding the Target," *New York*

Times, January 25, 1964, 49; Val Adams, " 'Week That Was' Will Be No More," *New York Times,* May 4, 1965, 87.

31. George Rosen, "Kintner: We'll Take Charge; Something New Happening in TV," *Variety,* December 11, 1963, 21.

32. See *That Was the Week That Was,* exec. prod. Leland Hayward; prod. Marshall Jamison; writ. Earl Doud, Robert Emmett, David Frost, Gerald Gardner; dir. Kirk Alexander, Marshall Jamison; perf. Elliot Reid, Henry Morgan, David Frost, et al.; NBC, January 10, 1964.

33. "That Was Weak, That Was," *Time,* January 17, 1964, 76.

34. Review of *That Was the Week That Was, Variety,* January 15, 1964, 35.

35. Cleveland Amory, review of *That Was the Week That Was, TV Guide,* March 21, 1964, 3.

36. Peter Bogdanovich, "That Was the Week That Was for TWTWTW," *TV Guide,* April 4, 1964, 24–28.

37. Ibid., 24. See also Gould, "TV: Finding the Target," 49; "As We See It," *TV Guide,* April 4, 1964, 1; "Follow Up Comment: *That Was the Week That Was," Variety,* May 13, 1964, 39.

38. Writer Gerald Gardner told *Variety* that the Republican preemptions of *TW3* made it appear as though the party was "out to get" the show. "Lament of TW3 Writer: 'Save Us from Friends,' " *Variety,* December 23, 1964, 20. Frost, for his part, has cited his angry response to an NBC representative who claimed that the only half-hour slots available for purchase by political parties were those occupied by *TW3, Hazel,* and *The Jack Benny Show.* Frost, *David Frost,* 133–34.

39. The logic of the absurd employed by the topical satirists of *TW3* inverts the ideological conventions John Fiske presents, tellingly, as "strategies of containment" that structure the television news programs from which they drew both their style and their content. See John Fiske, *Television Culture* (New York: Routledge, 1989), 283–96.

40. Bernard Hollowood, "Britain's 'New Wave' of Satire Ebbs," *New York Times Magazine,* January 24, 1964, 17.

41. Ibid. Hollowood cited the "with-it-ness" of *TW3*'s cultural literacy as proof that the claim that Britain was becoming a classless society was sheer "idiocy."

42. NBC was evidently aware of the very specific nature of the relationship between the show's creators and audience from its inception, as one network spokesman made clear at the time of its cancellation: "It was presented for a limited audience, but it hasn't rung the bell enough to keep even that audience interested." Quoted in Adams, " 'Week That Was,' " 87.

43. In addition to the United States, a national version of *TW3* operating under the same title began in France in 1964. See Hollowood, "Britain's 'New Wave,' " 71.

44. See Mikhail Bakhtin, *Problems of Dostoevsky's Poetics,* ed. and trans. Caryl Emerson (Minneapolis: University of Minnesota Press, 1984), 122–37; also Mikhail Bakhtin,

Rabelais and His World, trans. Helene Iswolsky (Bloomington: Indiana University Press, 1984), 1–58.

45. Robert Stam, *Subversive Pleasures: Bakhtin, Cultural Criticism and Film* (Baltimore: Johns Hopkins University Press, 1989), 95.

46. Ibid., 89; see also 26–56.

47. Ibid., 220, 221.

48. See Bakhtin, *Problems of Dostoevsky's Poetics,* 126–30.

49. Palmer's "logic of the absurd," as previously noted, allows for this ambivalence: the *peripeteia* can be read as a moment of liberation from the norm. It should also be noted, following his logic, that those who are not socially positioned in such a way as to "get" the comedy would not find anything liberating about it; thus the actions of the Conservative Party in Britain and the Republican Party in the United States.

50. Gitlin, *The Sixties,* 36.

51. On the role of verisimilitude in film and television comedy, see Neale and Krutnik, *Popular Film,* 83–94; Stam, *Subversive Pleasures,* 236–39.

52. Wilmut, *From Fringe to Flying Circus,* 75–79; Frost, *David Frost,* 137–54.

53. Wilmut, *From Fringe to Flying Circus,* 136–48; Frost, *David Frost,* 161–87.

54. On Frost's career as a talk-show host and interviewer, see Tim Brooks and Earle Marsh, *The Complete Directory to Prime Time Network TV Shows: 1946–Present,* 5th ed. (New York: Ballantine, 1992), 211; Hal Erickson, *Syndicated Television: The First Forty Years, 1947–1987* (Jefferson, N.C.: McFarland, 1989), 159–60; Frost, *David Frost,* 362–530.

55. Frost, *David Frost,* 167–68; 180–81; Wilmut, *From Fringe to Flying Circus,* 137–52.

56. Wilmut, *From Fringe to Flying Circus,* 46–51.

57. Ibid., 38–40.

58. Ibid., 120–34. *I'm Sorry, I'll Read That Again* featured several other *Cambridge Circus* veterans and was produced by another central figure in the Oxbridge comedy network, Humphrey Barclay. I was a regular listener when the program was broadcast on public radio in Iowa and California in the late 1970s and early 1980s.

59. Ibid., 144–50, 181–86.

60. Wilmut uses the term *Oxbridge Mafia* throughout *From Fringe to Flying Circus,* as does another of its dons, Bamber Gascoigne, in the book's preface. See also Tony Bennett and Janet Woollacott, *Bond and Beyond: The Political Career of a Popular Hero* (London: Methuen, 1987).

61. Crisell connects the rise of satire in Britain during the 1950s with the postwar rise in the standard of living—a rise that also increased leisure time for consumption of media among the upper classes and as a result also increased the cultural capital in currency ("Filth, Sedition and Blasphemy," 146–47).

62. Wilmut, *From Fringe to Flying Circus,* 146–49.

63. Ibid., 144, 183.

64. Although the BBC had made deals in the late 1960s with distributors who had entrée into the American market, it was not until early 1970 that it reorganized to allow programming heads of individual departments to negotiate export deals, rather than having to run decisions through a labyrinthine bureaucracy—a change suggested by an American management consultant. As Jack Pitman noted in *Variety:* "[BBC] product isn't angled to hook the Nielsen sample. BBC shows are styled, and always have been, first and foremost for domestic consumption—there never has been any effort to shape a series with a 'mid-Atlantic' accent." Jack Pitman, "BBC Gandering US Sales Push under New Setup Giving Program Tappers Authority to Make Deals," *Variety,* January 14, 1970, 45. See also "BBC-TV's $7-Mil Deal With H&W," *Variety,* March 19, 1969, 74.

65. As had been the case with other British imports, American audiences gained some advance knowledge about *Monty Python* from *TV Guide.* Robert Musel gave the show a positive mention in a 1970 article about the state of British television, and *Observer* critic Clive James, writing of the third season of *Python* shows at home, complained that the comics seemed to be running out of ideas. "I should add," he continued, "I wouldn't dream of missing their act—a larger confession than it looks, since I front a taped show on the commercial channel at the same time." Robert Musel, "How to Offend Everybody," *TV Guide,* February 7, 1970, 26; Clive James, "Good Old Boring Best-in-the-World," *TV Guide,* March 10, 1973, 29.

66. George Perry, *Life of Python* (Boston: Little, Brown, 1983), 93–94; Wilmut, *From Fringe to Flying Circus,* 121.

67. Wilmut, *From Fringe to Flying Circus,* 187–88. The sitcom, based on a series of novels about London medical students by Richard Gordon, was produced by Cleese's and Chapman's *I'm Sorry I'll Read That Again* colleague Humphrey Barclay. As Chapman was a licensed doctor, the team was a particularly apt choice for the assignment. One of Cleese's later scripts for the show, involving a trip to a resort hotel, proved to be the inspiration for his series *Fawlty Towers. Variety* said of *Doctor*'s premiere episode: "Working against it is the ancient bugaboo of limited acceptance of the British accent and product by American viewers. But based on the opening show... 'Doctor' seems to have better prospects than most previous importations." Review of *Doctor in the House, Variety,* September 22, 1971, 34.

68. The estimated audience for the 1969–70 *Python* series was three million viewers, according to Perry, *Life of Python,* 131–33. One problem with building and maintaining a British audience was the BBC programming schedule, which made its time of broadcast dependent upon whatever else the network was showing that night: a late soccer game might push it back to 11:30, or an early movie might have it running at 10:40.

69. According to a 1975 *New Yorker* piece, the records "sold surprisingly well, creating a fanatical cult"; none of the albums, however, tracked on any *Billboard* Top 200 album chart prior to 1975. "Talk of the Town," *New Yorker,* May 12, 1975, 35.

70. Perry, *Life of Python,* 161.

71. Ibid., 136–38. It should be noted that whereas *And Now for Something Completely Different* preceded the American import of *Monty Python's Flying Circus* by two years, the group's second film, *Monty Python and the Holy Grail,* released in spring 1975, also preceded the arrival of the television series in several markets, with a much broader band of publicity.

72. Simon argued that the movie was both more pointed and funnier than concurrent American satires, including Woody Allen's *Everything You Always Wanted to Know about Sex* and Robert Downey's *Greaser's Palace:* "It reeks with what might be prejudice, but resounds with what is certainly laughter. It dares to offend in pursuit of comic truth." John Simon, "And Now for Something Truly Funny," *New York Times,* September 10, 1972, II, 1.

73. "TV Syndication: 'Python Captures 64 Pub TV Outlets," *Variety,* April 23, 1975, 33; Les Brown, "BBC's 'MP' Surprise Hit on Public TV," *New York Times,* March 15, 1975, II, 23. Iowa and New York were among the first markets in the country to pick up *Monty Python*; among others to purchase the show early were such relatively unsophisticated markets as Omaha, Sacramento, and Scranton. See also David Littlejohn, "British TV Doesn't Mind Stepping on Toes," *New York Times,* December 29, 1974, II, 1.

74. Brown, "BBC's 'MP,' " II, 55.

75. Carlin's 1972 album *AM & FM* sold more than five hundred thousand units and received the Grammy Award for best comedy album of the year. Pryor's *That Nigger's Crazy* (1974) and *Is It Something I Said?* (1975) both won Grammies, with the latter selling more than one million copies. Ronald Smith, *Comedy on Record: The Complete Critical Discography* (New York: Garland, 1988), 118–22, 505–508; Joel Whitburn, *The Billboard Book of Top 40 Albums* (New York: Billboard, 1995), 54, 349.

76. Of particular interest here is the *Lampoon,* founded in 1970 by a group of writers and editors with the *Harvard Lampoon* in Cambridge, Massachusetts — much as Britain's *Private Eye* had been founded a decade earlier by a group of writers and editors (and performers) from Cambridge University. Indeed, one of the editors of the early *Lampoon* was Tony Hendra, a colleague of Chapman's and Cleese's in the Cambridge Footlights Club. See Smith, *Comedy on Record,* 463–64; Wilmut, *From Fringe to Flying Circus,* 33–34.

77. American Council on Education, *The Fact Book on Higher Education, 1986–87,* ed. Cecilia Ottinger (New York: Macmillan, 1987), 59.

78. In his sour recapitulation of paths followed by those who left political activism after the 1960s, Todd Gitlin cites the popularity of *Saturday Night Live,* the American offspring of *Monty Python* (as will be discussed in Chapter 6), as proof of the "normalization" of a "loose antiauthoritarianism" that spoke to the ideals of cultural plurality and participatory democracy that motivated the activists of the 1960s (*The Sixties,* 431).

79. New York's WNET brought Chapman, Gilliam, Jones, and Palin to its studios in April 1975 to assist in taking viewer pledges, part of an ongoing plan to utilize the show

to attract a younger audience to the station. See John O'Connor, "Silliness Made Sublime," *New York Times*, April 6, 1975, 25; Les Brown, "TV Station Chases Money and Ratings—It's Channel 13," *New York Times*, November 3, 1975, 70.

80. This elitism was not lost on some of those responsible for bringing the show to the United States: the vice president of programming at WNET told the *New York Times* that his initial impression of the show was that it was "a highly stylized program, dealing in humor that is typically British undergraduate." Quoted in Brown, "BBC's 'MP,' " II, 55. See also Neale and Krutnik, *Popular Film*, 206–7.

81. For thorough discussion of *Monty Python's Flying Circus*, see Wilmut, *From Fringe to Flying Circus*, 195–232; Neale and Krutnik, *Popular Film*, 196–208. Their analyses are supported by Python member Terry Gilliam, who states in the film *Life of Python:* "We were conscious of not trying to be satirical and topical aside from using funny names of politicians. The stuff holds up because of that."

82. The sketch ends with the friend committing suicide and Timmy asking the reporters interviewing him: "I think it shows I'm human, don't you? Super, super!" At the same time, the camera pulls back, revealing the coffee shop to be a studio set, a Frost visual trademark from *TW3* on. Quotes from Episode 19, *Monty Python's Flying Circus*, prod.-dir. Ian MacNaughton; writ.-perf. Graham Chapman, John Cleese, Terry Gilliam, et al.; BBC-TV, October 20, 1970. See also Graham Chapman et al., *The Complete Monty Python's Flying Circus: All the Words*, vol. 1 (New York: Pantheon, 1989), 255–57.

83. On this point, see Hendrik Hertzberg, "Onward and Upward with the Arts: Naughty Bits," *New Yorker*, March 29, 1976, 69–70.

84. Wilmut, *From Fringe to Flying Circus*, 198–99; Neale and Krutnik, *Popular Film*, 201–2.

85. Wilmut, *From Fringe to Flying Circus*, 198–99; Neale and Krutnik, *Popular Film*, 200–202.

86. All quotations here and in following paragraphs, unless noted otherwise, are from Episode 27, *Monty Python's Flying Circus*, prod.-dir. Ian MacNaughton; writ.-perf. Graham Chapman, John Cleese, Terry Gilliam, et al.; BBC-TV, October 19, 1972.

87. The visual denaturalization is helped by the music, which diminuendoes and ends as the Viking figure enters the screen, a cue that the character is going to speak.

88. For further discussion of the representation and presentational modes and their role in constructing televisual narratives as "realism," see Fiske, *Television Culture*, 21–47.

89. Graham Chapman et al., *The Complete Monty Python's Flying Circus: All the Words*, vol. 2 (New York: Pantheon, 1989), 57. This sketch, too, rises out of the "Njorl's Saga" metasketch: the first Whicker is introduced on the coast of Iceland, when the old women come in search of Sartre. Whicker's monologue there quickly turns into another promotion for North Malden; the scene then cuts back to the BBC head of drama, who is telling someone on the phone that they would be better off "sticking with the Caribbean islands." The other parody in the show is of a stock market report, in which the reporter's

business jargon turns first into pornographic descriptions and then childish singsong gobbledygook. Unlike every other sketch, it is not subsumed into "Njorl's Saga."

90. Slashes indicate where trade-offs are made between Whickers.

91. Cleveland Amory, review of *Monty Python's Flying Circus, TV Guide,* May 17, 1975, 32.

92. "Talk of the Town," *New Yorker,* May 12, 1975, 35.

93. Thomas Meehan, "And Now for Something Completely Different," *New York Times Magazine,* April 18, 1976, 35.

94. "Killer Joke Triumphs," *Time,* May 26, 1975, 58; Richard Schickel, "Legendary Lunacy," *Time,* May 26, 1975, 58.

95. The American popularity of *Monty Python,* along with the concomitant success of the film *Monty Python and the Holy Grail* and the troupe's earlier recordings and books, established a narrative image for later programs made by individual members of the group. John Cleese's situation comedy *Fawlty Towers* inherited an American Python audience, thanks to Cleese's choleric portrayal of resort hotel owner Basil Fawlty, yet another incompetent authority figure. Michael Palin's anthology series *Ripping Yarns* also received several showings on public television during the late 1970s, and Eric Idle and Neil Innes's mock Beatles documentary *All You Need Is Cash,* which began as an episode of the BBC series *Rutland Weekend Television,* was run as an NBC special in 1978. For a lengthy analysis of *Fawlty Towers* in terms of the "logic of the absurd," see Palmer, *The Logic of the Absurd,* 115–40. See also Wilmut, *From Fringe to Flying Circus,* 237–47.

96. In October 1975, ABC presented a ninety-minute compilation of three of the final six episodes of *Monty Python's Flying Circus*—episodes without John Cleese that had not been sold to public broadcasting outlets. Unfortunately for all concerned, the ninety minutes included twenty-four minutes of commercials and announcements. In cutting the three thirty-minute programs to fit commercial network requirements, the network excised a number of lines and scenes containing what it deemed offensive material, deletions that destroyed the flow of the programs and removed several sketches from the realm of understanding. After a loud protest by the show's American fans, Monty Python filed suit against the network for copyright infringement. Although it lost its effort to keep the network from broadcasting a second "edited" compilation, the group won back the distribution rights to all of its programs, establishing a legal precedent for other artists in copyright struggles with the American communication industry. See Hertzberg, "Onward and Upward," 69–85; Robert Hewison, *Monty Python: The Case Against* (London: Methuen, 1981), 41–58.

97. Most of the "women" in *Monty Python* sketches, like Mrs. Premise and Mrs. Conclusion, were portrayed by the men in drag; the "real" women—usually actresses Carol Cleveland and Connie Booth (Cleese's wife)—often appeared as busty sex objects (the only woman in the "Njorl's Saga" show is a BBC secretary, who is seen spraying perfume on her sizable chest). Complaints by women about their portrayal in the series have been taken seriously by members of the group, who look back on those sketches with some

chagrin: "The problem with Python about women was that I don't think we knew very much about women," John Cleese says in the documentary *Life with Python* (1989).

98. The responses of American audiences to the Python stage performances in New York were more similar to those at a pop concert than at a comedy gig, according to John Cleese: "Almost every performance you got applause at the start of the sketch, when they recognized it; during the sketch you got very few laughs because people knew it so well; and then at the end you'd get an enormous amount of applause." Quoted in Wilmut, *From Fringe to Flying Circus*, 228.

6. All in the Anglo-American Family

1. Dialogue from "Crossed Swords," *Steptoe and Son*, prod. Duncan Wood; writ. Ray Galton, Alan Simpson; perf. Wilfrid Brambell, Harry Corbett; BBC, October 11, 1965.

2. Dialogue from "Crossed Swords," *Sanford and Son*, exec. prod. Norman Lear; writ./prod. Aaron Ruben; dir. Bud Yorkin; perf. Redd Foxx, Demond Wilson; NBC, January 14, 1972.

3. Horace Newcomb and Paul Hirsch, "Television as a Cultural Forum," in *Television: The Critical View*, 4th ed., ed. Horace Newcomb (New York: Oxford University Press, 1987), 457–58, 463.

4. William Read, *America's Mass Media Merchants* (Baltimore: Johns Hopkins University Press, 1976), 90–92; Joseph Straubhaar, "Asymmetrical Interdependence and Cultural Proximity: A Critical Review on the International Flow of TV Programs," unpublished manuscript, 1992. I discuss Straubhaar's research on the Dominican Republic in particular in greater detail in Chapter 7.

5. Kaaren Nordenstreng and Tapio Varis note in *Television Traffic: A One-Way Street?* (New York: UNESCO, 1974) that the United States did not become a leading export market for the BBC until the late 1960s. (They do not provide data for British commercial producers.) By 1974, American sales constituted some 20 percent of the BBC's exports, roughly the same percentage as sales to Asia, Australia, and New Zealand; Europe accounted for about 10 percent of BBC trade. Here again, however, attention to political economics obfuscates cultural matters: Nordenstreng and Varis elide the fact that most American distribution of BBC programming was through PBS, which appealed to a small and distinctive audience, and which in many markets was consigned to UHF channels serving only a fraction of households using television. Moreover, they calculate the amount of BBC programming received in the United States by counting every hour of exported programming in every market, a standard applied to no other nation or region. Finally, they do not consider the role of adaptations of BBC programming in any market (29–34).

6. Barry Curtis, "Aspects of Sitcom," in *BFI Dossier 17: Television Sitcom*, ed. Jim Cook (London: British Film Institute, 1982), 7–9.

7. Steve Neale and Frank Krutnik, *Popular Film and Television Comedy* (London: Routledge, 1990), 236–42. Neale and Krutnik also provide useful prehistories of the television sitcom form in both Britain and the United States (209–26).

8. Robert Mulligan, "Sitcom Still Runs Amuck in UK ('Till Death Us Do Part' Cues New Battle of Britain)," *Variety,* January 24, 1968, 32.

9. As was the case with several programs, *TV Guide* introduced *Till Death* to the United States before the show itself arrived. In a 1967 article, Robert Musel praised the show as an example of BBC programming that was "pushing the horizons of television out a little bit further"—even though the lack of export success for *Till Death* proved that "the rest of the TV world is not yet ready for the comedy of social comment." See Robert Musel, "A Situation Comedy about a Bigot?" *TV Guide,* December 30, 1967, 15–17.

10. Thomas Pryor, "Norman Lear—Friend of Originals," *Variety,* May 3, 1967, 20.

11. Quoted in "BBC's Needling Comedy 'Till Death' Preparing US Version via Tandem," *Variety,* February 14, 1968, 26.

12. Quoted in Richard Adler, All in the Family: *A Critical Appraisal* (New York: Praeger, 1979), xix–xx. See also Todd Gitlin, *Inside Prime Time* (New York: Pantheon, 1985), 212; Donna McCrohan, *Archie & Edith, Mike & Gloria: The Tumultuous History of* All in the Family (New York: Workman, 1987), 11–12.

13. Quoted in McCrohan, *Archie & Edith,* 32.

14. The humor of *Till Death Us Do Part* and *All in the Family,* to follow Neale and Krutnik's argument to the fullest, is one that violates verisimilitude less than it does the decorum—what is proper and fitting—of social life and television convention. Alf's and Archie's railings against "coons," "Hebes," "wogs," and "micks," the audible flushing of toilets, and references to biological functions usually kept private all work to violate norms of both actual public behavior and the expectations incumbent upon television situation comedy. See Neale and Krutnik, *Popular Film,* 84–86.

15. On the early production history of *All in the Family,* see Les Brown, *The Business Behind the Box* (New York: Harcourt Brace Jovanovich, 1971), 128–30; Adler, All in the Family, xix–xx; Gitlin, *Inside Prime Time,* 212; McCrohan, *Archie & Edith,* 14–17. ABC's unfortunate nod to late-1960s relevance was the show *Turn On,* a version of the hip and hit *Laugh-In* series that spawned such critical and public hostility that it was canceled after a single episode.

16. The demographic shift engineered by Wood at CBS is the major subplot in Brown, *The Business Behind the Box.*

17. According to McCrohan, CBS programming vice president Fred Silverman jumped to his feet after viewing the pilot and shouted, "Don't let that tape out of the building!" (*Archie & Edith,* 20).

18. As Les Brown puts it: "Public consciousness of the ideological polarity in the country had increased between the fall of 1969 and the spring of 1970, as it had with the sensitivities between the races, the classes, the generations and the sexes. ABC tested the pilot when there was still some national disbelief in the rift; CBS when the national anxiety over it had become serious" (*The Business Behind the Box,* 130).

19. David Marc and Ella Taylor both point out that *All in the Family* was in fact not very different from the sitcoms that preceded it, particularly those, such as *The Honey-*

mooners and *The Flintstones,* featuring loud, blustery blue-collar workers as their pro-tagonists, and those, such as *I Love Lucy,* relying as much on body language, mugging, and slapstick as they did on verbal gags. See David Marc, *Comic Visions* (Boston: Unwin Hyman, 1989), 174–80; Ella Taylor, *Prime-Time Families: Television Culture in Postwar America* (Berkeley: University of California Press, 1989), 72–73.

20. See McCrohan, *Archie & Edith,* 38–40.

21. Lear told *TV Guide* at the time that videotaping helped "convey the *spontaneity* of family life." Quoted in Richard Barber, "Bellowing, Half-Baked, Fire-Breathing Bigotry," *TV Guide,* May 29, 1971, 32. See also "Dialogue on Film: Norman Lear," *American Film,* June 1977, 47.

22. "Lew Grade's Example May Stir Brit. Vidfilmers to Pursue O'Seas Loot," *Variety,* July 28, 1965, 34.

23. Barber, "Bellowing, Half-Baked," 35; McCrohan, *Archie & Edith,* 7.

24. All quotations and citations in this section are from "A House with Love in It," *Till Death Us Do Part,* prod. Dennis Main Wilson; writ. Johnny Speight; perf. Warren Mitchell, Dandy Nichols, Anthony Booth, Una Stubbs; BBC, June 20, 1966; and "Meet the Bunkers," writ.-prod. Norman Lear; dir. John Rich; perf. Carroll O'Connor, Jean Stapleton, Rob Reiner, Sally Struthers; CBS, January 12, 1971.

25. David Marc, *Demographic Vistas* (Philadelphia: University of Pennsylvania Press, 1984), 180–81.

26. On the background of the Michael Stivic character, see McCrohan, *Archie & Edith,* 17–18, 47–54. For more on the difference between the American and British Michaels, see Dick Fiddy, "Brit. Sits. Hit Blitz," *Primetime* 12 (spring/summer 1987): 15–16.

27. Marc, *Demographic Vistas,* 177–78. As Marc points out, the WASPishness of the Bunkers continued the de-ethnicization of sitcom characters from the days of *The Gold-bergs* and *Amos 'n' Andy* in the 1950s and served as another conventional element of Lear's allegedly revolutionary new show.

28. Credits for the episode note: "Based on 'Till Death Us Do Part,' created by Johnny Speight."

29. Marc refers to Lear's use of space as "precinematic, almost Victorian telethe-ater . . . so busy and tight with players and props and doors and staircases that it serves as an aesthetic counterweight to the show's self-consciously progressive narrative didacticism" (*Demographic Vistas,* 183).

30. Over the years, the other rooms of the Bunker house, as well as its front porch, the neighbors' house, and Kelsey's bar (later Archie Bunker's Place), became familiar to *All in the Family* viewers. Even so, it was the living room, dining room, and kitchen that confined and defined the Bunkers.

31. The harridan working-class mother in British films of the 1950s and 1960s, according to John Hill, is part of those films' representations of the decline of the (male) working class and the rise of (female) consumerism. The mother figures in those films, Hill argues, were outright castrators who fed off the decline into impotence and death of their

husbands and would threaten to do the same to their sons and sons-in-law. Else Garnett did not occupy the same position in *Till Death Us Do Part* that mums in films such as *Saturday Night and Sunday Morning* and *The Loneliness of the Long Distance Runner* did; nonetheless, the character's ragings against her husband and her protective relationship with her daughter can be seen to come from the same sources. See John Hill, *Sex, Class and Realism: British Cinema: 1956–1963* (London: British Film Institute, 1986), 158–62.

32. Kathleen Rowe defines the "unruly woman" as one who "through body and speech . . . violates the unspoken feminine sanction against 'making a spectacle' of herself." Else Garnett was just such a figure in *Till Death*; Lear managed to contain her in Edith Bunker. Kathleen Rowe, "Roseanne: Unruly Woman as Domestic Goddess," in *Television: The Critical View*, 5th ed., ed. Horace Newcomb (New York: Oxford University Press, 1994), 204.

33. Quoted in McCrohan, *Archie & Edith*, 67, emphasis added.

34. For more on the careers of Galton and Simpson, see Curtis, "Aspects of Sitcom," 6.

35. "The Offer," *Comedy Playhouse*, prod. Duncan Wood; writ. Ray Galton, Alan Simpson; perf. Wilfrid Brambell, Harry Corbett; BBC, May 1, 1962. See also Fred Cooke, "The Story of TV's Steptoe and Son," *Sunday Citizen* (London), February 3, 1963.

36. "US Pays £100,000 for 'Steptoe' Scripts; TV Cast of Americans," *Daily Telegraph* (London), May 8, 1964.

37. Quoted in Asa Brooks, *The BBC: The First Fifty Years* (Oxford: Oxford University Press, 1985), 340.

38. On the success of Flip Wilson, see Brown, *The Business Behind the Box*, 291–94.

39. W. E. B. Du Bois, *The Souls of Black Folk* (New York: Vintage, 1990), 8; "Meet the Bunkers," CBS, January 12, 1971. Readings of *All in the Family* by African Americans varied considerably. The June 1972 issue of *Ebony* featured a cover story on Archie Bunker and the show — the first time a white man had occupied the cover of the magazine — titled "Is Archie Bunker the Real White America?" Author Charles Sanders argued that "St. Archie," whether real or not, represented a genuine threat to gains made by black Americans in the previous decade. The magazine later printed thirty-four letters in response to the article, with opinions ranging from complete agreement ("The AITF show is a sick, sick, sick show, and I wish somehow there could be some concerted effort to take it off the air") to complete disagreement ("We are devoted fans of the *All in the Family* television show. Incidentally, we are black") to anger with the magazine for placing O'Connor/Bunker's face on the cover ("Many blacks, including myself, don't feel that this man should be on the cover of the leading black magazine in the nation"). Charles Sanders, "Is Archie Bunker the Real White America?" *Ebony*, June 1972, 186–94; "Letters to the Editor," *Ebony*, August 1972, 14–18; "Letters to the Editor," *Ebony*, September 1972, 18–20

40. Bud Yorkin supervised day-to-day production on *Sanford and Son* while Lear continued work on *All in the Family*.

41. Richard Adler, "Look What They Found in a Junkyard," *TV Guide,* May 13, 1972, 28–29.

42. The fact that *Sanford and Son* was shot, like *All in the Family,* in color on videotape, which flattened shadows and added to the brightness, was a technological help here as well, and continued Lear's establishment of British videotaping as a viable production technique for American television.

43. Newcomb and Hirsch, "Television as a Cultural Forum," 457.

44. Adler, "Look What They Found," 30. In Britain, the BBC ran clips of the two shows together, showing instances in which the dialogue was identical. See "Brits Galton & Simpson Talk about 'Steptoe & Son' Which Inspired 'Sanford,'" *Variety,* May 24, 1972, 46.

45. Quoted in Adler, "Look What They Found," 29.

46. Descriptions and dialogue from "Crossed Swords," BBC, October 11, 1965; and "Crossed Swords," NBC, January 14, 1972.

47. Adler, "Look What They Found," 30.

48. Herman Gray, *Watching Race: Television and the Struggle for "Blackness"* (Minneapolis: University of Minnesota Press, 1995), 77; Marc, as cited in McCrohan, *Archie & Edith,* 139.

49. Newcomb and Hirsch, "Television as a Cultural Forum," 461.

50. Gitlin, *Inside Prime Time,* 63–85.

51. As originally planned, the scene was to be played with Archie and Edith walking in on the kids coming down the stairs in the afterglow; CBS Standards and Practices objected, and Lear changed the script to indicate that the deed had yet to be done. See Brown, *The Business Behind the Box,* 138.

52. Tony Bennett and Janet Woollacott, *Bond and Beyond: The Political Career of a Popular Hero* (London: Methuen, 1987), 231–32, 241–47.

53. Bonnie Dow, "Hegemony, Feminist Criticism and *The Mary Tyler Moore Show,*" *Critical Studies in Mass Communication* 7 (1990): 261–74.

54. She would also become the protagonist in a similar program, *Get Christie Love!,* also broadcast in 1974 — except that the beautiful blonde was a beautiful black woman. *Christie Love* lasted only one season, however, a failure that supports the contention of J. Fred MacDonald, among others, that the mass middle-class white American audience was willing to accept blacks only in comedies in which they appeared as minstrel show stereotypes. See J. Fred MacDonald, *Blacks and White TV* (Chicago: Nelson-Hall, 1983), 176–77.

55. Susan Douglas, *Where the Girls Are: Growing Up Female with the Mass Media* (New York: Times Books, 1994), 209–12.

56. John Fiske, *Television Culture* (New York: Routledge, 1989), 45; Douglas, *Where the Girls Are,* 212–16.

57. For discussion of the contributions of Nicholl, Ross, and West to *All in the Family,* see McCrohan, *Archie & Edith,* 111–20.

58. Labor Day week was the week before the networks began their new seasons. Their reruns of reruns, then, allowed the independent station to promote the Thames shows not just as something completely different but as something completely new. See Bill Greeley, "Thames Overflows Banks, Cleanses Hudson Pollution," *Variety,* September 8, 1976, 63; Eric Levin, "The Week New York Had Its Own English Channel," *TV Guide,* November 20, 1976, 28–30.

59. Levin, "The Week New York Had," 30. See also "US TV Execs Evaluate the 'Thames on 9' Week," "Rock Follies Sold by Thames to PBS," and "Thames Ratings Hit Targeted 10 Share," all in *Variety,* September 8, 1976, 54.

60. "New York's TTC Has Thames Sitcom for Development in US," *Variety,* September 8, 1976, 55.

61. Quotations from "Three's a Crowd," *Man about the House,* prod. Peter Frazer-Jones; writ. Johnnie Mortimer, Brian Cooke; perf. Richard O'Sullivan, Paula Wilcox, Sally Thomsett; Thames Television, September 5, 1973; and "A Man about the House," *Three's Company,* exec. prod. Don Taffner; prod.-writ. Don Nicholl, Michael Ross, Bernie West; perf. John Ritter, Joyce DeWitt, Suzanne Somers; ABC, March 22, 1977.

62. Some examples of dialogue: George Roper to Mildred (U.K.): "It's a pity you don't live in India—you'd be sacred there"; Stanley Roper to Helen (U.S.): "It's a shame you don't live in India—you'd be sacred there." Chrissy to Robin (U.K.) "Eleanor didn't leave the recipe for toast"; Janet to Jack (U.S.): "Chrissy can't make toast—Eleanor didn't leave the recipe." Mildred to George (U.K.): "I think I should know what a man looks like—mostly from memory"; Helen to Stanley (U.S.): "I know a man when I see one—though it's been a long time."

63. Review of *Three's Company, Variety,* March 28, 1977, 58. See also Fiddy, "Brit. Sits. Hit Blitz," 18.

64. On the industry use of "tits and ass," see Gitlin, *Inside Prime Time,* 71.

65. Marc, *Demographic Vistas,* 215. The male character in *Man about the House* was named Robin Tripp.

66. Marc, *Comic Visions,* 213.

67. Terry Lovell, "A Genre of Social Disruption?" in *BFI Dossier 17: Television Sitcom,* ed. Jim Cook (London: British Film Institute, 1982), 22–25.

68. Marc, *Demographic Vistas,* 33; see also Jane Feuer, "Genre Study," *Channels of Discourse,* ed. Robert Allen (Chapel Hill: University of North Carolina Press, 1987), 127–28.

69. *The Benny Hill Show* was also a part of the Thames week in New York. The cherubic, rubber-faced Hill had been a fixture on British television since 1955 and was widely regarded as the first British comic to apply the production techniques of television to what were essentially decades-old music hall comedy routines. By 1971, at the same time *Monty Python* was winning critics and devotees to its brand of humor, Hill's regular comedy specials for Thames were the top-rated programs in Britain. Hill's 1979 arrival and suc-

cess, both critical and popular, in the United States can be attributed to both the carniva-lesque nature of his humor and the retrograde, "antifeminist" shift in American television's signification of women previously discussed. See Jane Harbord and Jeff Wright, *40 Years of British Television* (London: Boxtree, 1992), 56; Tom Shales, "Delightfully Bad Benny," *Washington Post*, April 25, 1979, D4; Tom Buckley, "TV: The 'Benny Hill Show' Stars British Comic," *New York Times*, April 29, 1979, C23; Michael Billington, "For Benny Hill, Vaudeville Still Lives," *New York Times*, July 29, 1979, II, 23.

70. Marc, *Demographic Vistas*, 143–50. For a further description and analysis of the rise and fall of *The Smothers Brothers Comedy Hour*, see Aniko Bodroghkozy, "*The Smothers Brothers Comedy Hour* and the Youth Rebellion," in *The Revolution Wasn't Televised: Sixties Television and Social Conflict*, ed. Lynn Spigel and Michael Curtin (New York: Routledge, 1997), 201–20.

71. Marc, *Demographic Vistas*, 150–52. Tim Brooks and Earle Marsh, in *The Complete Directory to Prime Time Network TV Shows: 1946–Present*, 5th ed. (New York: Ballantine, 1992), describe *Laugh-In* as "a cross between Olsen & Johnson's *Hellzapoppin'* . . . and the highly topical satire of *That Was the Week That Was*" (768).

72. Quoted in Doug Hill and Jeff Weingrad, *Saturday Night* (New York: Random House, 1986), 38.

73. Ibid., 18.

74. *Saturday Night Live* star Chevy Chase would later say that the limit of the *Python* influence on his show lay in the fact that "they could edit, while we had to write endings." In *Life of Python*, exec. prod. Charles Brand; prod.-dir. Mark Redhead; BBC/Devillier Donegan Enterprises, 1989.

75. Ibid.

76. Roger Wilmut, *From Fringe to Flying Circus* (London: Eyre Methuen, 1980), 237–38.

77. On the development of the TV Western, see Horace Newcomb, *TV: The Most Popular Art* (New York: Anchor, 1974), 59–82; on the decline of the form, see Brown, *The Business Behind the Box*, 47–58.

78. Michael Ryan, "The Decline and Fall of *Beacon Hill*," *TV Guide*, March 20, 1976, 12–16; "As We See It," *TV Guide*, November 1, 1975, A-2.

79. Ryan, "The Decline and Fall," 14; Cleveland Amory, review of *Beacon Hill*, *TV Guide*, September 30, 1975, 26; "CBS Axes 'Beacon' & 'Road,' May Re-switch 'MASH' & '5-0,'" *Variety*, October 29, 1975, 47.

80. "PBS 'Adams' Series Secures in Ratings," *Variety*, April 14, 1976, 53.

81. Bruce Cook, "Public Television's Big Splash," *American Film*, December 1975, 6–13; Henry Waters, "One Man's Family," *Newsweek*, January 19, 1976, 78–79.

82. In July 1998, Mobil Oil, WGBH, and PBS announced that *Mobil Masterpiece Theatre* would begin presenting American-produced versions of American literary classics in the 1999–2000 season, marking the first time since *The Adams Chronicles* that American public television (and Mobil Oil) would venture into domestic production of serialized

historical/literary drama. "Mobil Collaborates with Public Television Leaders Bringing American Drama to Mobil Masterpiece Theatre," Mobil press release (on-line), July 14, 1998 (www.mobil.com/news).

83. Quoted in Dwight Whitney, "The Book Covers 23 Years," *TV Guide*, January 31, 1976, 30. See also Philip Schlesinger, "Trading in Fictions: What Do We Know about British Television Imports and Exports?" *European Journal of Communication* 1 (1986): 264.

84. Brooks and Marsh, *The Complete Directory*, 1102.

85. Ibid., 1075–76.

86. Erik Barnouw, in *Tube of Plenty*, 2d ed. (New York: Oxford University Press, 1990), cites the celebration of the American Bicentennial as an important utterance shaping national television culture, a balm to ease the pain of the long televisual nightmares of Vietnam and Watergate. Even programming such as *Roots* and *Holocaust*, he argues, both follow and encourage "the spirit of reexamination and rededication furthered by the Bicentennial" (464–66).

87. Marshall Sahlins, *Culture and Practical Reason* (Chicago: University of Chicago Press, 1976), 217, as cited in Newcomb and Hirsch, "Television as a Cultural Forum," 457.

88. Horace Newcomb and Robert Alley, *The Producers' Medium* (New York: Oxford University Press, 1983), 34–38.

89. Roland Barthes, *Image, Music, Text* (New York: Hill & Wang, 1977), 142–48; Michel Foucault, "What Is an Author?" in *The Foucault Reader*, ed. Paul Rabinow (New York: Pantheon, 1984), 101–20.

90. David Wolper and Quincy Troupe, *The Inside Story of TV's* Roots (New York: Warner, 1977), 1–41; Sally Bedell, *Up the Tube: Prime Time TV and the Silverman Years* (New York: Viking, 1981), 168–70.

91. Fred Silverman scheduled *Roots* for the last week in January because he was not convinced that it would do well enough in the ratings to mandate its broadcast during the network "sweeps" period in February; he chose to present it over eight consecutive evenings both to heighten "the impact of the work" and to minimize any ratings damage that might be done by spreading it out over two months. Bedell, *Up the Tube*, 170–71; Wolper and Troupe, *The Inside Story*, 130–41.

92. In addition to readings focusing on the portrayal of blackness and whiteness in *Roots*, viewers and critics also noted its attention to familiar American ideals of family and the achievement of success over great odds through personal responsibility and initiative: "the Horatio Alger myth in black," as MacDonald puts it, which "allowed viewers to rededicate themselves to a myth fundamental to American culture and society" (*Blacks and White TV*, 220–21). For similar comments concerning the focus on family and success as opposed to racial subordination and exploitation, see Gray, *Watching Race*, 77–79; Lauren Tucker and Hemant Shah, "Race and the Transformation of Culture: The Making of the Television Miniseries *Roots*," *Critical Studies in Mass Communication* 9 (1992): 325–36. Other readings of the show at the time commented on its sex and violence;

Richard Schickel, for instance, referred to the show as "rooted in the paperback mentality... *Mandingo* for the middlebrows." Richard Schickel, review of *Roots, Time,* January 24, 1977, 56. See also Bedell, *Up the Tube,* 170–71.

93. Wolper and Troupe, *The Inside Story,* 141.

94. Among those working in the miniseries genre in the late 1970s were Abby Mann, responsible for *Judgment at Nuremberg* and *Kojak,* with *King,* a biography of Martin Luther King Jr.; Herbert Brodkin, producer of *The Defenders* and *The Nurses,* with *Holocaust*; and Roy Huggins, creator of *77 Sunset Strip* and *The Rockford Files,* with *The Captains and the Kings.*

95. Michener's comments on the success of *Roots* offer an ironic backdrop to the presentation of *Centennial:* "Encouraged by [*Roots's*] success, television managers will seek other books... if these books are required to match the performance of *Roots,* dreadful mistakes are bound to be made. Television should find good books, handle them in a good way, and expect moderately good results." James Michener, "The Guest Word: 'Roots,' Unique in Its Time," *New York Times Book Review,* February 27, 1977, 39.

96. *The Waltons* was actually created and produced by Earl Hamner, who worked for Rich's company (Lorimar) and also served as the show's head writer and narrator. Newcomb and Alley cite Hamner as "the purest example" of the producer as auteur; his next major success, however — the prime-time serial *Falcon Crest* — bore the hallmarks of Rich's success with *Dallas* and its spin-off *Knots Landing.* See Newcomb and Alley, *The Producers' Medium,* 154–61.

97. Advertisement for *Dallas, TV Guide* (Michigan ed.), April 1, 1978, A-47. On Sundays in April 1978, viewers could choose among the BBC/*Masterpiece Theatre* adaptation of *Anna Karenina* on PBS, *Holocaust* on NBC, and *Dallas* on CBS — a measure of the degree to which the British serialized drama form had come to shape American viewing patterns.

98. Both the *TV Guide* premiere episode description and a *Variety* ad for the show referred to it as a "five-hour, five-part miniseries." Program description of *Dallas, TV Guide* (Michigan ed.), April 1, 1978, A-46; advertisement for *Dallas, Variety,* April 19, 1978, 56.

7. British Television and American Culture

1. William Carlos Williams, *In the American Grain* (New York: New Directions, 1956), 207.

2. For figures, see Kirsten Beck, *Cultivating the Wasteland* (New York: American Council for the Arts, 1983), 15; J. Fred MacDonald, *One Nation under Television* (New York: Pantheon, 1990), 228.

3. Harry Waters, "Cable TV: Coming of Age," *Newsweek,* August 24, 1981, 45. By the end of the decade, that figure was 57 percent. See MacDonald, *One Nation under Television,* 228.

4. Beck, *Cultivating the Wasteland,* 18–20; MacDonald, *One Nation under Television,* 253–54.

5. Beck, *Cultivating the Wasteland*, 52–53. The English Channel was purchased by the USA network in 1980 and subsumed into that network's programming as Ovation. The British component of USA's programming faded during the 1980s as the network increasingly focused on a young male demographic.

6. Ibid., 61–64.

7. Ibid., 53.

8. Sally Bedell, "Cable TV Channel, Subsidiary of RCA, to Close with Loss," *New York Times*, February 23, 1983, 1.

9. Beck, *Cultivating the Wasteland*, 80–86.

10. Peter Kerr, "Cultural Channels Join Forces," *New York Times*, December 18, 1983, II, 39; N. R. Kleinfeld, "A&E: A Cable Success Story," *New York Times*, April 16, 1989, II, 31.

11. Kleinfeld, "A&E," II, 31. When A&E began programming in 1984, it had one advertiser: Ford. By 1989, 350 advertisers were purchasing time on the channel.

12. Andrew Goodwin's discussion of the British "origins" of music video in *Dancing in the Distraction Factory: Music Television and Popular Culture* (Minneapolis: University of Minnesota Press, 1992) also presents at length the ideological shifts within British pop music that led to the popularity of music video as commodity and genre (29–41). The first video shown on MTV, "Video Killed the Radio Star," featured the British band the Buggles.

13. BBC America is a joint venture of the BBC with Discovery Communications, the American parent company of the Discovery Channel. The deal also includes a number of BBC-produced nonfiction programs for the Discovery Channel and other American outlets (including A&E and PBS). The cable deal does not foreclose the BBC's ongoing relationship with PBS. See Adam Dawtrey, "BBC, Discovery Allies in U.S.," *Daily Variety* (on-line), March 20, 1998 (www.variety.com).

14. See Ron Miller, "*Mystery!* History" (on-line) (www.mystery!.com). See also Laurence Jarvik, "PBS and the Politics of Quality: Mobil Oil's *Masterpiece Theatre*," *Historical Journal of Film, Radio and Television* 12, no. 3 (1992): 268.

15. In a production development reminiscent of Lew Grade's mid-Atlantic approach, NBC had the voice of the lead character in *Stressed Eric* redubbed by American actor Hank Azaria — the character became an American expatriate — in order to avoid the old (perceived) problem of British accents. CBS, for its part, continued to revisit British sitcom successes with another remake of *Fawlty Towers*. *Payne*, starring John Larroquette in the Cleese role (this time named Royal Payne), came and went in spring 1999.

16. Herbert I. Schiller, *Mass Communications and American Empire* (New York: Augustus M. Kelley, 1969).

17. Joseph Straubhaar and Gloria Viscasillas, "Class, Genre, and the Regionalization of Television Programming in the Dominican Republic," *Journal of Communication* 41, no. 1 (1991): 53–69. Straubhaar and Viscasillas's research echoes William Read's characterization of transnational communication with the United States as exporter: "Foreign

systems began with a wealthy elite audience whose tastes tended to be more cosmopolitan than those of the middle class who later greatly enlarged the viewing audience.... But as foreign television systems matured, just as had the American system, their audience base broadened, they increased the number of telecasting hours, and they acquired more wherewithal to do their own productions that had greater local appeal." William Read, *America's Mass Media Merchants* (Baltimore: Johns Hopkins University Press, 1976), 91. Read also points out that part of the reason elite audiences were attracted to foreign (American) programming was that those audiences could afford the technology. Again, that situation is visible in the American reception of British programs, particularly those shown on PBS stations. Individual educational and public stations were mostly located in the UHF broadcasting spectrum, which during the period in question required different reception capabilities and more money per television set than did VHF stations.

18. Schiller, *Mass Communications,* 8–9.

19. Pierre Bourdieu, *Distinction: A Social Critique of the Judgement of Taste,* trans. Richard Nice (Cambridge: Harvard University Press, 1984).

20. Celeste Condit, "The Rhetorical Limits of Polysemy," in *Television: The Critical View,* 5th ed., ed. Horace Newcomb (New York: Oxford University Press, 1994), 426–47.

21. Todd Gitlin, *The Whole World Is Watching: Mass Media in the Making and Unmaking of the New Left* (Berkeley: University of California Press, 1980), 256.

22. Roland Barthes, *Mythologies* (New York: Noonday, 1972), 151–52. For an application of Barthes's concept to television, see John Fiske, *Television Culture* (New York: Routledge, 1989), 290–91.

23. Richard Adler collects many of the voices of the critical debate on the meaning(s) of *All in the Family* in All in the Family: *A Critical Appraisal* (New York: Praeger, 1979), 69–120. See also Donna McCrohan, *Archie & Edith, Mike & Gloria: The Tumultuous History of* All in the Family (New York: Workman, 1987), 177–98; Charles Sanders, "Is Archie Bunker the Real White America?" *Ebony,* June 1972, 186–94; "Letters to the Editor," *Ebony,* August 1972, 14–18; "Letters to the Editor," *Ebony,* September 1972, 18–20.

24. Raymond Williams, *Marxism and Literature* (Oxford: Oxford University Press, 1977), 113–14.

25. Tony Bennett and Janet Woollacott, *Bond and Beyond: The Political Career of a Popular Hero* (London: Methuen, 1987).

26. Williams, *Marxism and Literature,* 114.

Index

Jeffrey S. Miller is assistant professor of English and journalism at Augustana College in Sioux Falls, South Dakota.